God Wants You Well

Andrew Wommack

God Wants You Well Study Guide
ISBN: 978-1-59548-200-6
Copyright © 2010 by Andrew Wommack Ministries, Inc.
P.O. Box 3333
Colorado Springs, CO 80934

Published by Andrew Wommack Ministries, Inc.

Item Code: 430

Table of Contents

Introduction

Although I don't know everything there is to know about healing, I have grown a lot in this area, and I consider it to be a real strength in my life. In fact, it's now been almost forty years since I've had sickness win in my body. That doesn't mean I've never had a problem. Along the way, I've had things attack me. One time, while I was making radio programs, all of the symptoms of the flu hit me. My sinuses stopped up, my nose ran, and I began to have aches, chills, and a fever—all within a very short period of time. It took me about an hour praying over it, but then it was gone.

Probably the worst sickness that's come against me these past forty years was the time I returned home from England and went right to work on my pond. Something happened with the drain in the pond I was building on my property, so although I'd gone thirty-four hours without sleep, I had to attend to it immediately. Standing chest deep in cold water and working for about six hours while I was so weak, tired, and depleted was stupid on my part. My nose began to run, and my ears plugged up. However, I was able to overcome that runny nose in just about a day's time. Although it took me a couple of days to get my ears unplugged, an outside observer probably wouldn't have been able to tell that anything had occurred. That's the worst illness that I can remember happening to me in almost forty years.*

At the very beginning of this period of time, I was actually diagnosed with an incurable disease. However, within three days, that same doctor pronounced me whole because I had received prayer and healing. I've seen God heal me of a number of things.

Healing is a strength in my life. The truths I share in this **Study Guide** are working for me and have for decades. Even though I don't understand everything there is to understand about healing, I know more than I'll be able to talk about here. Please refer to the *Recommended Teachings* section for additional resources that will complement and expand on the truths contained here. My purpose in this **Study Guide** isn't to teach healing in an exhaustive manner but to lay a firm foundation.

How about You?

You need to consider the truths of God's Word contained in this **Study Guide**. Although I've personally walked in divine health for a long time, it's not because nothing has ever happened to me. I've been hurt, had accidents, and been attacked by sickness. I've had problems, but I've overcome them—and I've seen health manifest in my own physical body for decades.

I've also ministered healing to multitudes of others. I've seen the blind receive sight. This includes both partially blind eyes that improved and totally blind eyes that couldn't even perceive light. I've seen both totally and partially deaf people hear. I remember praying for people whose eardrums had deteriorated and even been surgically removed. God restored their hearing. I've seen individuals receive a miracle and start speaking in tongues who couldn't even talk because their larynx was gone. I've seen thousands of people healed of arthritis and all kinds of pain. One man had a metal rod in his back that made it physically impossible for him to bend over, yet he received healing and bent over just fine. I've seen deformities healed, diseases cured, and people come out of wheelchairs.

I've personally seen three people raised from the dead, including my own son. He'd been dead for almost five hours and had already turned black. His toe was tagged, and he was lying on a slab in the hospital morgue, but the Lord raised him up—glory to His name!

I don't share any of this to promote myself. I'm still learning about healing. There have been—and still are—times when I pray for people and they aren't healed. But I'm getting better results today than ever before. I haven't arrived, but I've left, and I've learned some important truths along the way.

How about you? Are you consistently walking in divine health? Are the people you pray for regularly healed? If not, then you ought to seriously consider the truths I share in this **Study Guide**.

God's Word Works!

Please don't mistake my confidence for arrogance, but this is an area of my life that works. I've personally ministered to tens and probably hundreds of thousands of people. I've trained others and seen these truths work for them. A lot of ministers have told me how receiving a revelation of these same truths has enabled them to see many people healed whom they have prayed for. Some of these ministers have seen nearly every single individual they prayed for healed, including multiple people raised from the dead. God's Word works!

I may not have it all figured out, but I know I'm going in the right direction. I've seen the power of God work again and again. If you're prejudiced against healing and refuse to consider what the Word says, I probably won't be able to help you. But if you genuinely desire to know about the divine healing that is available through the Lord Jesus Christ and faith in what He's done, this **Study Guide** could literally change your life. At the very least, these truths can bring you to a level of success and victory in this area of healing that is equal to what God has brought me to. Again, I don't claim to know it all, but healing is working pretty well in my life—not only just for me but also for the people I've ministered to.

As you humble yourself to receive God's Word, I believe these truths will really help you too.

*Author's Note: Since this *Introduction* was first written, I fought a sinus infection that lasted about three days. This, too, was stupidity induced. I had ministered forty-one times during one week and then forty times the next. Physically, this wore me out. I was so weak, I opened a door to sickness. Faith doesn't always overcome stupidity. I've taken steps to correct this.

How to Use Your Study Guide

Whether you are teaching a class, leading a small group, discipling an individual, or studying *God Wants You Well* on your own, this **Study Guide** is designed for you! Here's how it works:

Each study consists of a **Lesson Outline, Teacher's Guide, Discipleship Questions, Answer Key,** and **Scriptures**. Some **Lessons** also have **Additional Information**.

The teacher reads the **Lesson** aloud. While the **Lesson** is being read, each student follows along with their own copy of the **Lesson Outline**.

Once the **Lesson** is read, the teacher then facilitates a group Bible study using the **Teacher's Guide**. Simply read aloud one numbered section at a time, ask the corresponding questions that follow, and have the group answer them. Then, repeat the process for the next numbered section. For your convenience, answers are provided in parentheses.

Except for the corresponding questions and answers, the information on the **Teacher's Guide** is the same as the **Lesson Outline**. Therefore, the group should use their **Lesson Outlines** to assist them in answering the questions.

Whenever a question mentions a specific scripture, be sure to have the group look it up in their Bibles and read it together before answering the question. Feel free to interact with the group over the scriptures and points from the **Lesson** as time allows. Don't let any individual dominate the discussion, but try to draw out the quieter ones for the group conversation. As much as possible, keep the discussion centered on the scriptures and the **Lesson** points at hand. Remember, the goal is understanding (Matt. 13:19).

Discipleship Questions are provided for further study and meditation. They are designed for use as "homework," but—according to the teacher's discretion—may be helpful during the group study sometimes as well. Each **Lesson** comes with an **Answer Key**. As a brief review before launching into the current **Lesson**, the teacher may wish to go over the **Answer Key** for the previous study's **Discipleship Questions** with the group.

Some **Lessons** also have **Additional Information**. This section, geared toward the teacher, contains resource recommendations for further study.

Scriptures from the *King James Version* of the Bible are included as another tool for reference and meditation.

For personal study, read the **Lesson** and review the **Teacher's Guide**. Then, answer the **Discipleship Questions** and check your work with the **Answer Key**. For maximum impact, be sure to utilize the **Additional Information** and **Scriptures** sections.

Printable files of the **Lesson Outline, Discipleship Questions,** and **Scriptures** can be found on the CD-ROM included with this book. Copies may be made for each person in the group.

Outline for Group Study:

I. Briefly review previous study by going over the **Answer Key** for the **Discipleship Questions** (homework).

II. Read the current **Lesson** aloud.

    A. Be sure that each student has a copy of the **Lesson Outline**.

    B. While the **Lesson** is being read, students should use their **Lesson Outlines** to follow along.

III. Once the **Lesson** is read, facilitate a group Bible study using the **Teacher's Guide**.

    A. Read one entire numbered section (top of page).

    B. Ask the corresponding questions (bottom of page).

    C. Have the group look up and read aloud each specifically mentioned scripture before answering the question.

    D. Discuss the scripture and the answer/point from the **Lesson** as desired.

    E. Repeat the process by reading the next numbered section (top of page).

IV. Distribute copies of the **Discipleship Questions** to be worked on as homework.

Materials Needed:

Study Guide, Bible, and enough copies of the **Lesson Outline** and **Discipleship Questions** for each student.

Outline for Personal Study:

I. Read **Lesson**.

    A. Read **Additional Information**, if any.

    B. Meditate on the given scriptures, as desired.

II. Review **Teacher's Guide**.

III. Answer **Discipleship Questions**.

IV. Check your work with the **Answer Key**.

Materials Needed:

Study Guide, Bible, and a writing utensil.

Miracles Confirm God's Word
Lesson 1

Many people criticize me for emphasizing healing. They say, "This isn't important. You don't have to be healed to go to heaven. You shouldn't spend any of your time on radio, television, or in print emphasizing healing. It's a secondary issue. You're making it greater than it is!"

In a letter forwarded to me from a certain radio station, one man threatened to take legal action against me. Basically, he said, "It's a big sin for you to take people's money, which is hard to come by, and preach something like healing!" This fellow was one of many people who contend that it's a waste of time to talk about healing. I strongly disagree!

Healing is part of Christ's Atonement. If Jesus died to provide healing for us, then it's not just incidental. If the Lord suffered and took stripes on His back for our physical healing, then it's not insignificant. If Jesus thought enough of healing to purchase it for us, then we ought to think enough of it to receive.

God the Father caused His Son to bear all of our sins and all of our sicknesses on the cross. Jesus took our diseases just as much as He took our sins. Therefore, it honors Him to promote healing. In fact, Jesus spent more time talking about healing than He did several other truths that many people consider to be essential—heaven-and-hell—issues today. Actually, the Lord used healing like a bell to get people's attention and to prove that He did have power on earth to forgive sins. Many scriptural examples illustrate this.

Healing and Forgiveness

In Mark 2, some friends of a man who suffered from the palsy couldn't get him into the house where Jesus was ministering, because of the great crowd. Undeterred, they took him up to the top of the house, removed some tiles from the roof, and lowered this man in his stretcher right down in front of Him.

> *When Jesus saw their faith, he said unto the sick of the palsy, Son, thy sins be forgiven thee.*
>
> **Mark 2:5**

Notice that Jesus said, "Son, your sins be forgiven you."

> *But there were certain of the scribes sitting there, and reasoning in their hearts, Why doth this man thus speak blasphemies? who can forgive sins but God only? And immediately when Jesus perceived in his spirit that they so reasoned within themselves, he said unto them, Why reason ye these things in your hearts? Whether is it easier to say to the sick of the palsy, Thy sins be forgiven thee; or to say, Arise, and take up thy bed, and walk?*
>
> **Mark 2:6-9**

If Jesus had only been a mere man, it would have been impossible for Him to say either, "Rise up and walk" or "Your sins are forgiven you." Only God can forgive sins, and man in his physical ability does not have the power to produce healing. However, Jesus, being both fully God and fully man, could actually say and do both these things—healing and forgiveness.

It's easier to say "Your sins be forgiven you" because you can't see a sin, and you can't see if a sin is forgiven and dealt with or not. If someone challenged you, saying, "You can't do that," you could just answer, "I'll prove it!"

Verification

Jesus was saying that it's easier to say "Your sins are forgiven" than "Rise up and walk" because they would immediately be able to tell if He had the power or not by whether this man rose up and walked. For the Lord to say to this man in front of this crowd, "Rise up and walk," was actually harder because instantly, there would be physical evidence whether it did or didn't work.

If you can do the greater work, then certainly you can do the lesser. If you can jump fifteen feet, then certainly you can jump two feet.

The people in the house were just sitting there in silence, not knowing how to respond. Then Jesus continued, saying,

> *But that ye may know that the Son of man hath power on earth to forgive sins, (he saith to the sick of the palsy,) I say unto thee, Arise, and take up thy bed, and go thy way into thine house. And immediately he arose, took up the bed, and went forth before them all; insomuch that they were all amazed, and glorified God, saying, We never saw it on this fashion.*
>
> **Mark 2:10-12**

Jesus made it very clear that the reason He healed this man was so people would know He also had power on earth to forgive sins. The Lord used healing as verification that He had power to deal with unseen things. If He could deal with physical bodies and meet the physical and emotional needs of people, then He could also deal with their spiritual needs. Jesus used healing like a bell to draw people to Himself and get their attention, and then He would tell them the truth.

Words Only?

Jesus also said that the miracles He did authenticated who He was and confirmed what He said.

> *But I have greater witness than that of John: for the works which the Father hath given me to finish, the same works that I do, bear witness of me, that the Father hath sent me.*
>
> **John 5:36**

Although Jesus pointed to the testimony that John the Baptist bore of Him, He wasn't counting on it. Christ was dependent on the miracles He performed to confirm to people that His Father had sent Him. If Jesus needed the witness of the miracles He performed to validate His authority, then how can we possibly do less? It is the height of arrogance to think that we can use words alone to persuade people, when Jesus had to have signs and miracles to confirm His words.

The Way it Should Be

Some folks say, "We don't need miracles today; we have the Word of God." Yet that's not what the Bible teaches. Mark 16 reveals to us some of the final instructions Jesus gave His disciples before He ascended back to heaven. Notice what He promised after commanding us to go into all the world and preach the Gospel:

And these signs shall follow them that believe; In my name shall they cast out devils; they shall speak with new tongues; They shall take up serpents; and if they drink any deadly thing, it shall not hurt them; they shall lay hands on the sick, and they shall recover. So then after the Lord had spoken unto them, he was received up into heaven, and sat on the right hand of God. And they went forth, and preached every where, the Lord working with them, and confirming the word with signs following.

Mark 16:17-20

In other words, God used miracles to confirm that it was really Him speaking through these people. This passage also reveals that the Lord confirms the true preaching and teaching of His Word with signs following.

Based on this, I can truthfully say today that if ministers do not have the miraculous power of God flowing through them, then I would be skeptical about whether or not God is truly speaking through them. Now, don't misunderstand me: I'm not saying that a person who doesn't have healings manifest in their ministry is not of God. Neither am I saying to just automatically trust all the words of anyone who performs a miracle. What people say must always be checked against God's Word. However, in God's system, when His Word is truly preached, there will be signs and wonders to confirm that it is the truth.

We live in a day and age where the message of salvation has been corrupted and divided into parts. Certain aspects are neglected and misunderstood by most of the body of Christ. Many people are preaching only the forgiveness of sins. God confirms all of His Word that we preach, but if all we preach are things having spiritual, eternal value and the forgiveness of sins, then all we'll see is people being born again. But if we preach and teach the whole counsel of God, He will confirm it with signs, wonders, and miracles. This is the way God has established it in the Scriptures, and this is the way it should be.

We Do Too!

Not all true people of God see miracles today, because they aren't preaching the whole counsel of God. Some people that I respect very much have been faithful with the revelation that they have. They've seen people born again and lives transformed. I definitely wouldn't say that they aren't true ministers. However, it's obvious that they aren't preaching the whole counsel of God. God's will is for His whole counsel to be preached, and He will confirm it with signs and wonders following.

Hebrews 2:3-4 says,

How shall we escape, if we neglect so great salvation; which at the first began to be spoken by the Lord, and was confirmed unto us by them that heard him; God also bearing them witness, both with signs and wonders, and with divers miracles, and gifts of the Holy Ghost, according to his own will?

This says that God confirmed with miracles the Word that Jesus preached. When He had ascended to heaven and the disciples took over the ministry on this earth, God also confirmed the Word that they spoke with signs, wonders, and gifts of the Holy Spirit according to His will.

No one today can claim they are operating better than Jesus did. In fact, most Christians aren't even regularly seeing the fullness of the manifestation of God's power the way the early apostles did. Who do we think we are, to believe that somehow or another, we have a superior anointing or ability to minister effectively in God's eyes without needing miracles today? That's the height of arrogance. If both Jesus and the early believers needed miracles, signs, and wonders to confirm the message from God that they preached, then we do too!

Miracles Confirm God's Word
Lesson 1 – Outline

I. Healing is part of Christ's Atonement.

   A. If He suffered and took stripes on His back for our physical healing, then it's not insignificant.

   B. If He thought enough of healing to purchase it for us, then we ought to think enough of it to receive.

   C. God the Father caused His Son to bear all of our sins and all of our sicknesses on the cross. Jesus took our diseases just as much as He took our sins.

II. The Lord used healing like a bell to get people's attention and to prove that He did have power on earth to forgive sins.

> *When Jesus saw their faith, he said unto the sick of the palsy, Son, thy sins be forgiven thee. But there were certain of the scribes sitting there, and reasoning in their hearts, Why doth this man thus speak blasphemies? who can forgive sins but God only? And immediately when Jesus perceived in his spirit that they so reasoned within themselves, he said unto them, Why reason ye these things in your hearts? Whether is it easier to say to the sick of the palsy, Thy sins be forgiven thee; or to say, Arise, and take up thy bed, and walk?*
>
> **Mark 2:5-9**

   A. Jesus was saying that it's easier to say "Your sins are forgiven" than "Rise up and walk" because they would immediately be able to tell if He had the power or not by whether this man rose up and walked.

   B. If you can do the greater work, then certainly you can do the lesser. If you can jump fifteen feet, then certainly you can jump two feet.

> *But that ye may know that the Son of man hath power on earth to forgive sins, (he saith to the sick of the palsy,) I say unto thee, Arise, and take up thy bed, and go thy way into thine house. And immediately he arose, took up the bed, and went forth before them all; insomuch that they were all amazed, and glorified God, saying, We never saw it on this fashion.*
>
> **Mark 2:10-12**

   C. Jesus made it very clear that the reason He healed this man was so people would know He also had power on earth to forgive sins.

III. Jesus also said that the miracles He did authenticated who He was and confirmed what He said.

> *But I have greater witness than that of John: for the works which the Father hath given me to finish, the same works that I do, bear witness of me, that the Father hath sent me.*

John 5:36

   A. If Jesus needed the witness of the miracles He performed to validate His authority, then how can we possibly do less?

   B. It is the height of arrogance to think that we can use words alone to persuade people, when Jesus had to have signs and miracles to confirm His words.

IV. Some folks say, "We don't need miracles today; we have the Word of God." Yet that's not what the Bible teaches.

> *And these signs shall follow them that believe; In my name shall they cast out devils; they shall speak with new tongues; They shall take up serpents; and if they drink any deadly thing, it shall not hurt them; they shall lay hands on the sick, and they shall recover. So then after the Lord had spoken unto them, he was received up into heaven, and sat on the right hand of God. And they went forth, and preached every where, the Lord working with them, and confirming the word with signs following.*

Mark 16:17-20

   A. What people say must always be checked against God's Word.

   B. In God's system, when His Word is truly preached, there will be signs and wonders to confirm that it is the truth.

V. If all we preach are things having spiritual, eternal value and the forgiveness of sins, then all we'll see is people being born again.

   A. But if we preach and teach the whole counsel of God, He will confirm it with signs, wonders, and miracles.

   B. If both Jesus and the early believers needed miracles, signs, and wonders to confirm the message from God that they preached, then we do too!

Miracles Confirm God's Word
Lesson 1 – Teacher's Guide

1. Healing is part of Christ's Atonement. If He suffered and took stripes on His back for our physical healing, then it's not insignificant. If He thought enough of healing to purchase it for us, then we ought to think enough of it to receive. God the Father caused His Son to bear all of our sins and all of our sicknesses on the cross. Jesus took our diseases just as much as He took our sins.

2. The Lord used healing like a bell to get people's attention and to prove that He did have power on earth to forgive sins (Mark 2:5-9). Jesus was saying that it's easier to say "Your sins are forgiven" than "Rise up and walk" because they would immediately be able to tell if He had the power or not by whether this man rose up and walked. If you can do the greater work, then certainly you can do the lesser. If you can jump fifteen feet, then certainly you can jump two feet. Jesus made it very clear that the reason He healed this man was so people would know that also had power on earth to forgive sins (Mark 2:10-12).

3. Jesus also said that the miracles He did authenticated who He was and confirmed what He said (John 5:36). If Jesus needed the witness of the miracles He performed to validate His authority, then how can we possibly do less? It is the height of arrogance to think that we can use words alone to persuade people, when Jesus had to have signs and miracles to confirm His words.

1. A. If Christ suffered and took stripes on His back for our physical healing, then it's not what? (Insignificant)
    B. Jesus took our _____ just as much as He took our sins. (Diseases)
2. A. Read Mark 2:5-9. Jesus used healing like a bell to prove what? (That He had power on earth to forgive sins)
    B. Why did Jesus say that it's easier to say "Your sins are forgiven" than "Rise up and walk"? (Because they would immediately be able to tell if He had the power or not by whether this man rose up and walked)
    C. Read Mark 2:10-12. What did Jesus make very clear? (That the reason He healed this man was so people would know that He also had power on earth to forgive sins.
3. A. Read John 5:36. What authenticated who Jesus was and confirmed what He said? (The miracles He did)
    B. Jesus had to have signs and miracles confirm His words, should we use words alone to persuade? (No)

4. Some folks say, "We don't need miracles today; we have the Word of God." Yet that's not what the Bible teaches (Mark 16:17-20). What people say must always be checked against God's Word. In God's system, when His Word is truly preached, there will be signs and wonders to confirm that it is the truth.

5. If all we preach are things having spiritual, eternal value and the forgiveness of sins, then all we'll see is people being born again. But if we preach and teach the whole counsel of God, He will confirm it with signs, wonders, and miracles. If both Jesus and the early believers needed miracles, signs, and wonders to confirm the message from God that they preached, then we do too!

4. A. Read Mark 16:17-20. Does the Bible teach that miracles are not needed today? (No)
   B. When God's Word is preached, there will be _____ and _____ to confirm that it is the truth. (Signs, wonders)
5. A. If all we preach are things having spiritual, eternal value and the forgiveness of sins, then all we'll see is what? (People being born again)
   B. If we preach and teach the whole counsel of God, He will confirm it with what? (Signs, wonders, and miracles)
   C. If both Jesus and the early believers needed miracles, signs, and wonders to confirm the message from God that they preached, then what? (We do too!)

Miracles Confirm God's Word
Lesson 1 – Discipleship Questions

1. Read Mark 2:5-9. What did Jesus see before He spoke?

2. What did the scribes reason in their hearts?

3. Jesus asked them what was easier, to say **"Thy sins be forgiven thee"** or what?

4. According to Mark 2:10-12, what did Jesus do to show that He had power on earth to forgive sins?

5. What did the sick of the palsy do immediately?

6. Read John 5:36. What bore witness of Jesus that the Father had sent Him?

7. According to Mark 16:17-20, what shall follow them that believe?

8. What shall believers do in Jesus' name?

   A. They shall cast out devils.

   B. They shall speak with new tongues.

   C. They shall take up serpents.

   D. If they drink any deadly thing, it shall not hurt them.

   E. They shall lay hands on the sick, and they shall recover.

   F. All of the above.

   G. None of the above.

9. They went forth and preached everywhere, the Lord working with them and confirming the Word with _____ following.

10. Read Hebrews 2:3-4. What first began to be spoken by the Lord?

11. What did God bear them witness with?

Miracles Confirm God's Word
Lesson 1 – Answer Key

1. Their faith.

2. **"Why doth this man thus speak blasphemies? who can forgive sins but God only?"**

3. **"Arise, and take up thy bed, and walk."**

4. He told the sick of the palsy to arise, take up his bed, and go his way into his house.

5. He arose, took up his bed, and went forth before them all.

6. The works that the Father gave Him to finish, the same works that Jesus did.

7. These signs.

8. F. All of the above.

9. Signs.

10. So great salvation.

11. Signs, wonders, divers (various) miracles, and gifts of the Holy Ghost.

Miracles Confirm God's Word
Lesson 1 – Scriptures

Mark 2:5-12
When Jesus saw their faith, he said unto the sick of the palsy, Son, thy sins be forgiven thee. [6] But there were certain of the scribes sitting there, and reasoning in their hearts, [7] Why doth this man thus speak blasphemies? who can forgive sins but God only? [8] And immediately when Jesus perceived in his spirit that they so reasoned within themselves, he said unto them, Why reason ye these things in your hearts? [9] Whether is it easier to say to the sick of the palsy, Thy sins be forgiven thee; or to say, Arise, and take up thy bed, and walk? [10] But that ye may know that the Son of man hath power on earth to forgive sins, (he saith to the sick of the palsy,) [11] I say unto thee, Arise, and take up thy bed, and go thy way into thine house. [12] And immediately he arose, took up the bed, and went forth before them all; insomuch that they were all amazed, and glorified God, saying, We never saw it on this fashion.

John 5:36
But I have greater witness than that of John: for the works which the Father hath given me to finish, the same works that I do, bear witness of me, that the Father hath sent me.

Mark 16:17-20
And these signs shall follow them that believe; In my name shall they cast out devils; they shall speak with new tongues; [18] They shall take up serpents; and if they drink any deadly thing, it shall not hurt them; they shall lay hands on the sick, and they shall recover. [19] So then after the Lord had spoken unto them, he was received up into heaven, and sat on the right hand of God. [20] And they went forth, and preached every where, the Lord working with them, and confirming the word with signs following. Amen.

Hebrews 2:3-4
How shall we escape, if we neglect so great salvation; which at the first began to be spoken by the Lord, and was confirmed unto us by them that heard him; [4] God also bearing them witness, both with signs and wonders, and with divers miracles, and gifts of the Holy Ghost, according to his own will?

Part of His Atonement
Lesson 2

If the body of Christ was fully presenting the Gospel—the whole counsel of God—we'd be making a much greater impact on the world today. God not only wants to forgive us of our sins; He also loves us dearly and desires to heal our bodies, bless us financially, and deliver us from discouragement and depression. Think about that!

One of the main reasons the modern-day church has been rendered so ineffective and irrelevant in many people's eyes is that it has only preached that God is for the life hereafter. It's made having a relationship with the Lord a heaven-and-hell issue, and it hasn't preached that He loves us right now. The church hasn't taught that God wants to give us dynamic and absolutely victorious lives at this present time. It hasn't ministered healing, prosperity, or deliverance.

Some statistics I've seen have said that as much as 85 percent of the population in the United States believes that there is a God, yet only 10 to 15 percent actually attend church on a regular basis. Out of all these people who say they believe in God, would there be enough evidence to convict them if they were accused of being Christians? There is a huge gap between the people who say that God exists and those who enjoy a vibrant relationship with Him.

Why is that? Why do so many people, who know God exists, not go on to obtain this intimate relationship with Him and make Him the center of their lives? Although there are probably several factors, one of the most obvious is that the church has presented relationship with God as a heaven-and-hell issue. It has preached, "Just get your sins forgiven so you won't go to hell."

Truly Relevant

Even though that's true—there is a heaven to gain and a hell to lose and you must have your sins forgiven to escape hell—most people are living in such a hell in this life that they aren't concerned with a hell in the afterlife. They're in strife, enduring divorce, suffering from sickness, and terrified of what's happening out in the world. They haven't heard or seen that the Lord deals with these issues in *this* life. They just think that God is for the hereafter, and they're shortsighted. They should be thinking about eternity, but they aren't because they're so occupied with trying to struggle through all of the terrible things they're facing right now. They know God exists, but they put Him off until just before they die, because they don't see His relevance to their present, everyday lives.

However, if the church were to represent the Lord more accurately by saying "God will heal you and keep you healthy. He'll deliver you from the depression, despair, and strife that you find yourself in. God will prosper you in a way that you could never accomplish just through your own effort," if we presented that God is not only for the forgiveness of sins but for all these other areas, too, then people would see that He is truly relevant to their daily lives.

If a sick person came to one of many "churches" today (I use that term loosely), the people there would ask, "Why are you coming to us? Go to the doctor." If a poor person came, they'd say, "Well, have you checked with the government agencies and tried welfare yet?" If someone came who was discouraged, depressed, and under some kind of demonic oppression, they'd refer that person to a psychiatrist or other professional who would prescribe them some kind of a drug. But that's not the attitude God wants us to have. We, as the church, should be meeting the needs of people! Our lack of doing so is one reason many folks see the church as irrelevant to their present lives. They don't doubt God's existence; they just don't see why they need Him until they get ready to die. That's wrong!

Our example—Jesus—emphasized healing. I am simply following Him. Everywhere Jesus went, He healed people. God the Father used these miracles to show people that Jesus had power on earth to forgive sins. This confirmed Christ's message and proved the validity of His words. Since that's the way God did it with Jesus, I'm following a good precedent.

A terrible signal is sent both to unbelievers and Christians when misled preachers say things like, "God doesn't care about the healing of your body" or "He's putting sickness on you to teach you a lesson." That's absolutely untrue!

Not Just an "Add-on"

My dad died just about a month after I turned twelve. He was in a coma for a period of time before that. So, as an eleven-year-old, I went through this grueling experience of my father being on the verge of death for months. The church that I grew up in said that the Lord put that sickness on him and that it was God's will that he died. I didn't rebel because of that, but deep down in my heart, something about that just didn't sit right.

However, I can give you examples of many other people that went through similar experiences who did rebel. One fellow is very famous. As a young boy, he knew that God existed, and he even sought Him. But his sister died, and the religious people told him that God did it. He turned completely away from the Lord and today is a very outspoken atheist. He cites this example in his life and says, "You can't tell me that if there is a God, He would put sickness on people!" This misrepresentation of God turns a lot of folks away from the Lord and embitters them against Him.

It's only the grace of God that kept me from rebelling when I was told, "God is the one who killed your dad." Many others haven't responded as well.

Countless people know God exists, but for whatever reason, they just don't want anything to do with Him, or they don't see His relevance to their everyday lives. That's why healing needs to be emphasized. We need to speak the truth of the whole counsel of God. Although healing shouldn't be elevated above forgiveness of sins, neither should it be diminished below it. Jesus provided healing for us at the same time as He provided forgiveness for our sins.

Healing isn't just an "add-on" or an "added benefit" that only happens sometimes; it's an essential part of what Christ came to do. Jesus died for the physical healing of our bodies just the same as He died for our forgiveness of sins. The Lord purchased healing for us just as He purchased forgiveness. It's all part of His Atonement.

A Done Deal

This truth about healing is not yet widely understood and believed across the body of Christ today, which explains why so few people are walking in it. Most Christians think that God could certainly heal if He wanted to, but they don't see that He has already redeemed man from sickness and disease. They view healing as something the Lord can do, but they don't know for sure that it is His will.

If you recognize that healing is part of the Atonement (which took place 2,000 years ago), then you'll comprehend that the Lord has already healed you. He's already purchased that blessing. That power has already been generated. Healing is a done deal and is available to you now, exactly the same as forgiveness of sins.

Part of His Atonement
Lesson 2 – Outline

I. If the body of Christ was fully presenting the Gospel—the whole counsel of God—we'd be making a much greater impact on the world today.

    A. God not only wants to forgive us of our sins; He also loves us dearly and desires to heal our bodies, bless us financially, and deliver us from discouragement and depression.

    B. Think about that!

II. One of the main reasons the modern-day church has been rendered so ineffective and irrelevant in many people's eyes is that it has only preached that God is for the life hereafter.

    A. It's made having a relationship with the Lord a heaven-and-hell issue, and it hasn't preached that He loves us right now.

    B. It has preached, "Just get your sins forgiven so you won't go to hell."

    C. However, if the church were to represent the Lord more accurately by saying "God will heal you and keep you healthy. He'll deliver you from the depression, despair, and strife that you find yourself in. God will prosper you in a way that you could never accomplish just through your own effort," if we presented that God is not only for the forgiveness of sins but for all these other areas, too, then people would see that He is truly relevant to their daily lives.

III. We need to speak the truth of the whole counsel of God.

    A. Although healing shouldn't be elevated above forgiveness of sins, neither should it be diminished below it.

    B. Jesus provided healing for us at the same time as He provided forgiveness for our sins.

    C. Healing isn't just an "add-on" or an "added benefit" that only happens sometimes; it's an essential part of what Christ came to do.

    D. The Lord purchased healing for us just as He purchased forgiveness. It's all part of His Atonement.

IV. This truth about healing is not yet widely understood and believed across the body of Christ today, which explains why so few people are walking in it.

    A. Most Christians think that God could certainly heal if He wanted to, but they don't see that He has already redeemed man from sickness and disease.

    B. They view healing as something the Lord can do, but they don't know for sure that it is His will.

    C. Healing is a done deal and is available to you now, exactly the same as forgiveness of sins.

Part of His Atonement
Lesson 2 – Teacher's Guide

1. If the body of Christ was fully presenting the Gospel—the whole counsel of God—we'd be making a much greater impact on the world today. God not only wants to forgive us of our sins; He also loves us dearly and desires to heal our bodies, bless us financially, and deliver us from discouragement and depression. We need to think about that!

2. One of the main reasons the modern-day church has been rendered so ineffective and irrelevant in many people's eyes is it has only preached that God is for the life hereafter. It's made having a relationship with the Lord a heaven-and-hell issue, and it hasn't preached that He loves us right now. It has preached, "Just get your sins forgiven so you won't go to hell."

   However, if the church were to represent the Lord more accurately by saying "God will heal you and keep you healthy. He'll deliver you from the depression, despair, and strife that you find yourself in. God will prosper you in a way that you could never accomplish just through your own effort," if we presented that God is not only for the forgiveness of sins but for all these other areas, too, then people would see that He is truly relevant to their daily lives.

3. We need to speak the truth of the whole counsel of God. Although healing shouldn't be elevated above forgiveness of sins, neither should it be diminished below it. Jesus provided healing for us at the same time as He provided forgiveness for our sins. Healing isn't just an "add-on" or an "added benefit" that only happens sometimes; it's an essential part of what Christ came to do. The Lord purchased healing for us just as He purchased forgiveness. It's all part of His Atonement.

1. A. If the body of Christ was fully presenting the Gospel—the whole counsel of God—what would we be making? (A much greater impact on the world today)
   B. What does God desire to do besides forgive our sins? (Heal our bodies, bless us financially, and deliver us from discouragement and depression)
2. A. What is one of the main reasons the modern-day church has been rendered so ineffective and irrelevant in many people's eyes? (It has only preached that God is for the life hereafter)
   B. If the church were to represent the Lord more accurately, what would people see? (That God is truly relevant to their daily lives)
3. A. What do we need to speak? (The truth of the whole counsel of God)
   B. Is healing just an "add-on" or an "added benefit"? (No)
   C. What is it part of? (His Atonement)

4. This truth about healing is not yet widely understood and believed across the body of Christ today, which explains why so few people are walking in it. Most of us as Christians think that God could certainly heal if He wanted to, but we don't see that He has already redeemed us from sickness and disease. We view healing as something the Lord can do, but we don't know for sure that it is His will. Healing is a done deal and is available to us now, exactly the same as forgiveness of sins.

4. A. Why are so few people are walking in healing? (Because the truth about healing is not widely understood and believed across the body of Christ today)
    B. Even though most of us as Christians think that God could certainly heal if He wanted to, what don't we see? (That He has already redeemed us from sickness and disease)

Part of His Atonement
Lesson 2 – Discipleship Questions

1. According to the opening paragraphs of **Lesson 2**, what is there between the people who say that God exists and those who enjoy a vibrant relationship with Him?

2. What is one of the most obvious factors for why people, who know God exists, don't go on to obtain an intimate relationship with Him?

   A. They're too busy.

   B. They'd rather watch "As the Stomach Turns" on television.

   C. The church has presented having a relationship with God as a heaven-and-hell issue.

   D. They're not sure it's God's will.

   E. All of the above.

3. According to the section titled "Truly Relevant," why aren't unsaved people concerned with a hell in the afterlife?

4. What haven't they heard or seen?

5. What kind of signal is sent both to unbelievers and Christians when misled preachers say things like, "God doesn't care about the healing of your body" or "He's putting sickness on you to teach you a lesson"?

6. In the section titled "Not Just an 'Add-on,'" when my dad died, what did the church tell me?

7. What kind of representation of God is this?

8. What does this do to people?

9. According the section titled, "A Done Deal," most Christians view healing as something the Lord can do, but they don't know for sure _____.

10. What blessing has the Lord already purchased?

Part of His Atonement
Lesson 2 – Answer Key

1. A huge gap.

2. C. The church has presented having a relationship with God as a heaven-and-hell issue.

3. Because they are living in such a hell in this life that they aren't concerned with a hell in the afterlife.

4. That the Lord deals with these issues in this life.

5. A terrible signal.

6. That the Lord put that sickness on his father and that it was His will that his father died.

7. A misrepresentation.

8. It turns people away from the Lord and embitters them against Him.

9. That it is His will.

10. The blessing of healing.

Sozo!
Lesson 3

[Jesus] gave himself for our sins, that he might deliver us from this present evil world, according to the will of God and our Father.

Galatians 1:4, brackets mine

Jesus gave Himself for our sins that He might deliver us from *this present* evil world—not just the evil world to come.

Many people think that what Jesus produced through His death, burial, and resurrection only affects the spiritual, eternal realm. Because of this, they come up with song lyrics referring to when all of us get to heaven, what a day it will be. Of course it will be glorious in heaven, but Jesus also came to deliver us from this present evil world. We're not just saved from hell, our sins, and future punishment—Jesus also came to deliver, protect, and provide for us in this physical world right now.

An All-Encompassing Word

The Greek word *sozo* was used over a hundred times in the New Testament. It's an all-encompassing word for salvation, often rendered "save" or "saved." However, a closer look at how this important word was translated makes it very clear that our salvation includes much more than just forgiveness of sins.

Sozo was translated "save" thirty-eight times in reference to the forgiveness of sins. Some examples include:

She shall bring forth a son, and thou shalt call his name JESUS: for he shall save [sozo] his people from their sins.

Matthew 1:21, brackets mine

For after that in the wisdom of God the world by wisdom knew not God, it pleased God by the foolishness of preaching to save [sozo] them that believe.

1 Corinthians 1:21, brackets mine

Wherefore he is able also to save [sozo] them to the uttermost that come unto God by him, seeing he ever liveth to make intercession for them.

Hebrews 7:25, brackets mine

Forgiven, Healed, and Delivered

Sozo was translated another fifty-three times as "saved" (past tense) in reference to forgiveness of sins. However, there were also times where this exact same Greek word was translated as "healed."

> *[Jairus] besought [Jesus] greatly, saying, My little daughter lieth at the point of death: I pray thee, come and lay thy hands on her, that she may be healed [sozo]; and she shall live.*
>
> ### Mark 5:23, brackets mine

This word **"healed"** is referring to physical healing. As the story unfolds, Jairus' daughter actually died, and Jesus raised her from the dead (Mark 5:35-43). So, in this instance, *sozo*—**"healed"**—refers to physical healing, even physical resurrection from the dead.

This same word that's used for both forgiveness of sins and physical healing also applies to deliverance from demons.

> *They also which saw it told them by what means he that was possessed of the devils was healed [sozo].*
>
> ### Luke 8:36, brackets mine

Commonly called the Gadarene demoniac, nobody could hold this man. In fact, he often broke the very chains he was bound by (Luke 8:26-29). Sometimes deliverance from demons is necessary for someone to receive healing. This is included in this word *sozo*.

> *The same heard Paul speak: who stedfastly beholding him, and perceiving that he had faith to be healed [sozo].*
>
> ### Acts 14:9, brackets mine

Paul beheld this crippled man and perceived that he had faith to be healed [*sozo*], and he was (Acts 14:8-10).

Christ's Saving Power

James 5:15 is a classic example of Christ's saving power manifesting in our lives both as healing and forgiveness of sins:

> *And the prayer of faith shall save [sozo] the sick, and the Lord shall raise him up; and if he have committed sins, they shall be forgiven him.*
>
> ### Brackets mine

In another instance, Jesus knew the thoughts of the scribes and Pharisees, so He asked,

Is it lawful on the sabbath days to do good, or to do evil? to save [sozo] life, or to destroy it?

Luke 6:9, brackets mine

When they didn't answer, Jesus turned and healed the man with the withered right hand (Luke 6:8-11). He wasn't just talking about forgiveness of sins; He meant the healing of the body.

Made Whole

This same word—*sozo*—was also translated "made whole" in reference to healing. Consider the example of the woman with an issue of blood:

But Jesus turned him about, and when he saw her, he said, Daughter, be of good comfort; thy faith hath made thee whole [sozo]. And the woman was made whole [sozo] from that hour.

Matthew 9:22, brackets mine

In faith, she touched the hem of Jesus' garment and received healing. She was *sozo*—made whole. This is that same Greek word that is synonymous with forgiveness of sins. Here, again, it's applied to being healed physically. This same instance, recorded in the book of Mark, reveals that right before she reached out to Him, she said,

If I may touch but his clothes, I shall be whole [sozo].

Mark 5:28, brackets mine

Sozo was translated "made whole" or "be whole" eleven times in Scripture. It's obvious from God's Word that salvation isn't limited only to the forgiveness of sins.

And whithersoever he entered, into villages, or cities, or country, they laid the sick in the streets, and besought him that they might touch if it were but the border of his garment: and as many as touched him were made whole [sozo].

Mark 6:56, brackets mine

When Jesus heard the news that Jairus' daughter had died, He answered him, saying,

Fear not: believe only, and she shall be made whole [sozo].

Luke 8:50, brackets mine

The Lord was referring to the healing of her physical body.

Abundantly Supplied

Salvation doesn't only mean forgiveness of sins, but it also includes healing, deliverance, and financial prosperity too. Many in the modern church have interpreted salvation only to be forgiveness of sins, but that's a misrepresentation of what the Lord did. Forgiveness of our sins is certainly the centerpiece, and I'm not minimizing it at all. However, at the same time Christ died to purchase our redemption from sin, He also freed us from sickness, disease, depression, and poverty.

Second Corinthians 8:9 is very clear concerning the Atonement and our redemption from poverty:

> *For ye know the grace of our Lord Jesus Christ, that, though he was rich, yet for your sakes he became poor, that ye through his poverty might be rich.*

Jesus became poor so that we through His poverty might be made rich—abundantly supplied. Through Christ's death, burial, and resurrection, God has provided everything we need in this life and in the life to come—forgiveness of sins, healing for our bodies, along with deliverance and prosperity. Isn't God good!

Sozo!
Lesson 3 – Outline

I. Jesus gave Himself for our sins that He might deliver us from *this present* evil world—not just the evil world to come:

> *[Jesus] gave himself for our sins, that he might deliver us from this present evil world, according to the will of God and our Father.*
>
> ### Galatians 1:4, brackets mine

  A. We're not just saved from hell, our sins, and future punishment—Jesus also came to deliver, protect, and provide for us in this physical world right now.

II. The Greek word *sozo* was used over a hundred times in the New Testament.

  A. It's an all-encompassing word for salvation, often rendered "save" or "saved."

  B. However, a closer look at how this important word was translated makes it very clear that our salvation includes much more than just forgiveness of sins.

   i. *Sozo* was translated "save" thirty-eight times in reference to the forgiveness of sins (e.g., Matt. 1:21, 1 Cor. 1:21, and Heb. 7:25,).

   ii. It was translated another fifty-three times as "saved" (past tense) in reference to forgiveness of sins.

   iii. There were also times where this exact same Greek word was translated as "healed" (Mark 5:23 and Acts 14:8-10).

   iv. This same word that's used for both forgiveness of sins and physical healing also applies to deliverance from demons (Luke 8:36).

   v. James 5:15 is a classic example of Christ's saving power manifesting in our lives both as healing and forgiveness of sins.

   vi. This same word was also translated "made whole" in reference to healing (Matt. 9:22, Mark 6:56, and Luke 8:50).

   vii. *Sozo* was translated "made whole" or "be whole" eleven times in Scripture (e.g., Mark 5:28)

  C. It's obvious from God's Word that salvation isn't limited only to the forgiveness of sins.

III. Many in the modern church have interpreted salvation only to be forgiveness of sins, but that's a misrepresentation of what the Lord did.

  A. Forgiveness of our sins is certainly the centerpiece, and I am not minimizing it at all.

  B. However, at the same time Christ died to purchase our redemption from sin, He also freed us from sickness, disease, depression, and poverty.

IV. Second Corinthians 8:9 is very clear concerning the Atonement and our redemption from poverty:

For ye know the grace of our Lord Jesus Christ, that, though he was rich, yet for your sakes he became poor, that ye through his poverty might be rich.

A. Through Christ's death, burial, and resurrection, God has provided everything we need in this life and in the life to come—forgiveness of sins, healing for our bodies, along with deliverance and prosperity. Isn't God good!

Sozo!
Lesson 3 – Teacher's Guide

1. Jesus gave Himself for our sins that He might deliver us from *this present* evil world—not just the evil world to come (Gal. 1:4) We're not just saved from hell, our sins, and future punishment—Jesus also came to deliver, protect, and provide for us in this physical world right now.

2. The Greek word *sozo* was used over a hundred times in the New Testament. It's an all-encompassing word for salvation, often rendered "save" or "saved." However, a closer look at how this important word was translated makes it very clear that our salvation includes much more than just forgiveness of sins.

   Sozo was translated "save" thirty-eight times in reference to the forgiveness of sins (e.g., Matt. 1:21, 1 Cor. 1:21, and Heb. 7:25). It was translated another fifty-three times as "saved" (past tense) in reference to forgiveness of sins. There were also times where this exact same Greek word was translated as "healed" (Mark 5:23 and Acts 14:8-10). This same word that's used for both forgiveness of sins and physical healing also applies to deliverance from demons (Luke 8:36). James 5:15 is a classic example of Christ's saving power manifesting in our lives both as healing and forgiveness of sins. This same word was also translated "made whole" in reference to healing (Matt. 9:22, Mark 6:56, and Luke 8:50). *Sozo* was translated "made whole" or "be whole" eleven times in Scripture e.g., Mark 5:28). It's obvious from God's Word that salvation isn't limited only to the forgiveness of sins.

3. Many in the modern church have interpreted salvation only to be forgiveness of sins, but that's a misrepresentation of what the Lord did. Forgiveness of our sins is certainly the centerpiece, and I am not minimizing it at all. However, at the same time Christ died to purchase our redemption from sin, He also freed us from sickness, disease, depression, and poverty.

1. A. Read Galatians 1:4. What did Jesus deliver us from? (This present evil world)
   B. Are we saved only from hell, our sins, and future punishment? (No)
2. A. The Greek word translated for "save" and "saved" makes it very clear that what? (Our salvation includes much more than just forgiveness of sins)
   B. Read Matthew 1:21, 9:22; Mark 5:23, 28, 6:56; Luke 8:36, 50; Acts 14:8-10; 1 Corinthians 1:21; Hebrews 7:25; and James 5:15. It's obvious from God's Word that salvation isn't limited only to what? (The forgiveness of sins)
   C. What else does it include? (Healing)
3. A. What is a misrepresentation of what the Lord did? (Interpreting salvation as only the forgiveness of sins)
   B. At the same time Christ died to purchase our redemption from sin, He also freed us from what? (Sickness, disease, depression, and poverty)

4.   Second Corinthians 8:9 is very clear concerning the Atonement and our redemption from poverty. Through Christ's death, burial, and resurrection, God has provided everything we need in this life and in the life to come—forgiveness of sins, healing of our bodies, along with deliverance and prosperity. Isn't God good!

4.   A. Read 2 Corinthians 8:9. How is this passage clear concerning the Atonement and our redemption from poverty? (Jesus, for our sakes, became poor so that we through His poverty might be rich)
       B. What has God provided through the death, burial, and resurrection of Christ? (Everything we need in this life and in the life to come—forgiveness of sins, healing of our bodies, along with deliverance and prosperity)

Sozo!
Lesson 3 – Discipleship Questions

1. Read Galatians 1:4. In order to deliver us from this present evil world, what did He (Jesus) give Himself for?

2. According to Matthew 1:21, why was the Son to be called Jesus?

3. Read 1 Corinthians 1:21. It pleased God by the _____ of preaching to save them that believe.

4. Read Hebrews 7:25. Because He (Jesus) ever lives to make intercession for people, what is He able to do?

5. According to Mark 5:23, Jairus begged Jesus, saying, **"I pray thee, come and lay thy hands on her, that she may be healed; and she _____ live."**

6. Read Mark 5:35-43. Once Jesus reached Jairus' house, He told the mourners that the child was not dead but _____.

7. What is the interpretation of "Talitha cumi"?

8. Who was greatly astonished when she arose?

9. According to Luke 8:36, he that was possessed of the devils was _____.

    A. Delivered.

    B. Crazy.

    C. Healed.

    D. All of the above.

10. Read Luke 8:26-29. What did Jesus command the unclean spirit to do?

11. Read Acts 14:8-10. What did Paul perceive that the crippled man had?

12. What happened after Paul said to the crippled man, **"Stand upright on thy feet"?**

13. According to James 5:15, what shall save the sick?

14. Read Luke 6:8-11. When the man with the withered hand stretched forth his hand, it was _____ whole as the other.

15. When Jesus healed the man with the withered hand, what were the scribes and Pharisees filled with?

16. According to Matthew 9:22, Jesus called the woman who was made whole _____.

17. Read Mark 5:28. Who said that if she touched but his clothes, she would be whole?

18.   According to Mark 6:56, who were made whole?

19.   Read Luke 8:50. In order for Jairus' daughter to be made whole, what did Jesus say?

20.   According to 2 Corinthians 8:9, "For ye know the _____ of our Lord Jesus Christ, that, though he was rich, yet for your sakes he became poor, that ye through his poverty might be rich."

Sozo!
Lesson 3 – Answer Key

1.   Our sins.

2.   Because He would save His people from their sins.

3.   Foolishness.

4.   Save them to the uttermost.

5.   **"Shall."**

6.   Sleeping.

7.   **"Damsel, I say unto thee, arise."**

8.   Peter, James, John, Jairus, and Jairus' wife.

9.   C. Healed.

10.   Come out of the man.

11.   Faith to be healed.

12.   The crippled man leaped and walked.

13.   The prayer of faith.

14.   Restored.

15.   Madness.

16.   Daughter.

17.   The woman with the issue of blood.

18.   As many as touched Him (Jesus).

19.   **"Fear not: believe only."**

20.   Grace.

Sozo!
Lesson 3 – Scriptures

Galatians 1:4
Who gave himself for our sins, that he might deliver us from this present evil world, according to the will of God and our Father.

Matthew 1:21
And she shall bring forth a son, and thou shalt call his name JESUS: for he shall save his people from their sins.

1 Corinthians 1:21
For after that in the wisdom of God the world by wisdom knew not God, it pleased God by the foolishness of preaching to save them that believe.

Hebrews 7:25
Wherefore he is able also to save them to the uttermost that come unto God by him, seeing he ever liveth to make intercession for them.

Mark 5:23
And besought him greatly, saying, My little daughter lieth at the point of death: I pray thee, come and lay thy hands on her, that she may be healed; and she shall live.

Mark 5:35-43
While he yet spake, there came from the ruler of the synagogue's house certain which said, Thy daughter is dead: why troublest thou the Master any further? [36] As soon as Jesus heard the word that was spoken, he saith unto the ruler of the synagogue, Be not afraid, only believe. [37] And he suffered no man to follow him, save Peter, and James, and John the brother of James. [38] And he cometh to the house of the ruler of the synagogue, and seeth the tumult, and them that wept and wailed greatly. [39] And when he was come in, he saith unto them, Why make ye this ado, and weep? the damsel is not dead, but sleepeth. [40] And they laughed him to scorn. But when he had put them all out, he taketh the father and the mother of the damsel, and them that were with him, and entereth in where the damsel was lying. [41] And he took the damsel by the hand, and said unto her, Talitha cumi; which is, being interpreted, Damsel, I say unto thee, arise. [42] And straightway the damsel arose, and walked; for she was of the age of twelve years. And they were astonished with a great astonishment. [43] And he charged them straitly that no man should know it; and commanded that something should be given her to eat.

Luke 8:36

They also which saw it told them by what means he that was possessed of the devils was healed.

Luke 8:26-29

And they arrived at the country of the Gadarenes, which is over against Galilee. [27] And when he went forth to land, there met him out of the city a certain man, which had devils long time, and ware no clothes, neither abode in any house, but in the tombs. [28] When he saw Jesus, he cried out, and fell down before him, and with a loud voice said, What have I to do with thee, Jesus, thou Son of God most high? I beseech thee, torment me not. [29] (For he had commanded the unclean spirit to come out of the man. For oftentimes it had caught him: and he was kept bound with chains and in fetters; and he brake the bands, and was driven of the devil into the wilderness.)

Acts 14:8-10

And there sat a certain man at Lystra, impotent in his feet, being a cripple from his mother's womb, who never had walked: [9] The same heard Paul speak: who sted-fastly beholding him, and perceiving that he had faith to be healed, [10] Said with a loud voice, Stand upright on thy feet. And he leaped and walked.

James 5:15

And the prayer of faith shall save the sick, and the Lord shall raise him up; and if he have committed sins, they shall be forgiven him.

Luke 6:8-11

But he knew their thoughts, and said to the man which had the withered hand, Rise up, and stand forth in the midst. And he arose and stood forth. [9] Then said Jesus unto them, I will ask you one thing; Is it lawful on the sabbath days to do good, or to do evil? to save life, or to destroy it? [10] And looking round about upon them all, he said unto the man, Stretch forth thy hand. And he did so: and his hand was restored whole as the other. [11] And they were filled with madness; and communed one with another what they might do to Jesus.

Matthew 9:22

But Jesus turned him about, and when he saw her, he said, Daughter, be of good comfort; thy faith hath made thee whole. And the woman was made whole from that hour.

Mark 5:28

For she said, If I may touch but his clothes, I shall be whole.

Mark 6:56

And whithersoever he entered, into villages, or cities, or country, they laid the sick in the streets, and besought him that they might touch if it were but the border of his garment: and as many as touched him were made whole.

Luke 8:50

But when Jesus heard it, he answered him, saying, Fear not: believe only, and she shall be made whole.

2 Corinthians 8:9

For ye know the grace of our Lord Jesus Christ, that, though he was rich, yet for your sakes he became poor, that ye through his poverty might be rich.

The Full Package
Lesson 4

Jesus didn't just die for our sins, and then healing was something He could do if He wanted to. No! Christ paid for the healing of our bodies as completely as He paid for the forgiveness of our sins. He purchased it all at once in His Atonement. This may be different than what much of the modern-day church presents, but scriptures bear it out.

Consider Psalm 103, which says,

Bless the LORD, O my soul: and all that is within me, bless his holy name. Bless the LORD, O my soul, and forget not all his benefits: Who forgiveth all thine iniquities; who healeth all thy diseases.

Psalm 103:1-3

Verse 2 specifically tells us not to forget ALL of His benefits. The Lord forgives all of our iniquities and heals all of our diseases (verse 3). In the New Testament, 1 Peter 2 agrees, saying,

Who his own self bare our sins in his own body on the tree, that we, being dead to sins, should live unto righteousness: by whose stripes ye were healed.

1 Peter 2:24

Both Psalm 103:3 and 1 Peter 2:24 mention the salvation benefits of forgiveness of sins and physical healing together in the same verse. Scripture does not separate what Jesus did in the Atonement; only people do that. As far as God is concerned, salvation is a package deal.

Fringe Benefits?

It's people—not God—who have said, "Let's not talk about healing, deliverance, or prosperity; let's just focus on forgiveness of sins. That's the part everyone can agree on. That's the main part of the Atonement. All these others are just fringe benefits." Fringe benefits? I believe that's offensive to God!

Suppose I had done all the things for you that Jesus did for us—I died for your sins to be forgiven, borne stripes on my body to produce healing for you, been separated from God my Father so that you would never have to be separated, became poor so that you might be made rich. Then you said to me, "Thank you for what you did, but I'm only going to take one-fourth of it. Forgiveness of sins is the most important, and that's what I really want to focus on. So I'm not going to take advantage of the healing for my body, the deliverance from demonic oppression, or the financial blessing. I just don't want those things. You did more than enough for me, so I'm going to humble myself and only take one-fourth of what you did." It sure wouldn't bless me for you to break it up in pieces.

That wouldn't please me. It would make me feel like saying, "What was the point in me suffering for these other things if you aren't going to take advantage of them?"

God so loved the world that He gave His only begotten Son. It wasn't only so that people wouldn't go to hell; Jesus saved us from sin, sickness, disease, and poverty. He gave Himself as the perfect atoning sacrifice that He might deliver us from this present evil world (Gal. 1:4).

It wouldn't please me for you to only take advantage of a small portion of everything I had suffered, bled, died, and resurrected to provide for you. If I were God, I'm sure that I'd still love you, but I wouldn't be pleased. I'm not saying God is angry with people, but I'm sure He finds it disappointing that He provided all of this for us, and so many of us simply aren't taking advantage of it.

Basically, Christianity has preached, "Forgiveness of sins is all that Jesus atoned for. Of course, since God is God, He could heal if He wants to, but that's like icing on the cake. That's extra. It isn't part of the basic package." No, God's Word clearly reveals that healing is an integral part of the salvation package.

Actively Fight Against

Healing is in the Atonement just as much as forgiveness of sins! Once you get this revelation firmly established in your heart, it'll cause you to reject this false teaching that says, "God is the one who causes people to die. He puts sickness on you to humble you for some redemptive purpose and to perfect you through all this suffering." No! Jesus died for the forgiveness of your sins and for the healing of your body. They're all part of one complete and finished Atonement. This means Jesus would no more put sickness on you than He would lead you to sin. When you understand this, you'll say, "I won't submit to sickness any more than I would go out and yield to sin." Once you get that mindset, you'll start seeing healing manifest in your body.

One reason people don't see a greater degree of healing is because they aren't committed to it. They embrace infirmity, thinking, *Well, this is just natural.* Even worse, many times they're told, "It's God making you sick." James 4:7 says,

> *Submit yourselves therefore to God. Resist the devil, and he will flee from you.*

The word **"resist"** means to actively fight against. How can you actively fight against the devil—and the sickness, infirmity, and disease that come from him—if you think that God is the one sending it instead? If Satan can convince you that the Lord wants you sick, then you won't actively fight against sickness. You may beg and plead for God to set you free, but you won't fight sickness until you know that He isn't its author. If you don't believe that Jesus purchased healing as part of His Atonement, then you won't resist infirmity and disease. If you aren't persuaded in your heart that God wants you well, you might ask for deliverance, but you won't actively fight against sickness or stand in faith for healing.

You need to get the same attitude toward sickness that you have toward sin! I'm not condemning you if you get sick any more than I would condemn you if you sin (Rom. 8:1-2). Christians are redeemed from sin. The power of sin has been broken over you, and you are dead to sin (Rom. 6:11-14). You should not be living in sin, but there is forgiveness. There is grace if you do sin, so I'm not condemning you. Every born-again believer has had to live with the fact that they haven't lived up to all that they want to, and I'm not condemning them for that. Likewise, I'm not condemning a Christian who is sick. However, I am condemning the attitude that says, "Sickness is something God wants for us." That attitude is just as bad as saying, "Sin is something God wants for us." No, that's wrong. Jesus redeemed us from sin, and at the very same time, He also redeemed us from sickness.

Now, you can learn something if you go out and sin. You could take drugs, blow out your mind, do stupid things, get in car wrecks, and be arrested. You could get drunk, participate in immorality and perversion, and get a sexually transmitted disease. You can learn from hard knocks that doing these kinds of things is stupid and that there are much better things you could do, but that doesn't mean God wanted you to get drunk, have a car wreck, and kill somebody to teach you that you should be seeking Him more. You could learn through such experiences as those, but did God want you to do that? No. Nobody would say, "God made me get drunk and high and then kill this person so He could humble me." They wouldn't say that because they recognize that Jesus died to set them free from sin.

Oppressed of the Devil

In the same way that Jesus died to set you free from sin, He also died to set you free from sickness. In the same way that Christ does not lead you into sin, neither does He bring you infirmity or disease. God is not the author of the sickness that comes against you!

In Acts 10, Peter was preaching the Gospel to Cornelius and his household. He summarized the life and ministry of Jesus, saying,

> *God anointed Jesus of Nazareth with the Holy Ghost and with power: who went about doing good, and healing all that were oppressed of the devil; for God was with him.*

Acts 10:38

Notice that the Word says that when Jesus went about healing people, it was good. Some religious churches today think that people who pray for others and claim that they're healed are of the devil. That's contrary to what the Word of God says here in this verse. When Jesus healed the sick, the Bible declares that it was good, and it brought glory to God. Things that bring glory to God and draw people closer to Him are not of the devil. Satan is not out healing people.

Jesus went about doing good—healing all that were oppressed of the devil. Notice that they were oppressed of the devil, not of God. God is not the author of sickness, infirmity, or disease.

Prophecy Fulfilled

Isaiah prophesied powerfully of the coming Messiah in chapter 53, saying,
> *He is despised and rejected of men; a man of sorrows, and acquainted with grief: and we hid as it were our faces from him; he was despised,*

and we esteemed him not. Surely he hath borne our griefs, and carried our sorrows: yet we did esteem him stricken, smitten of God, and afflicted. But he was wounded for our transgressions, he was bruised for our iniquities: the chastisement of our peace was upon him; and with his stripes we are healed.

Isaiah 53:3-5

Earlier in my life, I always heard this passage changed and interpreted to say, "This isn't talking about physical healing; it's just speaking of emotional and spiritual healing. In a symbolic sense, we were all cripples limping through life because of the damage sin had done to us. Jesus came to set us free from that." However, if you study the Hebrew meanings of the words in the original language here, especially in verse 4, they clearly refer to physical healing.

In fact, Matthew 8 describes Jesus actually fulfilling this prophecy from Isaiah 53:4:

When the even was come, they brought unto him many that were possessed with devils: and he cast out the spirits with his word, and healed all that were sick: That it might be fulfilled which was spoken by Esaias [Isaiah] the prophet, saying, Himself took our infirmities, and bare our sicknesses.

Matthew 8:16-17, brackets mine

Notice how Matthew in the New Testament, quoting Isaiah 53:4 under the inspiration of the Holy Spirit, interpreted **"griefs"** and **"sorrows"** to mean **"infirmities"** and **"sicknesses."** This scripture makes it very clear that Isaiah wasn't speaking of spiritual and emotional healing. Of course, spiritual and emotional healing are included in our salvation benefits, but these verses are speaking specifically about the physical healing of our bodies. The context in Matthew proves this. When Jesus cast these demons out and healed all that were sick, the Bible says this was the fulfillment of Isaiah's prophecy.

In light of Matthew 8:16-17, it's clear that when Isaiah 53:4-5 says that He bore our griefs and carried our sorrows and that by His stripes we are healed, this is not just referring to some kind of spiritual or emotional healing; it's talking about the physical healing of our bodies. Matthew 8's commentary on Isaiah 53 verifies this powerful truth.

Slicing Up the Atonement

We've already looked at many scriptures that clearly reveal physical healing as an important part of Christ's Atonement. Since it's part of what Jesus bled, died, and resurrected to provide, it's not optional. That's why it's incorrect to say, "Let's not preach healing; let's just focus on the forgiveness of sins." That's slicing up the Atonement into different parts and saying, "Some parts of what Jesus did are important and others aren't." Not true. All of what Jesus did for us—all that He suffered, died, and rose again to provide—is important.

We are not honoring the Lord by picking and choosing and presenting a less-than-true picture of the message He really wants us to communicate. We are not glorifying God by ignoring, neglecting, and/or disbelieving an important part of the full salvation package He has provided. We've made the Gospel message irrelevant to many people because they see it as only applying to the future. They perceive salvation as having no relevance to their present-day situations, which is absolutely incorrect.

The Full Package
Lesson 4 – Outline

I. Jesus didn't just die for our sins, and then healing was something He could do if He wanted to.

   A. This may be different than what much of the modern-day church presents, but scriptures bear it out.

   Bless the LORD, O my soul: and all that is within me, bless his holy name. Bless the LORD, O my soul, and forget not all his benefits: Who forgiveth all thine iniquities; who healeth all thy diseases.

   Psalm 103:1-3

   B. Verse 2 specifically tells us not to forget ALL of His benefits.

   C. In the New Testament, 1 Peter 2 says,

   Who his own self bare our sins in his own body on the tree, that we, being dead to sins, should live unto righteousness: by whose stripes ye were healed.

   1 Peter 2:24

   D. Both Psalm 103:3 and 1 Peter 2:24 mention the salvation benefits of forgiveness of sins and physical healing together in the same verse.

   E. As far as God is concerned, salvation is a package deal.

   F. It's people—not God—who have said, "Let's not talk about healing, deliverance, or prosperity; let's just focus on forgiveness of sins. That's the part everyone can agree on. That's the main part of the Atonement. All these others are just fringe benefits." believe that's offensive to God!

II. Healing is in the Atonement just as much as forgiveness of sins!

   A. Once you get this revelation firmly established in your heart, it'll cause you to reject this false teaching that says, "God is the one who causes people to die. He puts sickness on you to humble you for some redemptive purpose and to perfect you through all this suffering."

   B. Jesus died for the forgiveness of your sins and for the healing of your body. They're all part of one complete and finished Atonement.

   C. This means Jesus would no more put sickness on you than He would lead you to sin.

   D. When you understand this, you'll say, "I won't submit to sickness any more than I would go out and yield to sin."

E. Once you get that mindset, you'll start seeing healing manifest in your body.

III. One reason people don't see a greater degree of healing is because they aren't committed to it.

A. They embrace infirmity, thinking, *Well, this is just natural.*

B. Even worse, many times they're told, "It's God making you sick."

> *Submit yourselves therefore to God. Resist the devil, and he will flee from you.*
>
> **James 4:7**

C. The word **"resist"** means to actively fight against.

D. How can you actively fight against the devil—and the sickness, infirmity, and disease that come from him—if you think that God is the one sending it instead?

E. If you aren't persuaded in your heart that God wants you well, you might ask for deliverance, but you won't actively fight against sickness or stand in faith for healing.

F. You need to get the same attitude toward sickness that you have toward sin!

IV. In the same way that Christ does not lead you into sin, neither does He bring you infirmity or disease.

> *God anointed Jesus of Nazareth with the Holy Ghost and with power: who went about doing good, and healing all that were oppressed of the devil; for God was with him.*
>
> **Acts 10:38**

A. Notice that the Word says that when Jesus went about healing people, it was good.

B. Notice that they were oppressed of the devil, not of God.

C. God is not the author of sickness, infirmity, or disease.

V. Isaiah prophesied powerfully of the coming Messiah.

> *He is despised and rejected of men; a man of sorrows, and acquainted with grief: and we hid as it were our faces from him; he was despised, and we esteemed him not. Surely he hath borne our griefs, and carried our sorrows: yet we did esteem him stricken, smitten of God, and afflicted. But he was wounded for our transgressions, he was bruised for our iniquities: the chastisement of our peace was upon him; and with his stripes we are healed.*
>
> **Isaiah 53:3-5**

A. Matthew 8 describes Jesus actually fulfilling this prophecy from Isaiah 53:4:

When the even was come, they brought unto him many that were possessed with devils: and he cast out the spirits with his word, and healed all that were sick: That it might be fulfilled which was spoken by Esaias [Isaiah] the prophet, saying, Himself took our infirmities, and bare our sicknesses.

Matthew 8:16-17, brackets mine

B. Notice how Matthew in the New Testament, quoting Isaiah 53:4 under the inspiration of the Holy Spirit, interpreted **"griefs"** and **"sorrows"** to mean **"infirmities"** and **"sicknesses."**

C. In light of Matthew 8:16-17, it's clear that when Isaiah 53:4-5 says that He bore our griefs and carried our sorrows and that by His stripes we are healed, this is not just referring to some kind of spiritual or emotional healing; it's talking about the physical healing of our bodies.

VI. We've already looked at many scriptures that clearly reveal physical healing as an important part of Christ's Atonement.

A. Since it's part of what Jesus bled, died, and resurrected to provide, it's not optional.

B. We are not honoring the Lord by picking and choosing and presenting a less-than-true picture of the message He really wants us to communicate.

C. We are not glorifying God by ignoring, neglecting, and/or disbelieving an important part of the full salvation package He has provided.

D. We've made the Gospel message irrelevant to many people because they see it as only applying to the future.

E. They perceive salvation as having no relevance to their present-day situations, which is absolutely incorrect.

The Full Package
Lesson 4 – Teacher's Guide

1.   Jesus didn't just die for our sins, and then healing was something He could do if He wanted to. This may be different than what much of the modern-day church presents, but scriptures bear it out (Ps. 103:1-3 and 1 Peter 2:24). Psalm 103:2 specifically tells us not to forget ALL of His benefits. Both Psalm 103:3 and 1 Peter 2:24 mention the salvation benefits of forgiveness of sins and physical healing together in the same verse. As far as God is concerned, salvation is a package deal. It's people—not God—who have said, "Let's not talk about healing, deliverance, or prosperity; let's just focus on forgiveness of sins. That's the part everyone can agree on. That's the main part of the Atonement. All these others are just fringe benefits." I believe that's offensive to God!

2.   Healing is in the Atonement just as much as forgiveness of sins! Once we get this revelation firmly established in our hearts, it'll cause us to reject this false teaching that says, "God is the one who causes people to die. He puts sickness on you to humble you for some redemptive purpose and to perfect you through all this suffering." Jesus died for the forgiveness of our sins and for the healing of our bodies. They're all part of one complete and finished Atonement. This means Jesus would no more put sickness on us than He would lead us to sin. When we understand this, we'll say, "I won't submit to sickness any more than I would go out and yield to sin." Once we get that mindset, we'll start seeing healing manifest in our bodies.

3.   One reason people don't see a greater degree of healing is because they aren't committed to it. They embrace infirmity, thinking, *Well, this is just natural.* Even worse, many times they're told, "It's God making you sick." In James 4:7, the word **"resist"** means to actively fight against. How can we actively fight against the devil—and the sickness, infirmity, and disease that come from him—if we think that God is the one sending it instead? If we aren't persuaded in our hearts that God wants us well, we might ask for deliverance, but we won't actively fight against sickness or stand in faith for healing. We need to get the same attitude toward sickness that we have toward sin!

1.   A. Read Psalm 103:1-3 and 1 Peter 2:24. What salvation benefits do both these passages mention? (Forgiveness of sins and physical healing)
     B. Who is it that says forgiveness of sins is the main part of the Atonement? (People)
2.   A. Forgiveness of sins and the healing of our bodies are all part of what? (One complete and finished Atonement)
     B. What does this mean? (That Jesus would no more put sickness on us than He would lead us to sin)
3.   A. What is one reason people don't see a greater degree of healing? (Because they aren't committed to it)
     B. We are to actively fight against the devil and what? (The sickness, infirmity, and disease that come from him)
     C. What kind of attitude do we need to get? (The same attitude toward sickness that we have toward sin)

4. In the same way that Christ does not lead us into sin, neither does He bring us infirmity or disease (Acts 10:38). Notice in this passage that when Jesus went about healing people, it was good. Notice that they were oppressed of the devil, not of God. God is not the author of sickness, infirmity, or disease.

5. Isaiah prophesied powerfully of the coming Messiah in Isaiah 53:3-5. Matthew 8:16-17 describes Jesus actually fulfilling this prophecy from Isaiah 53:4. Notice how Matthew in the New Testament, quoting Isaiah 53:4 under the inspiration of the Holy Spirit, interpreted **"griefs"** and **"sorrows"** to mean **"infirmities"** and **"sicknesses."** In light of Matthew 8:16-17, it's clear that when Isaiah 53:4-5 says that He bore our griefs and carried our sorrows and that by His stripes we are healed, this is not just referring to some kind of spiritual or emotional healing; it's talking about the physical healing of our bodies.

6. We've already looked at many scriptures that clearly reveal physical healing as an important part of Christ's Atonement. Since it's part of what Jesus bled, died, and resurrected to provide, it's not optional. We are not honoring the Lord by picking and choosing and presenting a less-than-true picture of the message He really wants us to communicate. We are not glorifying God by ignoring, neglecting, and/or disbelieving an important part of the full salvation package He has provided. We've made the Gospel message irrelevant to many people because they see it as only applying to the future. They perceive salvation as having no relevance to their present-day situations, which is absolutely incorrect.

4. A. In the same way that Christ does not lead us into sin, neither does He bring us what? (Infirmity or disease)
   B. Read Acts 10:38. God is not the _____ of sickness, infirmity, or disease. (Author)
5. A. Read Isaiah 53:3-5 and Matthew 8:16-17. What does Matthew interpret "griefs" and "sorrows"? ("Infirmities" and "sickness")
   B. In light of Matthew 8:16-17, what is clear? (That when Isaiah 53:4-5 says that He bore our sorrows and carried our griefs and that by His stripes we are healed, this is not just referring to some kind of spiritual or emotional healing; it's talking about the physical healing of our bodies)
6. A. Since Jesus bled, died, and resurrected to provide physical healing, is it optional? (No)
   B. What are we not doing by picking and choosing and presenting a less-than-true picture of the message the Lord really wants us to communicate? (We are not honoring Him)
   C. What are we doing by ignoring, neglecting, and/or disbelieving an important part of the full salvation package God has provided? (We are not glorifying Him)

The Full Package
Lesson 4 – Discipleship Questions

1. Read Psalm 103:1-3. **"Bless the LORD, O my _____."**

2. What are we not to forget?

3. What are His benefits?

4. Read 1 Peter 2:24. Why did Jesus bear our sins in His own body on the tree?

5. Read Galatians 1:4. According to whose will did Jesus give Himself for our sins?

6. Read James 4:7. What happens when we resist the devil?

7. According to Romans 8:1-2, there is no condemnation to whom?

8. What has made us free from the law of sin and death?

9. Read Romans 6:11-14. We are to reckon ourselves dead to sin but _____.

10. What should we not let reign in our mortal bodies?

11. Why shouldn't sin have dominion over us?

12. According to Acts 10:38, God anointed Jesus of Nazareth with what?

    A. Peanut butter.

    B. The Holy Ghost

    C. Power.

    D. A. and C.

    E. B. and C.

13. Read Isaiah 53:3-5. Was Jesus liked and accepted of men?

14. Why was He wounded?

15. Why was He bruised?

16. The chastisement of our _____ was upon Him.

17. With His stripes, what are we?

18. According to Matthew 8:16-17, what did Jesus cast the spirits out with?

19. What else did He do?

The Full Package
Lesson 4 – Answer Key

1. **"Soul."**

2. His benefits.

3. He forgives all our iniquities and heals all our diseases.

4. That we, being dead to sins, should live unto righteousness.

5. God and our Father.

6. He will flee from us.

7. Them which are in Christ Jesus.

8. The law of the Spirit of life in Christ Jesus.

9. Alive unto God through Jesus Christ our Lord.

10. Sin.

11. Because we are not under the Law but under grace.

12. E.

13. No.

14. For our transgressions.

15. For our iniquities.

16. Peace.

17. Healed.

18. His word.

19. He healed all that were sick.

The Full Package
Lesson 4 – Scriptures

Psalm 103:1-3
Bless the LORD, O my soul: and all that is within me, bless his holy name. [2] Bless the LORD, O my soul, and forget not all his benefits: [3] Who forgiveth all thine iniquities; who healeth all thy diseases.

1 Peter 2:24
Who his own self bare our sins in his own body on the tree, that we, being dead to sins, should live unto righteousness: by whose stripes ye were healed.

Galatians 1:4
Who gave himself for our sins, that he might deliver us from this present evil world, according to the will of God and our Father.

James 4:7
Submit yourselves therefore to God. Resist the devil, and he will flee from you.

Romans 8:1-2
There is therefore now no condemnation to them which are in Christ Jesus, who walk not after the flesh, but after the Spirit. [2] For the law of the Spirit of life in Christ Jesus hath made me free from the law of sin and death.

Romans 6:11-14
Likewise reckon ye also yourselves to be dead indeed unto sin, but alive unto God through Jesus Christ our Lord. [12] Let not sin therefore reign in your mortal body, that ye should obey it in the lusts thereof. [13] Neither yield ye your members as instruments of unrighteousness unto sin: but yield yourselves unto God, as those that are alive from the dead, and your members as instruments of righteousness unto God. [14] For sin shall not have dominion over you: for ye are not under the law, but under grace.

Acts 10:38
How God anointed Jesus of Nazareth with the Holy Ghost and with power: who went about doing good, and healing all that were oppressed of the devil; for God was with him.

Isaiah 53:3-5
He is despised and rejected of men; a man of sorrows, and acquainted with grief: and we hid as it were our faces from him; he was despised, and we esteemed him not. [4] Surely he hath borne our griefs, and carried our sorrows: yet we did esteem him stricken, smitten of God, and afflicted. [5] But he was wounded for our transgressions, he was bruised for our iniquities: the chastisement of our peace was upon him; and with his stripes we are healed.

Matthew 8:16-17

When the even was come, they brought unto him many that were possessed with devils: and he cast out the spirits with his word, and healed all that were sick: [17] That it might be fulfilled which was spoken by Esaias the prophet, saying, Himself took our infirmities, and bare our sicknesses.

Sickness and Sin
Lesson 5

It's always God's will to heal us. We know this because Jesus only did what He saw His Father do:

Then answered Jesus and said unto them, Verily, verily, I say unto you, The Son can do nothing of himself, but what he seeth the Father do: for what things soever he doeth, these also doeth the Son likewise.

John 5:19

And God the Son is the express image of God the Father:

Who being the brightness of his glory, and the express image of his person, and upholding all things by the word of his power, when he had by himself purged our sins, sat down on the right hand of the Majesty on high.

Hebrews 1:3

The Greek word translated **"express image"** speaks of an identical copy or a perfect representation. Therefore, God's Word reveals that Jesus Christ is the identical copy and perfect representation of His Father. He only spoke what He heard His Father say, and He only did what He saw His Father do. So we can be confident in determining God's will concerning healing by looking at the life of Jesus.

Perfect Representation

In the Gospels, there is not one example of Jesus ever putting sickness on anyone. The modern church that preaches "God makes people sick" is representing Him completely contrary to the perfect representation of Christ. It's totally opposite the exact image Jesus gave us of His Father. Not one single time did Jesus ever make anyone sick. Not once did He ever refuse to heal someone. Now, there are a couple of times where someone refused to receive healing from Him, but it wasn't because Jesus didn't want to minister it to them. They wouldn't receive it (I'll deal with this more later). There isn't one single time that Jesus said, "No, God wants you sick." He never laid hands on a person and gave them an infirmity or a disease. That's not the way Jesus represented God the Father.

There are seventeen times in the Gospels where Jesus healed all of the sick who were present. There are forty-seven other instances where Christ healed at least one or two people at a time (see the **Is it Always God's Will to Heal?** section at the back of this **Study Guide**). However, you cannot find even one instance where Jesus refused to heal a person or put sickness on someone.

God anointed Jesus of Nazareth with the Holy Ghost and with power: who went about doing good, and healing all that were oppressed of the devil; for God was with him.

Acts 10:38

God is not the author of sickness—He's the author of healing.

Blessing or Curse?

Even under the Old Testament Law, sickness, infirmity, and disease were never considered "blessings." Deuteronomy 28:1-14 lists the blessings promised to those who would keep God's commandments, and 28:15-68 describes the curses that would come upon those who didn't.

Now, you need to understand that we're in the New Covenant today. We don't have to keep all of the Old Testament Law in order to receive the blessings of God. Jesus redeemed us from the curse of the Law so that the blessing can come upon us by faith in Him.

Christ hath redeemed us from the curse of the law, being made a curse for us: for it is written, Cursed is every one that hangeth on a tree: That the blessing of Abraham might come on the Gentiles through Jesus Christ; that we might receive the promise of the Spirit through faith.

Galatians 3:13-14

Therefore, in Christ we have access by faith to the blessings listed in Deuteronomy 28, and in Christ we have been redeemed and delivered from the curses listed in Deuteronomy 28. However, this chapter of the Bible still shows us what God considers "blessings" and "curses."

Imagine a chalkboard with a line drawn down the middle, dividing it into two columns. At the top of the left column is the word "Blessings." At the top of the right column is the word "Curses." According to Deuteronomy 28, "health" would be listed on the left in the "Blessings" column, and "sickness" would be listed on the right in the "Curses" column. Yet many people in the church today reverse this, saying, "Oh, no. It's really a blessing that God gave me this sickness." That's not true.

Roadblocks

Now, can some good come out of people being sick? Certainly. It's just like those who learned from the hard knocks of sin. While doing something terribly wrong, they realize, *Man, my life is totally out of balance. I'm a messed-up person. I might even be demonized. I need to turn to God!* So they call on the name of the Lord in faith, receive salvation, and get delivered. I've actually talked with individuals who are in prison for murder and are on death row who have turned to the Lord and were born again. Several inmates in this situation have heard my radio programs and written to me. God used what was happening in their lives to bring them to the end of themselves and cause them to be born again. Now their whole lives are changed, and they are gloriously saved and serving God. I'm sure you can see that this could happen, but is it correct to say that the Lord caused them to go commit that murder? No, that wasn't God. I can guarantee you that the Lord tried to put restraints on them and obstacles in their way.

God tried to stop those two teenage boys from doing what they did at Columbine High School. They killed twelve fellow students, a teacher, and then themselves while wounding twenty-three others. One of those boys was in a youth Bible study the week before he did that. The minister conducting the Bible study received a word of knowledge from the Lord, interrupted the study, and said, "Somebody here is either thinking about killing themselves or killing someone else." He gave an invitation for a long period of time and pleaded for that person to respond, but he didn't. The very next week, this boy and another went out and killed all of these people. God was putting a roadblock in that young man's life. He was dealing with him and trying to turn him from that course of action. It wasn't God that led him to kill people, then kill himself, and send himself to hell. No, God tried to stop him.

However, there are other individuals who have killed someone and then at some point afterward turned to the Lord in repentance and faith. The Lord can use even the things that the devil does in our lives, but that doesn't mean He caused them.

In the same way, Satan has caused people to be sick, infirmed, and diseased. Yet, when they get into these terrible situations, they cry out to God, turning wholeheartedly to Him, and He answers their prayers. After being gloriously saved, these people may learn that they were just self-centered before. They didn't care about God or other people. They may learn important lessons through their infirmity, and because of that, they mistakenly begin to credit God with giving them that sickness. God would no more give people sickness to humble them than He would cause them to murder somebody to humble them.

Resist Sickness

Healing is part of Christ's Atonement just as much as forgiveness of sins. In the same way that I should resist sin, I should resist sickness. I shouldn't accept infirmity or disease just the same as I wouldn't say, "Well, God, I know that You could help me not to sin, but I don't know if You want me not to sin. Maybe it's Your will for me to sin." Nobody would advocate that type of an attitude, but Christians today do exactly that when it comes to healing: "God, we know You can if it's Your will. We ask You to heal us." If they get healed, then it must have been God's will. If they don't, then it must not have been His will. That's as wrong as people praying, "God, if You don't want me to go out and commit adultery, then stop me." And if they don't commit adultery, they say, "Thank You, God, for stopping me." But if they do it, then they say, "It must have been God's will for me to commit adultery." We would never say that, because adultery is sin. But they see sickness as something that is optional. No, healing is paid for and available just as much as forgiveness of sin. Therefore, we ought to hate sickness and disease as much as we hate sin.

As long as you can tolerate sickness, you will. As long as you can tolerate sin, you will. But once you reach the place of saying, "I'm not living like this. I will not do it. I'll die before I go out and do this"; once you reach this point, you'll start seeing sin diminished in your life. Once you get this attitude that *I will not put up with sickness, infirmity, and disease. I resist it in Jesus' name*, you'll start seeing healing manifest in your life.

Of course, there's more to it than just this. Among other things, there are laws that govern healing. There's much to learn about receiving healing from God, but this has to be your foundation: Healing is included in Christ's Atonement.

God's Will Is Clear

I am seeing a tremendous amount of victory in the area of healing personally and in ministering to others. Unless you are having better results, you ought to consider these truths I'm sharing. This is a foundational truth that makes everything else work: Jesus bore your stripes on His body to heal your body just as much as He died to forgive your sins.

Without exception, all of the people I've studied who have had the healing power of God manifest in their lives and ministries on a regular basis have had this same foundational belief. I'm not talking about someone who just every once in a while see healing. Even an old blind squirrel will come up with a nut sometimes. I'm talking about the people who walk in divine health and consistently see miracles of healing. Every single one of them has believed that healing is part of the Atonement of the Lord Jesus Christ. They believe it's always God's will to heal just the same as it's always God's will to save.

Until you get that attitude, Satan will always be able to make you passive. You have to resist—actively fight against—the devil before he'll flee from you (James 4:7). You need to understand and believe that healing is from God, and sickness is from Satan. Once you make this clear distinction in your heart, then you must resist the devil—and all the sickness, infirmity, and disease he sends your way. You can't just passively say, "Lord, if it's Your will, heal me." You must be persuaded in your heart of the truth of God's Word concerning healing and then actively stand against the devil.

God's Word is His will, and it's very clear:

> *Beloved, I wish above all things that thou mayest prosper and be in health, even as thy soul prospereth.*
>
> **3 John 2**

God wants you well!

Sickness and Sin
Lesson 5 – Outline

I.   It's always God's will to heal us.

    A. We know this because Jesus only did what He saw His Father do:

> *Then answered Jesus and said unto them, Verily, verily, I say unto you,*
> *The Son can do nothing of himself, but what he seeth the Father do:*
> *for what things soever he doeth, these also doeth the Son likewise.*
>
> **John 5:19**

    B. And God the Son is the express image of God the Father:

> *Who being the brightness of his glory, and the express image of his person,*
> *and upholding all things by the word of his power, when he had by himself*
> *purged our sins, sat down on the right hand of the Majesty on high.*
>
> **Hebrews 1:3**

    C. The Greek word translated **"express image"** speaks of an identical copy or a perfect representation.

    D. So we can be confident in determining God's will concerning healing by looking at the life of Jesus.

II.   In the Gospels, there is not one example of Jesus ever putting sickness on anyone.

    A. The modern church that preaches "God makes people sick" is representing Him completely contrary to the perfect representation of Christ.

    B. It's totally opposite the exact image Jesus gave us of His Father.

    C. (See *Is it Always God's Will to Heal?* section at the back of this **Study Guide**.)

    D. God is not the author of sickness—He's the author of healing.

III.   Even under the Old Testament Law, sickness, infirmity, and disease were never considered "blessings."

    A. Yet many people in the church today reverse this, saying, "Oh, no. It's really a blessing that God gave me this sickness." That's not true.

    B. Now, can some good come out of people being sick? Certainly. It's just like those who learned from the hard knocks of sin.

    C. God used what was happening in their lives to bring them to the end of themselves and cause them to be born again.

D. The Lord can use even the things that the devil does in our lives, but that doesn't mean He caused them.

E. In the same way, Satan has caused people to be sick, infirmed, and diseased. They may learn important lessons through their infirmity, and because of that, they mistakenly begin to credit God with giving them that sickness.

F. God would no more give people sickness to humble them than He would cause them to murder somebody to humble them.

IV. As long as you can tolerate sickness, you will.

A. Once you get this attitude that *I will not put up with sickness, infirmity, and disease. I resist it in Jesus' name*, you'll start seeing healing manifest in your life.

B. There's much to learn about receiving healing from God, but this has to be your foundation: Healing is included in Christ's Atonement.

C. I am seeing a tremendous amount of victory in the area of healing personally and in ministering to others.

D. Unless you are having better results, you ought to consider these truths I'm sharing.

V. Without exception, all of the people I've studied who have had the healing power of God manifest in their lives and ministries on a regular basis have had this same foundational belief.

A. Every single one of them has believed that healing is part of the Atonement of the Lord Jesus Christ.

B. They believe it's always God's will to heal just the same as it's always God's will to save.

C. Until you get that attitude, Satan will always be able to make you passive.

VI. You must be persuaded in your heart of the truth of God's Word concerning healing and then actively stand against the devil.

A. God's Word is His will, and it's very clear:

Beloved, I wish above all things that thou mayest prosper and be in health, even as thy soul prospereth.

3 John 2

B. God wants you well!

Sickness and Sin
Lesson 5 – Teacher's Guide

1. It's always God's will to heal us. We know this because Jesus only did what He saw His Father do (John 5:19). And God the Son is the express image of God the Father (Heb. 1:3). In Hebrews 1:3, the Greek word translated **"express image"** speaks of an identical copy or a perfect representation. So we can be confident in determining God's will concerning healing by looking at the life of Jesus.

2. In the Gospels, there is not one example of Jesus ever putting sickness on anyone. The modern church that preaches "God makes people sick" is representing Him completely contrary to the perfect representation of Christ. It's totally opposite the exact image Jesus gave us of His Father. (See *Is it Always God's Will to Heal?* section at the back of this **Study Guide**.) God is not the author of sickness—He's the author of healing.

3. Even under the Old Testament Law, sickness, infirmity, and disease were never considered "blessings." Yet many people in the church today reverse this, saying, "Oh, no. It's really a blessing that God gave me this sickness." That's not true. Now, can some good come out of people being sick? Certainly. It's just like those who learned from the hard knocks of sin. God used what was happening in their lives to bring them to the end of themselves and cause them to be born again. The Lord can use even the things that the devil does in our lives, but that doesn't mean He caused them. In the same way, Satan has caused people to be sick, infirmed, and diseased. They may learn important lessons through their infirmity, and because of that, they mistakenly begin to credit God with giving them that sickness. God would no more give people sickness to humble them than He would cause them to murder somebody to humble them.

1. A. Read John 5:19 and Hebrews 1:3. How do we know it is God's will to heal us? (Because Jesus only did what He saw His Father do and He—God the Son—is the express image of God the Father)
    B. What can we be confident about? (Determining God's will concerning healing by looking at the life of Jesus)
2. A. In the Gospels, are there any examples of Jesus ever putting sickness on anyone? (No)
    B. God is not the author is sickness but of what? (Healing)
3. A. Under the Old Testament Law, were sickness, infirmity, and disease ever considered "blessings"? (No)
    B. The Lord can use even the things the devil does in our lives, but that doesn't mean _____. (He caused them)
    C. When people learn important lessons through their infirmity, how do they begin to credit God with giving them that sickness? (Mistakenly)

4. As long as we can tolerate sickness, we will. Once we get this attitude that *We will not put up with sickness, infirmity, and disease. We resist it in Jesus' name*, we'll start seeing healing manifest in our lives. There's much to learn about receiving healing from God, but this has to be our foundation: Healing is included in Christ's Atonement. I am seeing a tremendous amount of victory in the area of healing personally and in ministering to others. Unless you are having better results, you ought to consider these truths I'm sharing.

5. Without exception, all of the people I've studied who have had the healing power of God manifest in their lives and ministries on a regular basis have had this same foundational belief. Every single one of them has believed that healing is part of the Atonement of the Lord Jesus Christ. They believe it's always God's will to heal just the same as it's always God's will to save. Until we get that attitude, Satan will always be able to make us passive.

6. We must be persuaded in our hearts of the truth of God's Word concerning healing and then actively stand against the devil. God's Word is His will, and it's very clear: He wants us well (3 John 2)!

4. A. What kind of attitude do we need to start seeing healing manifest in our lives? (An attitude that we will not put up with sickness, infirmity, and disease. We resist it in Jesus' name)
   B. What has to be our foundation? (That healing is included in Christ's Atonement)
5. A. All of the people I've studied who have had the healing power of God manifest in their lives and ministries on a regular basis believed what? (That healing is part of the Atonement of the Lord Jesus Christ)
   B. What else did they believe? (That it's always God's will to heal just the same as it's always God's will to save)
   C. Until we get that attitude, Satan will always what? (Be able to make us passive)
6. A. What must we be persuaded of? (The truth of God's Word concerning healing)
   B. Then what must we do? (Actively stand against the devil)
   C. Since God's Word is His will, what is very clear? (That He wants us well)

Sickness and Sin
Lesson 5 – Discipleship Questions

1. Read John 5:19. What does the Son do?

2. Read Hebrews 1:3. What is upheld by the word of God's power?

3. Did Jesus and someone else purge our sins?

4. Read Acts 10:38. Who was with Jesus?

5. According to Deuteronomy 28:1-14, how were the people to hearken?

    A. Lethargically.

    B. Hastily.

    C. Diligently.

    D. All of the above.

    E. None of above.

6. Were these suggestions or commandments?

7. What would come upon the people and overtake them?

8. According to Deuteronomy 28:15-68, what would happen if the people did not hearken unto the voice of the Lord their God, to observe to do all His commandments and His statutes that He commanded them that day?

9. Which section is larger: the blessings or the curses?

10. Are the curses desirable things?

11. Read Galatians 3:13-14. What has Christ redeemed us from?

12. Why was He made a curse for us?

13. Read James 4:7. **"Submit _____ therefore to God. Resist the devil, and he will flee from you."**

14. According to 3 John 2, God wishes above all things that we might prosper and be in health even as what?

Sickness and Sin
Lesson 5 – Answer Key

1.   What He sees the Father do.

2.   All things.

3.   No.

4.   God.

5.   C. Diligently.

6.   Commandments.

7.   All the blessings listed.

8.   All the curses listed would come upon them and overtake them.

9.   The curses.

10. No.

11. The curse of the Law.

12. That the blessing of Abraham might come on the Gentiles, that we might receive the promise of the Spirit through faith.

13. **"Yourselves."**

14. Our souls prosper.

Sickness and Sin
Lesson 5 – Scriptures

John 5:19
Then answered Jesus and said unto them, Verily, verily, I say unto you, The Son can do nothing of himself, but what he seeth the Father do: for what things soever he doeth, these also doeth the Son likewise.

Hebrews 1:3
Who being the brightness of his glory, and the express image of his person, and upholding all things by the word of his power, when he had by himself purged our sins, sat down on the right hand of the Majesty on high.

Acts 10:38
How God anointed Jesus of Nazareth with the Holy Ghost and with power: who went about doing good, and healing all that were oppressed of the devil; for God was with him.

Deuteronomy 28:1-68
And it shall come to pass, if thou shalt hearken diligently unto the voice of the LORD thy God, to observe and to do all his commandments which I command thee this day, that the LORD thy God will set thee on high above all nations of the earth: [2] And all these blessings shall come on thee, and overtake thee, if thou shalt hearken unto the voice of the LORD thy God. [3] Blessed shalt thou be in the city, and blessed shalt thou be in the field. [4] Blessed shall be the fruit of thy body, and the fruit of thy ground, and the fruit of thy cattle, the increase of thy kine, and the flocks of thy sheep. [5] Blessed shall be thy basket and thy store. [6] Blessed shalt thou be when thou comest in, and blessed shalt thou be when thou goest out. [7] The LORD shall cause thine enemies that rise up against thee to be smitten before thy face: they shall come out against thee one way, and flee before thee seven ways. [8] The LORD shall command the blessing upon thee in thy storehouses, and in all that thou settest thine hand unto; and he shall bless thee in the land which the LORD thy God giveth thee. [9] The LORD shall establish thee an holy people unto himself, as he hath sworn unto thee, if thou shalt keep the commandments of the LORD thy God, and walk in his ways. [10] And all people of the earth shall see that thou art called by the name of the LORD; and they shall be afraid of thee. [11] And the LORD shall make thee plenteous in goods, in the fruit of thy body, and in the fruit of thy cattle, and in the fruit of thy ground, in the land which the LORD sware unto thy fathers to give thee. [12] The LORD shall open unto thee his good treasure, the heaven to give the rain unto thy land in his season, and to bless all the work of thine hand: and thou shalt lend unto many nations, and thou shalt not borrow. [13] And the LORD shall make thee the head, and not the tail; and thou shalt be above only, and thou shalt not be beneath; if that thou hearken unto the commandments of the LORD thy God,

which I command thee this day, to observe and to do them: [14] And thou shalt not go aside from any of the words which I command thee this day, to the right hand, or to the left, to go after other gods to serve them. [15] But it shall come to pass, if thou wilt not hearken unto the voice of the LORD thy God, to observe to do all his commandments and his statutes which I command thee this day; that all these curses shall come upon thee, and overtake thee: [16] Cursed shalt thou be in the city, and cursed shalt thou be in the field. [17] Cursed shall be thy basket and thy store. [18] Cursed shall be the fruit of thy body, and the fruit of thy land, the increase of thy kine, and the flocks of thy sheep. [19] Cursed shalt thou be when thou comest in, and cursed shalt thou be when thou goest out. [20] The LORD shall send upon thee cursing, vexation, and rebuke, in all that thou settest thine hand unto for to do, until thou be destroyed, and until thou perish quickly; because of the wickedness of thy doings, whereby thou hast forsaken me. [21] The LORD shall make the pestilence cleave unto thee, until he have consumed thee from off the land, whither thou goest to possess it. [22] The LORD shall smite thee with a consumption, and with a fever, and with an inflammation, and with an extreme burning, and with the sword, and with blasting, and with mildew; and they shall pursue thee until thou perish. [23] And thy heaven that is over thy head shall be brass, and the earth that is under thee shall be iron. [24] The LORD shall make the rain of thy land powder and dust: from heaven shall it come down upon thee, until thou be destroyed. [25] The LORD shall cause thee to be smitten before thine enemies: thou shalt go out one way against them, and flee seven ways before them: and shalt be removed into all the kingdoms of the earth. [26] And thy carcase shall be meat unto all fowls of the air, and unto the beasts of the earth, and no man shall fray them away. [27] The LORD will smite thee with the botch of Egypt, and with the emerods, and with the scab, and with the itch, whereof thou canst not be healed. [28] The LORD shall smite thee with madness, and blindness, and astonishment of heart: [29] And thou shalt grope at noonday, as the blind gropeth in darkness, and thou shalt not prosper in thy ways: and thou shalt be only oppressed and spoiled evermore, and no man shall save thee. [30] Thou shalt betroth a wife, and another man shall lie with her: thou shalt build an house, and thou shalt not dwell therein: thou shalt plant a vineyard, and shalt not gather the grapes thereof. [31] Thine ox shall be slain before thine eyes, and thou shalt not eat thereof: thine ass shall be violently taken away from before thy face, and shall not be restored to thee: thy sheep shall be given unto thine enemies, and thou shalt have none to rescue them. [32] Thy sons and thy daughters shall be given unto another people, and thine eyes shall look, and fail with longing for them all the day long: and there shall be no might in thine hand. [33] The fruit of thy land, and all thy labours, shall a nation which thou knowest not eat up; and thou shalt be only oppressed and crushed alway: [34] So that thou shalt be mad for the sight of thine eyes which thou shalt see. [35] The LORD shall smite thee in the knees, and in the legs, with a sore botch that cannot be healed, from the sole of thy foot unto the top of thy head. [36] The LORD shall bring thee, and thy king which thou shalt set over thee, unto a nation which neither thou nor thy fathers have known; and there shalt thou serve other gods, wood and stone. [37] And thou shalt become an astonishment, a proverb, and a byword, among all nations whither the LORD shall lead thee. [38] Thou shalt carry much seed out into the field, and shalt gather but little in; for the locust shall consume it. [39] Thou shalt plant vineyards, and dress them, but shalt neither drink of the wine, nor gather the grapes; for the worms shall eat them. [40] Thou shalt have olive trees throughout all thy coasts, but thou shalt not anoint thyself with the oil; for thine olive shall cast his fruit. [41] Thou shalt beget sons and daughters, but thou shalt not enjoy them; for they shall go into captivity. [42] All thy trees and fruit of thy land shall the locust consume. [43] The stranger that is within thee shall get up above thee very high; and thou shalt come down very low. [44] He shall lend to thee, and thou shalt not lend to him: he shall be the head, and thou shalt be the tail. [45] Moreover all these curses shall come upon thee, and shall pursue thee, and overtake thee, till thou be destroyed; because thou hearkenedst not unto the voice of the LORD thy God, to keep his commandments and his statutes which he commanded thee: [46] And they shall be upon thee for a sign and for a wonder, and upon thy seed for ever. [47] Because thou servedst not the LORD thy God with joyfulness, and with gladness of heart, for the abundance of all things; [48] Therefore shalt thou serve thine enemies which the LORD shall send against thee, in hunger, and in thirst, and in nakedness, and in want of all things: and he shall put a yoke of iron upon thy neck, until he have destroyed thee. [49] The LORD shall bring a nation against thee from far, from the end of the earth, as swift as the eagle flieth; a nation whose tongue thou shalt not understand; [50] A nation of fierce countenance, which shall not regard the person of the old, nor shew favour to the young: [51] And he shall eat the fruit of thy cattle, and the fruit of thy land, until thou be destroyed: which also shall not leave thee either corn, wine, or oil, or the increase of thy kine, or flocks of thy sheep, until he have destroyed thee. [52] And he shall besiege thee in all thy gates, until thy high and fenced walls come down, wherein thou trustedst, throughout all thy land: and he shall besiege thee in all thy gates throughout all thy land, which the LORD thy God hath given thee. [53] And thou shalt eat the fruit of thine own body, the flesh of thy sons and of thy daughters, which the LORD thy God hath given thee, in the siege, and in the straitness, wherewith thine enemies shall distress thee: [54] So that the man that is tender among you, and very delicate, his eye shall be evil toward his brother, and toward the wife of his bosom, and toward the remnant of his children which he shall leave: [55] So that he will not give to any of them of the flesh of his children whom he shall eat: because he hath nothing left him in the siege, and in the straitness, wherewith thine enemies shall distress thee in all thy gates. [56] The tender and delicate woman among you, which would not adventure to set the sole of her foot upon the ground for delicateness and tenderness, her eye shall be evil toward the husband of her bosom, and toward her son, and toward her daughter, [57] And toward her young one that cometh out from between her feet, and toward her children which she shall bear: for she shall eat them for want of all things secretly in the siege and straitness, wherewith thine enemy shall distress thee in thy gates. [58] If thou wilt not observe to do all the words of this law that are written in this book, that thou mayest fear this glorious and fearful name, THE LORD THY GOD; [59] Then the LORD will make thy plagues wonderful, and the plagues of thy seed, even great

*plagues, and of long continuance, and sore sicknesses, and of long continuance.
[60] Moreover he will bring upon thee all the diseases of Egypt, which thou wast
afraid of; and they shall cleave unto thee. [61] Also every sickness, and every
plague, which is not written in the book of this law, them will the LORD bring
upon thee, until thou be destroyed. [62] And ye shall be left few in number,
whereas ye were as the stars of heaven for multitude; because thou wouldest not
obey the voice of the LORD thy God. [63] And it shall come to pass, that as the
LORD rejoiced over you to do you good, and to multiply you; so the LORD will
rejoice over you to destroy you, and to bring you to nought; and ye shall be
plucked from off the land whither thou goest to possess it. [64] And the LORD
shall scatter thee among all people, from the one end of the earth even unto the
other; and there thou shalt serve other gods, which neither thou nor thy fathers
have known, even wood and stone. [65] And among these nations shalt thou find
no ease, neither shall the sole of thy foot have rest: but the LORD shall give thee
there a trembling heart, and failing of eyes, and sorrow of mind: [66] And thy life
shall hang in doubt before thee; and thou shalt fear day and night, and shalt have
none assurance of thy life: [67] In the morning thou shalt say, Would God it were
even! and at even thou shalt say, Would God it were morning! for the fear of thine
heart wherewith thou shalt fear, and for the sight of thine eyes which thou shalt
see. [68] And the LORD shall bring thee into Egypt again with ships, by the way
whereof I spake unto thee, Thou shalt see it no more again: and there ye shall be
sold unto your enemies for bondmen and bondwomen, and no man shall buy you.*

Galatians 3:13-14
*Christ hath redeemed us from the curse of the law, being made a curse for us: for
it is written, Cursed is every one that hangeth on a tree: [14] That the blessing of
Abraham might come on the Gentiles through Jesus Christ; that we might receive
the promise of the Spirit through faith.*

James 4:7
Submit yourselves therefore to God. Resist the devil, and he will flee from you.

3 John 2
*Beloved, I wish above all things that thou mayest prosper and be in health, even as thy
soul prospereth.*

A Cop-out
Lesson 6

Healing is part of Christ's Atonement. It's not a separate issue from salvation. The very Greek word associated with salvation over a hundred times in the New Testament was also translated "healed," "made whole," and "saved" in reference to healing the sick. God never intended for what Jesus accomplished through His death, burial, and resurrection to be broken up and separated into different elements.

Some people have said, "We're going to accept forgiveness of sins but reject healing, prosperity, and deliverance." No, it's actually all a package deal. It's wrong for the church to present healing as some fringe benefit that "could happen but certainly isn't part of our salvation. It's just up to the Lord whether He chooses to heal or not." God's will is to heal you just as much as it is to forgive you. He wants you to resist sickness and disease just as much as He wants you to resist sin.

Part of the Fall

I've often thought about why anybody would fight against healing. Being well seems to be a universal desire. Consider the effort people put into getting their bodies well. They spend untold amounts of money on doctors' visits, medications, and operations. Medications alone are huge in today's society. People are taking drugs that produce all kinds of side effects. I've seen advertisements on television for different medications that caused so many terrible side effects that I've thought in my heart, *I'd rather be sick than have all of those side effects.* Yet many people will put up with them. They take radiation and chemotherapy that causes their hair to fall out. They'll take drugs that make them swell. People will literally have parts of their bodies cut off in an effort to live. Nobody likes sickness!

Even hypochondriacs don't like it. They may have a fear of sickness that draws them into it and causes them to obsess over it, but they don't like it.

People universally hate sickness and disease. That's because God didn't create mankind to die. Death was something man chose, but it wasn't something God chose. The Lord originally intended for our bodies to live forever. I've actually read some medical reports that say that the body is capable of healing and repairing itself. The medical profession really cannot understand why the body doesn't live forever. Of course, there are these invaders, like germs and viruses, but we have the capacity to overcome them. God's original plan was for us never to be sick. Sickness was not a part of God's plan—it was part of what we unknowingly chose in the Fall.

We were created with a God-given desire on the inside of every one of us for health. People don't like sickness. God doesn't like it. Why, then, do some people fight against God being our Healer? They'll actually say "You are of the devil" if you believe that the Lord heals today. Why would somebody argue that when health is a universal need and desire? Everybody wants health. Why would we credit God with wanting something less than the best for our health?

There are also lesser manifestations of this same attitude. These people may not say you're of the devil if you believe for healing. They may not reject you for laying hands on the sick and believing for them to recover (Mark 16:18). But they would certainly say that it's not God's will to heal every single time. Why would they think that? I've already proven earlier in this book that healing is part of the Atonement. God provided healing for our bodies just as much—and at the very same time—as He provided forgiveness of sins. With this being so obvious, why do people fight against healing?

A Common Root

Although there are many reasons why people are prejudiced, biased, and teach against healing, I believe they all stem from a common root. People resist the truth that healing is in the Atonement and they resist that it is God's will to heal every time, because it's convenient to believe that way. There may be some sincere people who have been taught wrong, but the bottom line of this teaching against healing is that it's a cop-out. It avoids the responsibility that becomes theirs when they accept that God wants them well.

If the Lord has provided healing for us—and it's obvious that not everybody is healed—then the question arises, "Why aren't we well?" If God wants us well and we aren't, this means we have to accept some degree of responsibility. I'll deal with this issue later in the book when I discuss why everyone isn't healed. However, for now, we need to realize that we must accept some responsibility. Yet in an effort to dodge responsibility and guilt, we often simply say, "Well, it must not have been God's will." That's not true.

Some people argue, "If God wanted someone healed, then they'd be healed whether you or I prayed for them or not." That's not true either. Consider the forgiveness of sins. God's Word says that...

> *The Lord is not slack concerning his promise, as some men count slackness; but is longsuffering to us-ward, not willing that any should perish, but that all should come to repentance.*
>
> **2 Peter 3:9**

You can't make it any clearer than that. God's will is for people to be saved. Yet not everybody is saved. Jesus Himself prophesied that more people would choose the broad gate that leads to destruction than the narrow gate that leads to everlasting life.

> *Enter ye in at the strait gate: for wide is the gate, and broad is the way, that leadeth to destruction, and many there be which go in there-at: Because strait is the gate, and narrow is the way, which leadeth unto life, and few there be that find it.*
>
> **Matthew 7:13-14**

God's will concerning salvation doesn't automatically come to pass. He's not willing that anyone perish but that all come to repentance and the knowledge of Him. The Lord doesn't will for anyone to die and go to hell, but He gave man a choice. People go to hell because they reject God's provision. Some reject it blatantly in open rebellion against the Lord. Others reject it because they are taught wrong, so they're trusting in their own good works, like attending church, being moral, or tithing (Rom. 10:2-3). Although they've been deceived, it's still their choices that caused them to miss it.

Accept Responsibility

God doesn't want people to go to hell, but they do. He doesn't want people to be sick either, but they are. Certainly, some people are in total rebellion toward the Lord and His ways, and they're reaping what they've sown. Yet other people desire healing, and they still fall short. This is because they don't understand how to receive healing properly. Some people think that being a good person, attending church, and being water baptized as an infant will produce salvation in their lives. They may be sincere, but they're sincerely wrong. Although it's not God's will for them to perish, people are perishing. It's not God's will for people to be sick either, but they are. They don't understand how to receive.

We need to understand and accept our part. It's our failure, not God's, that sends people to hell and causes us to be sick. It's our failure to accept this responsibility that's the root of why we fight against healing. We do not want to accept responsibility. We don't want to confront the truth that as believers in Christ, we could have done something to prevent that loved one from suffering under sickness and dying.

I'm not saying it's our fault directly, although in some cases it could be. Often it's not an individual's sin that brought sickness and disease, but mankind's sin that has corrupted this world. It's the sin that caused germs and viruses, fungi and infections, and the like that were never a part of God's original plan for mankind. They're perversions of nature that happened through sin, not necessarily individual sin, but the collective sin that has corrupted the entire system. Even though it might not be something we did individually that caused sickness, there is always something we can do individually to overcome that perversion and walk in health.

Not God's Will

Back in the early 1970s, I pastored a church in a small town in Texas. A couple in this church had a child who was born mongoloid. (That's not intended as a slur. I realize that we don't use that term anymore, but that's what the parents called it. I'm just repeating what they said.) She was a very small woman, and they had been living in Guatemala at the time of his birth. She delivered this baby in a taxi on the way to the hospital, and it caused brain damage. Because the baby was born mongoloid, his immune system was deficient. The doctor said that if the child ever got a cold, he would die because there was nothing they could do for him. They didn't expect him to live, but he did. When I met them, he was four years old.

Finally, he did get a cold. So I went to their house and prayed over him to be healed. While holding the child in my arms, he died. We sat there with the parents and prayed for hours for this child to be raised from the dead. We did everything I knew to do. Eventually, we finally called the authorities. The police showed up, and it was a miracle that we didn't all get sent to jail. Really, the only reason they didn't arrest us was because the parents had doctors' reports proving that they had said, "If he ever gets sick or has an infection, just keep him at home because there's nothing we can do for him." Because they had those, the police let us go. It was a very tragic situation.

The parents asked me to do his funeral. I was groping for something that would comfort both them and me. I had taken this personally. It would have been comforting momentarily to have just said, "Well, it couldn't have been us that missed it. We gave it everything we've got." The parents were grieving, and I certainly didn't want to point the finger at them by saying, "It's your fault." It would have been comforting to say, "God works in mysterious ways. He must have wanted your son in heaven. God needed him there." It would have been comforting to come up with some of these clichés that are commonly heard given in religion, but I had to be honest with the Word.

I told those parents, "I don't believe this was God's will. The Lord did not kill your son. He didn't allow this to happen. Satan was the one who snuffed his life out. Even though the devil may have won this battle, he didn't win the war." Then I shared from 2 Samuel 12:23 and other scriptures how this child was now in the presence of God. I ministered hope, and the reality that this boy was with Jesus.

"The Truth Shall Make You Free"

But when it came to why it happened, I basically said, "It's either my fault, your fault, both of our faults, or things that we don't understand. I don't know what it is, but I can guarantee you, it's not God." That wasn't as comforting as if I would have said, "Well, God works in mysterious ways. He allowed it. The Lord did this for some reason." That might have given momentary comfort, but the Bible says,

Ye shall know the truth, and the truth shall make you free.

John 8:32

God's Word is true, and I couldn't find in there where Jesus made people sick. I just had to tell them, "I don't know where the problem is, but it's not God. Satan beat us. He won a battle, but he didn't win the war. Your son is now with Jesus, but it wasn't God's will for him to go now, due to sickness." Because I told these people the truth, they prayed and God showed them some things where they had allowed fear, doubt, and unbelief in. This had hindered their faith and kept them from receiving the miracle they needed. Because they received the truth, they repented and were able to overcome that fear.

The doctors had told this woman that the reason her child was mongoloid was because she was so small. They said the baby should have been taken by a C-section. They concluded that if she ever got pregnant again, the baby would probably have to be taken by C-section and that both she and the child would probably lose their lives. So they told her never to have another child again.

That was back in the early 1970s. Since then, she's had three or four more children. She recently sent me a picture of all of her kids. They had graduated from high school and were in college. She had all natural childbirths at home without any doctor's help, because she knew that no doctor, after seeing her records, would ever allow her to have a baby again. So she just believed God. Instead of going childless and living her entire life in bitterness, wondering *God, why did You do this?* she found out that God wasn't the author of sickness, disease, and death. This precious sister was able to go on and have other children because she took hold of the truth, and the truth set her free.

We Fail to Receive

I understand why we want to say, "Surely this must have been God's will." It's because it makes us look good. It doesn't make us failures. But it's an easy way out—a cop-out. I understand it, and I have been tempted to do the same thing, but it's not God who makes people sick. It's not God who fails to heal us; it's us who fail to receive.

A Cop-out
Lesson 6 – Outline

I. God never intended for what Jesus accomplished through His death, burial, and resurrection to be broken up and separated into different elements.

    A. No, it's actually all a package deal.

    B. God's will is to heal you just as much as it is to forgive you.

    C. He wants you to resist sickness and disease just as much as He wants you to resist sin.

II. Being well seems to be a universal desire.

    A. Consider the effort people put into getting their bodies well.

    B. People universally hate sickness and disease.

    C. That's because God didn't create mankind to die. Death was something man chose, but it wasn't something God chose.

    D. The Lord originally intended for our bodies to live forever.

    E. The medical profession really cannot understand why the body doesn't live forever.

    F. God's original plan was for us never to be sick.

    G. Sickness was not a part of God's plan—it was part of what we unknowingly chose in the Fall.

    H. We were created with a God-given desire on the inside of every one of us for health.

III. Why, then, do some people fight against God being our Healer?

    A. They'll actually say "You are of the devil" if you believe that the Lord heals today.

    B. Others may not reject you for laying hands on the sick and believing for them to recover (Mark 16:18). But they would certainly say it's not God's will to heal every single time.

    C. Although there are many reasons why people are prejudiced, biased, and teach against healing, I believe they all stem from a common root.

IV. People resist the truth that healing is in the Atonement and they resist that it is God's will to heal every time, because it's convenient to believe that way.

    A. There may be some sincere people who have been taught wrong, but the bottom line of this teaching against healing is that it's a cop-out.

    B. It avoids the responsibility that becomes theirs when they accept that God wants them well.

C. If the Lord has provided healing for us—and it's obvious that not everybody is healed—then the question arises, "Why aren't we well?"

D. If God wants us well and we aren't, this means we have to accept some degree of responsibility.

V. Some people argue, "If God wanted someone healed, then they'd be healed whether you or I prayed for them or not."

A. That's not true either. Consider the forgiveness of sins:

> *The Lord is not slack concerning his promise, as some men count slackness; but is longsuffering to us-ward, not willing that any should perish, but that all should come to repentance.*
>
> **2 Peter 3:9**

B. God's will is for people to be saved. Yet not everybody is saved.

C. He doesn't want people to be sick either, but they are.

D. Certainly, some people are in total rebellion toward the Lord and His ways, and they're reaping what they've sown.

E. Yet other people desire healing, and they still fall short.

F. They don't understand how to receive.

G. We need to understand and accept our part.

VI. It's our failure to accept this responsibility that's the root of why we fight against healing.

A. I'm not saying it's our fault directly, although in some cases it could be.

B. Often it's not an individual's sin that brought sickness and disease, but mankind's sin that has corrupted this world.

C. It's the sin that caused germs and viruses, fungi and infections, and the like that were never a part of God's original plan for mankind.

D. They're perversions of nature that happened through sin, not necessarily individual sin, but the collective sin that has corrupted the entire system.

E. Even though it might not be something we did individually that caused sickness, there is always something we can do individually to overcome that perversion and walk in health.

F. It's not God who fails to heal us; it's us who fail to receive.

A Cop-Out
Lesson 6 – Teacher's Guide

1. God never intended for what Jesus accomplished through His death, burial, and resurrection to be broken up and separated into different elements. No, it's actually all a package deal. God's will is to heal us just as much as it is to forgive us. He wants us to resist sickness and disease just as much as He wants us to resist sin.

2. Being well seems to be a universal desire. Consider the effort people put into getting their bodies well. People universally hate sickness and disease. That's because God didn't create mankind to die. Death was something man chose, but it wasn't something God chose. The Lord originally intended for our bodies to live forever. The medical profession really cannot understand why the body doesn't live forever. God's original plan was for us never to be sick. Sickness was not a part of God's plan—it was part of what we unknowingly chose in the Fall. We were created with a God-given desire on the inside of every one of us for health.

3. Why, then, do some people fight against God being our Healer? They'll actually say "You are of the devil" if we believe that the Lord heals today. Others may not reject us for laying hands on the sick and believing for them to recover (Mark 16:18). But they would certainly say that it's not God's will to heal every single time. Although there are many reasons why people are prejudiced, biased, and teach against healing, I believe they all stem from a common root.

1. A. Did God ever intend for what Jesus accomplished through His death, burial, and resurrection to be broken up and separated into different elements? (No)
    B. He wants us to resist sickness just as much as we resist what? (Sin)
2. A. What seems to be a universal desire? (Being well)
    B. What did the Lord originally intend? (For our bodies to live forever)
    C. What was God's original plan? (For us to never be sick)
    D. What was every one of us created with? (A God-given desire for health)
3. Although there are many reasons why people are prejudiced, biased, and teach against healing, what do the reasons have in common? (They all stem from a common root)

4. People resist the truth that healing is in the Atonement and they resist that it is God's will to heal every time, because it's convenient to believe that way. There may be some sincere people who have been taught wrong, but the bottom line of this teaching against healing is that it's a cop-out. It avoids the responsibility that becomes theirs when they accept that God wants them well. If the Lord has provided healing for us—and it's obvious that not everybody is healed—then the question arises, "Why aren't we well?" If God wants us well and we aren't, this means we have to accept some degree of responsibility.

5. Some people argue, "If God wanted certain people healed, then they'd be healed whether you or I prayed for them or not." That's not true either. Consider the forgiveness of sins (2 Pet. 3:9). God's will is for people to be saved. Yet not everybody is saved. He doesn't want anyone to be sick either, but they are. Certainly, some people are in total rebellion toward the Lord and His ways, and they're reaping what they've sown. Yet other people desire healing, and they still fall short. They don't understand how to receive. We need to understand and accept our part.

6. It's our failure to accept this responsibility that's the root of why we fight against healing. I'm not saying it's our fault directly, although in some cases it could be. Often it's not an individual's sin that brought sickness and disease, but mankind's sin that has corrupted this world. It's the sin that caused germs and viruses, fungi and infections, and the like that were never a part of God's original plan for mankind. They're perversions of nature that happened through sin, not necessarily individual sin, but the collective sin that has corrupted the entire system. Even though it might not be something we did individually that caused sickness, there is always something we can do individually to overcome that perversion and walk in health. It's not God who fails to heal us; it's us who fail to receive.

4. A. Why do people resist the truth that healing is in the Atonement and that it is God's will to heal every time? (Because it's convenient to believe that way)
    B. Is it a cop-out? (Yes)
    C. If God wants us well and we aren't, what does this mean? (We have to accept some degree of responsibility)
5. A. Is it true that if God wanted certain people healed, they'd be healed whether you or I prayed for them or not? (No)
    B. What do we need to understand and accept? (Our part)
6. A. If it's often not an individual sin that brought sickness and disease, what is it? (Mankind's sin that has corrupted this world)
    B. Even though it might not be something we did individually that caused sickness, there is always something we can do individually to what? (Overcome that perversion and walk in health)
    C. It's not God who fails to heal us; it's us who what? (Fail to receive)

A Cop-out
Lesson 6 – Additional Information

My teaching entitled *You've Already Got It!* expands and expounds on these concepts more than I'm able to here. Even though it's applied generally to the Christian life, I give many examples of healing and teaching about healing that prove how God has already healed us. It's not a matter of God giving us healing; it's a matter of us reaching out and by faith receiving healing.

A Cop-out
Lesson 6 – Discipleship Questions

1. Read Mark 16:18. Who is saying this?

2. **"They shall lay hands on the sick, and they _____ recover."**

3. According to 2 Peter 3:9, who is the Lord long-suffering to?

4. If He is not willing that any should perish, what is His will?

5. Read Matthew 7:13-14. Where does Jesus instruct us to enter?

6. How many people find the way that leads to life?

7. According to Romans 10:2-3, the zeal that the Jewish people had was not according to _____.

8. If a person, ignorant of God's righteousness, goes about to establish their own righteousness, what have they done?

    A. They have bought the farm.

    B. They have not submitted to the righteousness of God.

    C. They have succeeded.

    D. All of the above.

    E. None of the above.

9. Read 2 Samuel 12:23. Why didn't David want to fast?

10. According to John 8:32, **"Ye shall know the truth, and the truth shall _____ you free."**

A Cop-out
Lesson 6 – Answer Key

1. Jesus.

2. **"Shall."**

3. Us-ward.

4. That all should come to repentance.

5. The strait gate.

6. Few.

7. Knowledge.

8. B. They have not submitted to the righteousness of God.

9. Because his son was dead, and David couldn't bring him back.

10. **"Make."**

A Cop-out
Lesson 6 – Scriptures

Mark 16:18
They shall take up serpents; and if they drink any deadly thing, it shall not hurt them; they shall lay hands on the sick, and they shall recover.

2 Peter 3:9
The Lord is not slack concerning his promise, as some men count slackness; but is longsuffering to us-ward, not willing that any should perish, but that all should come to repentance.

Matthew 7:13-14
Enter ye in at the strait gate: for wide is the gate, and broad is the way, that leadeth to destruction, and many there be which go in thereat: [14] Because strait is the gate, and narrow is the way, which leadeth unto life, and few there be that find it.

Romans 10:2-3
For I bear them record that they have a zeal of God, but not according to knowledge. [3] For they being ignorant of God's righteousness, and going about to establish their own righteousness, have not submitted themselves unto the righteousness of God.

2 Samuel 12:23
But now he is dead, wherefore should I fast? can I bring him back again? I shall go to him, but he shall not return to me.

John 8:32
And ye shall know the truth, and the truth shall make you free.

Paul's Thorn in the Flesh
Lesson 7

Anytime I minister on physical healing, someone brings up Paul's thorn in the flesh. They say, "God gave Paul a thorn in the flesh. He made him sick. Paul tried to believe the Lord for healing but wasn't healed. Since Paul was such a great man of God—and the Lord didn't heal him—who are we to think that God will heal us?" This misconception is based on a misinterpretation of Scripture.

The Bible does not say that Paul's thorn in the flesh was sickness. You can't find that. You can listen to people who argue that, but it's not what the Word really says.

> *And lest I should be exalted above measure through the abundance of the revelations, there was given to me a thorn in the flesh, the messenger of Satan to buffet me, lest I should be exalted above measure. For this thing I besought the Lord thrice, that it might depart from me. And he said unto me, My grace is sufficient for thee: for my strength is made perfect in weakness. Most gladly therefore will I rather glory in my infirmities, that the power of Christ may rest upon me. Therefore I take pleasure in infirmities, in reproaches, in necessities, in persecutions, in distresses for Christ's sake: for when I am weak, then am I strong.*
>
> **2 Corinthians 12:7-10**

In verse 7, Paul made it very clear that this thorn in the flesh was a messenger from Satan, not from God. The Greek word translated **"messenger"** here is also rendered **"angel"** elsewhere in the New Testament (Luke 1:13, 2 Cor. 11:14, and Gal. 4:14, for instance.) Therefore, this was a demonic messenger, a dark angel, sent from the devil to buffet Paul.

From the Devil

Some people erroneously suppose that God gave this thorn in the flesh to Paul because this kept him from being exalted above measure. They just automatically think that this is saying the thorn in the flesh was sent from God to keep him humble. Not true.

Humility is important, but there's also a godly type of exaltation that is mentioned many times in both the Old and New Testament scriptures. One example is 1 Peter 5:6, which says,

> *Humble yourselves therefore under the mighty hand of God, that he may exalt you in due time.*

Being exalted, being lifted up, is good when God does it. However, some people assume that Paul was speaking about pride in 2 Corinthians 12:7. They argue, "Paul had a real problem with pride and arrogance, so God gave him this thorn in the flesh to break him and keep him humble." That's not a godly principle. The Bible says to humble yourself (1 Pet. 5:6). If God does it to you, that's not humility; it's humiliation. Humility is not something you can force on a person; it has to come from the inside out.

Second Corinthians 12:7 is talking about Paul being glorified everywhere he went. He saw people raised from the dead (Acts 20:9-12), demons cast out (Acts 16:16-18), and many other miracles (Acts 19:11-12). The people in one city where he ministered exclaimed, "Those that have turned the world upside down have come here also!" (see Acts 17:6). There was so much power and anointing flowing through Paul's life and ministry that it was drawing many people to the Lord. They were saying, "I want to be like Paul. I want to have the ability to overcome adversity. If I'm thrown in jail for preaching the Gospel, I want an earthquake to come and set me free too!" (Acts 16:25-33). Every time something happened, Paul saw it turn around for his good. People noticed this and were saying, "I want that kind of power in my life too!" Satan recognized that Paul was drawing many people to the Lord because he was walking in such absolute victory and being exalted by God. The devil wanted to debase him and do something to keep him from being exalted. That's what 2 Corinthians 12:7 is talking about. Lest Paul be exalted above measure, Satan gave him a thorn in the flesh. It was from the devil, not God.

I've had people who were sick tell me, "I'm like the Apostle Paul. God has given me a thorn in the flesh, and I'm just supposed to bear it." Remember, it was because of the abundance of the revelations that this thorn came. With those revelations, Paul wrote half of the New Testament. Therefore, anybody who hasn't had an abundance of revelations like Paul did shouldn't be hiding behind Paul's thorn in the flesh today. Besides, this thorn was from Satan, not God.

When I've talked to drug addicts, prostitutes, and adulterers about receiving from God, many of them have told me, "Well, like the Apostle Paul, I've just got a thorn in the flesh." They didn't even have a relationship with God, yet they're claiming Paul's thorn in the flesh. If you have been using this thorn-in-the-flesh thing as an excuse, too, you need to quit hiding behind it unless you have so much revelation that you could write half of the New Testament.

Paul's thorn in the flesh was not sickness. It was a demonic messenger sent from Satan to buffet him.

A Weakness or Inadequacy

Another reason some people think it was sickness is because the word **"infirmities"** is used twice in this passage. Verses 9 and 10 say,

> *And he said unto me, My grace is sufficient for thee: for my strength is made perfect in weakness. Most gladly therefore will I rather glory in my infirmities, that the power of Christ may rest upon me. Therefore I take pleasure in infirmities, in reproaches, in necessities,*

in persecutions, in distresses for Christ's sake: for when I am weak,
then am I strong.

2 Corinthians 12:9-10

The word *infirmity* is used nearly universally nowadays to refer to some type of a sickness. People say, "This person has an infirmity." We even call the place where we send sick people "the infirmary." Although it has an almost exclusive connotation with sickness in its popular use today, the meaning of the word "infirmity" wasn't limited to sickness at the time the *King James* Bible was written. Take, for example, Romans 8:

Likewise the Spirit also helpeth our **infirmities: for we know not**
what we should pray for as we ought*: but the Spirit itself maketh*
intercession for us with groanings which cannot be uttered.

Romans 8:26, emphasis mine

Notice the colon (:) after the word **"infirmities"** and again after the word **"ought."** This verse is saying that it is an infirmity not to know what we should pray for as we ought. If you were to look up the word "infirmity" in the dictionary, you'd find that it not only means a sickness; it could also be any weakness or inadequacy. This is how it was used in Romans 8:26. Not knowing how to pray for something is a weakness, an inadequacy, an infirmity—not a sickness or a disease.

Not Sickness

Some people suppose that Paul was talking about sickness here in 2 Corinthians when he said, "I glory in my infirmities." But as we look at the context, we'll see that it wasn't sickness. We must remember that man put in the chapter and verse divisions later for the purpose of reference. There's nothing wrong with that. But we need to remember that the book we call 2 Corinthians was all one letter. It wasn't broken up by chapter and verse divisions. In what we call 2 Corinthians 11, Paul talked about his infirmities. He said,

If I must needs glory, I will glory of the things which concern mine
infirmities.

2 Corinthians 11:30

Starting in verse 23, Paul defined, explained, and listed what he was calling **"infirmities"**:

Are they ministers of Christ? (I speak as a fool) I am more; in labours
more abundant.

2 Corinthians 11:23

As this list continues, keep in mind that these are all the things that just a few verses later Paul summarized by saying, "I'm going to glory in these infirmities" (2 Cor. 11:30 and 12:9).

He called **"labours more abundant"** (hard work) an infirmity. It caused weakness, stress, and problems in his life.

> *In stripes above measure, in prisons more frequent, in deaths oft. Of the Jews five times received I forty stripes save one.*
>
> **2 Corinthians 11:23-24**

Five times Paul was whipped with thirty-nine stripes.

> *Thrice was I beaten with rods.*
>
> **2 Corinthians 11:25**

Three times he was cruelly beaten with an instrument similar to a metal rod. This was often done on the feet, resulting in broken bones.

> *Once was I stoned.*
>
> **2 Corinthians 11:25**

This happened in Acts 14:19. I personally believe he died. We'll take a closer look at it in the next **Lesson**, but for now...

> *Thrice I suffered shipwreck, a night and a day I have been in the deep; In journeyings often, in perils of waters, in perils of robbers, in perils by mine own countrymen, in perils by the heathen, in perils in the city, in perils in the wilderness, in perils in the sea, in perils among false brethren; In weariness and painfulness, in watchings often, in hunger and thirst, in fastings often, in cold and nakedness. Beside those things that are without, that which cometh upon me daily, the care of all the churches. Who is weak, and I am not weak? who is offended, and I burn not? If I must needs glory, I will glory of the things which concern mine infirmities.*
>
> **2 Corinthians 11:25-30**

Persecutions & Hardships

All of these things listed were talking about persecution and hardships that Paul endured for the cause of Christ. Then, just a few verses later, he declared,

> *Most gladly therefore will I rather glory in my infirmities.*
>
> **2 Corinthians 12:9**

In context, **"infirmities"** here is talking about all of the hardships he suffered for the Gospel. It's a wrong assumption to just take the word "infirmity" and assume that it refers to sickness when, in context of other verses, Paul made it very clear that it didn't. Romans 8:26 used the same word—**"infirmities"**—to refer to a lack of knowledge or understanding about how to pray.

Paul's thorn in the flesh was a messenger from Satan (2 Cor. 12:7). Many people jump to the conclusion of sickness because of this word "infirmity." Yet, in context, it was used in a different way here, to describe the persecutions and hardships Paul suffered because of the Gospel. Verse 10 goes on to make it very clear, saying,

> *Therefore I take pleasure in infirmities, in reproaches, in necessities, in persecutions, in distresses for Christ's sake: for when I am weak, then am I strong.*
>
> **2 Corinthians 12:10**

Although some people assume the word **"infirmities"** here means physical sickness, the other four things listed in this verse and the context of 2 Corinthians 11:23-33 immediately before this reveal otherwise. The other four things listed in 2 Corinthians 12:10 are reproaches, necessities, persecutions, and distresses. Every one of these makes it very clear that this is not talking about some kind of physical sickness. Rather, it was speaking of a hardship or persecution that Paul had to deal with. **"Reproaches"** were insults, injuries, harms, and hurts. **"Necessities"** refers to doing without certain things for the Gospel's sake. **"Persecutions"** and **"distresses"** are easily understood. All of these are consistent with the context of this passage. If Paul was using this word "infirmity" to mean physical sickness, it would be inconsistent with the other things he listed here. **"Infirmities"** here is referring to the hardships he suffered for the cause of the Lord.

Old Testament Imagery

Also, the people with a Jewish background in the church that Paul was writing to would recognize the phrase **"thorn in the flesh"** from the early books of the Old Testament:

> *But if ye will not drive out the inhabitants of the land from before you; then it shall come to pass, that those which ye let remain of them shall be pricks in your eyes, and thorns in your sides, and shall vex you in the land wherein ye dwell.*
>
> **Numbers 33:55**

Moses told the Israelites that if they did not drive out the inhabitants of the land from before them, then these heathen people would persecute and corrupt them. They would be stained and tainted through these pagan people if they let them live.

> *Know for a certainty that the LORD your God will no more drive out any of these nations from before you; but they shall be snares and traps unto you, and scourges in your sides, and thorns in your eyes,*

until ye perish from off this good land which the LORD your God hath given you.

Joshua 23:13

The Israelites hadn't obeyed God. So the Lord said, "All right, the prophecy that Moses gave in Numbers 33:55 is going to come to pass." Once again He referred to people as being scourges in their sides or thorns in their eyes.

Wherefore I also said, I will not drive them out from before you; but they shall be as thorns in your sides, and their gods shall be a snare unto you.

Judges 2:3

When Paul used the terminology **"thorn in the flesh,"** their minds immediately went back to the imagery in the Old Testament scriptures of Numbers 33:55, Joshua 23:13, and Judges 2:3. In each case, it referred to people who were antagonistic toward God's people. This is further biblical evidence that Paul's thorn in the flesh was a demonic personality, a dark angel, a messenger from Satan that stirred up persecutions everywhere Paul went. He made reference to this in 1 Corinthians 4, saying, in essence, "We apostles suffer more than anybody else. The people we minister to are esteemed and blessed, but we are despised and considered the scourges of the earth…"

For I think that God hath set forth us the apostles last, as it were appointed to death: for we are made a spectacle unto the world, and to angels, and to men. We are fools for Christ's sake, but ye are wise in Christ; we are weak, but ye are strong; ye are honourable, but we are despised. Even unto this present hour we both hunger, and thirst, and are naked, and are buffeted, and have no certain dwellingplace; And labour, working with our own hands: being reviled, we bless; being persecuted, we suffer it: Being defamed, we entreat: we are made as the filth of the world, and are the offscouring of all things unto this day.

1 Corinthians 4:9-13

In other words, Paul was talking about the hardships and persecution that he endured. It's apparent in the Word that this demonic messenger worked hard to influence people to persecute Paul wherever he went. Paul walked in victory, but he also endured more persecution, shipwrecks, beatings, imprisonment, rejection, and criticism than anyone else. Satan used this opposition against him. Even though the power of God was manifest in Paul's life, it was not without a price. This made other people think twice. The devil was doing this to turn people away from Paul's message. They may have even reasoned in their hearts, *What he's saying is true, but I'm not sure I'd like to suffer the way he suffered in order to be able to walk in it.*

"My Grace Is Sufficient"

So Paul sought the Lord three times to remove this thorn in the flesh, this demonic angel that stirred up persecution through people. As we saw in the Old Testament, that's what a thorn in the flesh is: persecution through people. Paul asked Jesus three times to remove it and the Lord answered,

> *My grace is sufficient for thee: for my strength is made perfect in weakness.*
>
> ## 2 Corinthians 12:9

Through Christ's Atonement, we have been redeemed from sickness, but not from persecution. Paul himself acknowledged this truth later in his life while writing to Timothy:

> *Yea, and all that will live godly in Christ Jesus shall suffer persecution.*
>
> ## 2 Timothy 3:12

Perhaps Paul didn't understand this yet when he asked God to take this thorn in the flesh away. He was pressing in as hard as he could to receive all that the Lord had for him (Phil. 3:14). He was even trying to get free from and stop the persecution. Finally, the Lord told him, "Paul, you aren't redeemed from persecution. But I'll give you My grace to deal with it."

Just think: If God had redeemed us from persecution and He stopped all of our persecutors, there never would have been an Apostle Paul. Paul himself had been a persecutor. Paul was there participating in the stoning death of Stephen (Acts 7:58). If God would have just wiped out all of the persecutors, there never would have been an Apostle Paul. God doesn't just stop all of our persecutors. Rather, He reveals Himself to people through us as we continue to love them, forgive them, turn the other cheek, and follow Jesus. It's a powerful testimony when we continue to love God despite their threats, and God uses it. We aren't redeemed from persecution, but we are redeemed from sickness.

Paul's Thorn in the Flesh
Lesson 7 – Outline

I. Anytime I minister on physical healing, someone brings up Paul's thorn in the flesh.

    A. They say, "God gave Paul a thorn in the flesh. He made him sick. Paul tried to believe the Lord for healing but wasn't healed."

    B. This misconception is based on a misinterpretation of Scripture.

> *And lest I should be exalted above measure through the abundance of the revelations, there was given to me a thorn in the flesh, the messenger of Satan to buffet me, lest I should be exalted above measure. For this thing I besought the Lord thrice, that it might depart from me. And he said unto me, My grace is sufficient for thee: for my strength is made perfect in weakness. Most gladly therefore will I rather glory in my infirmities, that the power of Christ may rest upon me. Therefore I take pleasure in infirmities, in reproaches, in necessities, in persecutions, in distresses for Christ's sake: for when I am weak, then am I strong.*
>
> **2 Corinthians 12:7-10**

    C. In verse 7, Paul made it very clear that this thorn in the flesh was a messenger from Satan, not from God.

    D. The Greek word translated **"messenger"** here is also rendered **"angel"** elsewhere in the New Testament (Luke 1:13, 2 Cor. 11:14, and Gal. 4:14).

    E. Therefore, this was a demonic messenger, a dark angel, sent from the devil to buffet Paul.

II. Some people erroneously suppose that God gave this thorn in the flesh to Paul because this kept him from being exalted above measure.

    A. They just automatically think this is saying the thorn in the flesh was sent from God to keep him humble. Not true.

> *Humble yourselves therefore under the mighty hand of God, that he may exalt you in due time.*
>
> **1 Peter 5:6**

    B. Being exalted, being lifted up, is good when God does it.

    C. The Bible says to humble yourself.

    D. If God does it to you, that's not humility; it's humiliation.

E. Humility is not something you can force on a person; it has to come from the inside out.

III. Satan recognized that Paul was drawing many people to the Lord because he was walking in such absolute victory and being exalted by God.

    A. Lest Paul be exalted above measure, Satan gave him a thorn in the flesh.

    B. It was from the devil, not God.

    C. I've had people who were sick tell me, "I'm like the Apostle Paul. God has given me a thorn in the flesh, and I'm just supposed to bear it."

    D. Remember, it was because of the abundance of the revelations that this thorn came.

    E. If you have been using this thorn-in-the-flesh thing as an excuse, too, you need to quit hiding behind it unless you have so much revelation that you could write half of the New Testament.

IV. Another reason some people think it was sickness is because the word **"infirmities"** is used twice here in 2 Corinthians 12:9-10.

    A. We must remember that man put in the chapter and verse divisions later for the purpose of reference. Second Corinthians wasn't broken up by chapter and verse divisions.

    B. Starting in 2 Corinthians 11:23, Paul defined, explained, and listed what he was calling **"infirmities."**

    C. All of these things listed were talking about persecution and hardships that Paul endured for the cause of Christ.

    D. Then, just a few verses later, he declared,

Most gladly therefore will I rather glory in my infirmities.

2 Corinthians 12:9

    E. In context, **"infirmities"** here is talking about all of the hardships he suffered for the Gospel.

    F. Verse 10 goes on to make it very clear, saying,

Therefore I take pleasure in infirmities, in reproaches, in necessities, in persecutions, in distresses for Christ's sake: for when I am weak, then am I strong.

2 Corinthians 12:10

    G. Every one of these makes it very clear that this is not talking about some kind of physical sickness. Rather, it was speaking of a hardship or persecution that Paul had to deal with.

V. Also, the people with a Jewish background in the church that Paul was writing to would recognize the phrase **"thorn in the flesh"** from the early books of the Old Testament.

    A. When Paul used the terminology **"thorn in the flesh,"** their minds immediately went back to the imagery in the Old Testament scriptures of Numbers 33:55, Joshua 23:13, and Judges 2:3.

    B. In each case, it referred to people who were antagonistic toward God's people.

VI. Paul walked in victory, but he also endured more persecution, shipwrecks, beatings, imprisonment, rejection, and criticism than anyone else.

    A. The devil was doing this to turn people away from Paul's message.

    B. So Paul sought the Lord three times to remove this thorn in the flesh, this demonic angel that stirred up persecution through people.

    C. The Lord answered,

> *My grace is sufficient for thee: for my strength is made perfect in weakness.*
>
> **2 Corinthians 12:9**

VII. Through Christ's Atonement, we have been redeemed from sickness, but not from persecution.

    A. Paul himself acknowledged this truth later in his life while writing to Timothy:

> *Yea, and all that will live godly in Christ Jesus shall suffer persecution.*
>
> **2 Timothy 3:12**

    B. God doesn't just stop all of our persecutors.

    C. Rather, He reveals Himself to people through us as we continue to love them, forgive them, turn the other cheek, and follow Jesus.

    D. It's a powerful testimony when we continue to love God despite their threats, and God uses it.

    E. We aren't redeemed from persecution, but we are redeemed from sickness.

Paul's Thorn in the Flesh
Lesson 7 – Teacher's Guide

1. Anytime I minister on physical healing, someone brings up Paul's thorn in the flesh. They say, "God gave Paul a thorn in the flesh. He made him sick. Paul tried to believe the Lord for healing but wasn't healed." This misconception is based on a misinterpretation of Scripture (2 Cor. 12:7-10). In verse 7, Paul made it very clear that this thorn in the flesh was a messenger from Satan, not from God. The Greek word translated **"messenger"** here is also rendered **"angel"** elsewhere in the New Testament (Luke 1:13, 2 Cor. 11:14, and Gal. 4:14). Therefore, this was a demonic messenger, a dark angel, sent from the devil to buffet Paul.

2. Some people erroneously suppose that God gave this thorn in the flesh to Paul because this kept him from being exalted above measure. They just automatically think this is saying the thorn in the flesh was sent from God to keep him humble. Not true (1 Pet. 5:6). Being exalted, being lifted up, is good when God does it. The Bible says to humble ourselves. If God does it to us, that's not humility; it's humiliation. Humility is not something we can force on a person; it has to come from the inside out.

3. Satan recognized that Paul was drawing many people to the Lord because he was walking in such absolute victory and being exalted by God. Lest Paul be exalted above measure, Satan gave him a thorn in the flesh. It was from the devil, not God. I've had people who were sick tell me, "I'm like the Apostle Paul. God has given me a thorn in the flesh, and I'm just supposed to bear it." Remember, it was because of the abundance of the revelations that this thorn came. If we have been using this thorn-in-the-flesh thing as an excuse, too, we need to quit hiding behind it unless we have so much revelation that we could write half of the New Testament.

1. A. Read 2 Corinthians 12:7-10. In verse 7, what did Paul make clear? (That this thorn in the flesh was a messenger from Satan, not from God)
    B. What was the demonic messenger sent to do? (Buffet Paul)
2. A. What do some people erroneously suppose? (That God gave this thorn in the flesh to Paul because this kept him from being exalted above measure)
    B. When is it good to be lifted up, exalted? (When God does it)
    C. Humility is not something we can force on a person, but it has to come from where? (The inside out)
3. A. Lest Paul be exalted above measure, what did Satan do? (Gave him a thorn in the flesh)
    B. Was it from God? (No)
    C. Unless we have so much revelation that we could write half of the New Testament, what do we need to do? (Quit hiding behind this thorn-in-the-flesh thing)

4. Another reason some people think it was sickness is because the word **"infirmities"** is used twice here in 2 Corinthians 12:9-10. We must remember that man put in the chapter and verse divisions later for the purpose of reference. Second Corinthians wasn't broken up by chapter and verse divisions. Starting in 2 Corinthians 11:23, Paul defined, explained, and listed what he was calling **"infirmities."** All of these things listed were talking about persecution and hardships that Paul endured for the cause of Christ. Then, just a few verses later, he declared, **"Most gladly therefore will I rather glory in my infirmities"** (2 Cor. 12:9). In context, **"infirmities"** here is talking about all of the hardships he suffered for the Gospel. Verse 10 goes on to make it very clear, saying, **"Therefore I take pleasure in infirmities, in reproaches, in necessities, in persecutions, in distresses for Christ's sake: for when I am weak, then am I strong"** (2 Cor. 12:10). Every one of these makes it very clear that this is not talking about some kind of physical sickness. Rather, it was speaking of a hardship or persecution that Paul had to deal with.

5. Also, the people with a Jewish background in the church that Paul was writing to would recognize the phrase **"thorn in the flesh"** from the early books of the Old Testament. When Paul used the terminology **"thorn in the flesh,"** their minds immediately went back to the imagery in the Old Testament scriptures of Numbers 33:55, Joshua 23:13, and Judges 2:3. In each case, it referred to people who were antagonistic toward God's people.

6. Paul walked in victory, but he also endured more persecution, shipwrecks, beatings, imprisonment, rejection, and criticism than anyone else. The devil was doing this to turn people away from Paul's message. So Paul sought the Lord three times to remove this thorn in the flesh, this demonic angel that stirred up persecution through people. The Lord answered, **"My grace is sufficient for thee: for my strength is made perfect in weakness"** (2 Cor. 12:9).

4. Starting in 2 Corinthians 11:23, what did Paul define, explain, and list as **"infirmities"**? (Persecution and hardships that he endured for the cause of Christ)
5. A. Is the phrase **"thorn in the flesh"** only found in the New Testament? (No)
   B. What did it refer to in the Old Testament? (People who were antagonistic toward God's people)
6. A. Why was the devil doing what he did to Paul? (To turn people away from Paul's message)
   B. When Paul had sought the Lord three times to remove this thorn in the flesh, what did He say? (**"My grace is sufficient for thee: for my strength is made perfect in weakness"**)

7.   Through Christ's Atonement, we have been redeemed from sickness, but not from persecution. Paul himself acknowledged this truth later in his life while writing to Timothy: **"Yea, and all that will live godly in Christ Jesus shall suffer persecution"** (2 Tim. 3:12). God doesn't just stop all of our persecutors. Rather, He reveals Himself to people through us as we continue to love them, forgive them, turn the other cheek, and follow Jesus. It's a powerful testimony when we continue to love God despite their threats, and God uses it. We aren't redeemed from persecution, but we are redeemed from sickness.

7.   A. Have we been redeemed from persecution? (No)
      B. What does God do instead of stopping our persecutors? (He reveals Himself to people through us as we continue to love them, forgive them, turn the other cheek, and follow Jesus)
      C. What is a powerful testimony? (When we continue to love God despite their threats)

Paul's Thorn in the Flesh
Lesson 7 – Discipleship Questions

1. Read 2 Corinthians 12:7-10. A thorn in the flesh was given to Paul lest he should be _____ through the abundance of the revelations.

    A. Paid above normal.

    B. Warmed and filled.

    C. Exalted above measure.

    D. All of the above.

    E. None of the above.

2. What was made perfect in Paul's weakness?

3. According to Luke 1:13, the angel greeted Zacharias by saying what?

4. Read 2 Corinthians 11:14. What can Satan be transformed into?

5. According to Galatians 4:14, was Paul despised or rejected because of the temptation in his flesh?

6. How was he received?

7. According to 1 Peter 5:6, if we humble ourselves, what will God do?

8. Read Acts 20:9-12. When did Eutychus fall asleep?

9. When Eutychus was raised from the dead, were the people only a little comforted?

10. According to Acts 16:16-18, whom did Paul speak to?

11. Read Acts 19:11-12. God worked _____ miracles by the hands of Paul.

12. According to Acts 17:6, whom were Jason and certain brethren taken to?

13. Read Acts 16:25-33. What did Paul and Silas answer the keeper of the prison?

14. He and his entire house were baptized when?

15. According to Romans 8:26, the Spirit makes intercession for us with groanings that cannot be _____.

16. Read 2 Corinthians 11:23-33. If Paul needed to glory, what was he going to glory in?

17. Read Acts 14:19. After stoning Paul, what did the people do to him?

18. Read Numbers 33:55. What would happen if the inhabitants of the land weren't driven out?

19. According to Joshua 23:13, was the Lord going to drive out the nations from before the Israelites anymore?

20. According to Judges 2:3, what would the gods be to the Israelites?

21. Read 1 Corinthians 4:9-13. Who were the apostles spectacles to?

22. Read 2 Timothy 3:12. Is this a guarantee?

23. Read Philippians 3:14. **"I _____ toward the mark for the prize of the high calling of God in Christ Jesus."**

24. According to Acts 7:58, at that time, Saul was a _____ man.

Paul's Thorn in the Flesh
Lesson 7 – Answer Key

1.   C. Exalted above measure.

2.   The Lord's strength.

3.   **"Fear not."**

4.   An angel of light.

5.   No.

6.   As an angel of God, even as Christ Jesus.

7.   Exalt us in due time.

8.   As Paul was long preaching.

9.   No.

10.   The spirit.

11.   Special.

12.   The rulers of the city.

13.   **"Believe on the Lord Jesus Christ, and thou shalt be saved, and thy house."**

14.   Straightway.

15.   Uttered.

16.   The things that concerned his infirmities.

17.   They dragged him out of the city, supposing he was dead.

18.   Those that remained would be pricks in the Israelites' eyes and thorns in their sides, and the inhabitants would vex them in the land where the Israelites dwelt.

19.   No.

20.   A snare.

21.   The world, angels, and people.

22.   Yes.

23.   Press.

24.   Young.

Paul's Thorn in the Flesh
Lesson 7 – Scriptures

2 Corinthians 12:7-10
And lest I should be exalted above measure through the abundance of the revelations, there was given to me a thorn in the flesh, the messenger of Satan to buffet me, lest I should be exalted above measure. [8] For this thing I besought the Lord thrice, that it might depart from me. [9] And he said unto me, My grace is sufficient for thee: for my strength is made perfect in weakness. Most gladly therefore will I rather glory in my infirmities, that the power of Christ may rest upon me. [10] Therefore I take pleasure in infirmities, in reproaches, in necessities, in persecutions, in distresses for Christ's sake: for when I am weak, then am I strong.

Luke 1:13
But the angel said unto him, Fear not, Zacharias: for thy prayer is heard; and thy wife Elisabeth shall bear thee a son, and thou shalt call his name John.

2 Corinthians 11:14
And no marvel; for Satan himself is transformed into an angel of light.

Galatians 4:14
And my temptation which was in my flesh ye despised not, nor rejected; but received me as an angel of God, even as Christ Jesus.

1 Peter 5:6
Humble yourselves therefore under the mighty hand of God, that he may exalt you in due time.

Acts 20:9-12
And there sat in a window a certain young man named Eutychus, being fallen into a deep sleep: and as Paul was long preaching, he sunk down with sleep, and fell down from the third loft, and was taken up dead. [10] And Paul went down, and fell on him, and embracing him said, Trouble not yourselves; for his life is in him. [11] When he therefore was come up again, and had broken bread, and eaten, and talked a long while, even till break of day, so he departed. [12] And they brought the young man alive, and were not a little comforted.

Acts 16:16-18
And it came to pass, as we went to prayer, a certain damsel possessed with a spirit of divination met us, which brought her masters much gain by soothsaying: [17] The same followed Paul and us, and cried, saying, These men are the servants of the most high God, which shew unto us the way of salvation. [18] And this did she many days. But Paul, being grieved, turned and said to the

spirit, I command thee in the name of Jesus Christ to come out of her. And he came out the same hour.

Acts 19:11-12
And God wrought special miracles by the hands of Paul: [12] So that from his body were brought unto the sick handkerchiefs or aprons, and the diseases departed from them, and the evil spirits went out of them.

Acts 17:6
And when they found them not, they drew Jason and certain brethren unto the rulers of the city, crying, These that have turned the world upside down are come hither also.

Acts 16:25-33
And at midnight Paul and Silas prayed, and sang praises unto God: and the prisoners heard them. [26] And suddenly there was a great earthquake, so that the foundations of the prison were shaken: and immediately all the doors were opened, and every one's bands were loosed. [27] And the keeper of the prison awaking out of his sleep, and seeing the prison doors open, he drew out his sword, and would have killed himself, supposing that the prisoners had been fled. [28] But Paul cried with a loud voice, saying, Do thyself no harm: for we are all here. [29] Then he called for a light, and sprang in, and came trembling, and fell down before Paul and Silas, [30] And brought them out, and said, Sirs, what must I do to be saved? [31] And they said, Believe on the Lord Jesus Christ, and thou shalt be saved, and thy house. [32] And they spake unto him the word of the Lord, and to all that were in his house. [33] And he took them the same hour of the night, and washed their stripes; and was baptized, he and all his, straightway.

Romans 8:26
Likewise the Spirit also helpeth our infirmities: for we know not what we should pray for as we ought: but the Spirit itself maketh intercession for us with groanings which cannot be uttered.

2 Corinthians 11:23-33
Are they ministers of Christ? (I speak as a fool) I am more; in labours more abundant, in stripes above measure, in prisons more frequent, in deaths oft. [24] Of the Jews five times received I forty stripes save one. [25] Thrice was I beaten with rods, once was I stoned, thrice I suffered shipwreck, a night and a day I have been in the deep; [26] In journeyings often, in perils of waters, in perils of robbers, in perils by mine own countrymen, in perils by the heathen, in perils in the city, in perils in the wilderness, in perils in the sea, in perils among false brethren; [27] In weariness and painfulness, in watchings often, in hunger and thirst, in fastings often, in cold and nakedness. [28] Beside those things that are without, that which cometh upon me daily, the care of all the churches. [29] Who is weak, and I am not weak? who is offended, and I burn not? [30] If

I must needs glory, I will glory of the things which concern mine infirmities. [31] The God and Father of our Lord Jesus Christ, which is blessed for evermore, knoweth that I lie not. [32] In Damascus the governor under Aretas the king kept the city of the Damascenes with a garrison, desirous to apprehend me: [33] And through a window in a basket was I let down by the wall, and escaped his hands.

Acts 14:19
And there came thither certain Jews from Antioch and Iconium, who persuaded the people, and, having stoned Paul, drew him out of the city, supposing he had been dead.

Numbers 33:55
But if ye will not drive out the inhabitants of the land from before you; then it shall come to pass, that those which ye let remain of them shall be pricks in your eyes, and thorns in your sides, and shall vex you in the land wherein ye dwell.

Joshua 23:13
Know for a certainty that the LORD your God will no more drive out any of these nations from before you; but they shall be snares and traps unto you, and scourges in your sides, and thorns in your eyes, until ye perish from off this good land which the LORD your God hath given you.

Judges 2:3
Wherefore I also said, I will not drive them out from before you; but they shall be as thorns in your sides, and their gods shall be a snare unto you.

1 Corinthians 4:9-13
For I know nothing by myself; yet am I not hereby justified: but he that judgeth me is the Lord. [5] Therefore judge nothing before the time, until the Lord come, who both will bring to light the hidden things of darkness, and will make manifest the counsels of the hearts: and then shall every man have praise of God. [6] And these things, brethren, I have in a figure transferred to myself and to Apollos for your sakes; that ye might learn in us not to think of men above that which is written, that no one of you be puffed up for one against another. [7] For who maketh thee to differ from another? and what hast thou that thou didst not receive? now if thou didst receive it, why dost thou glory, as if thou hadst not received it? [8] Now ye are full, now ye are rich, ye have reigned as kings without us: and I would to God ye did reign, that we also might reign with you. [9] For I think that God hath set forth us the apostles last, as it were appointed to death: for we are made a spectacle unto the world, and to angels, and to men. [10] We are fools for Christ's sake, but ye are wise in Christ; we are weak, but ye are strong; ye are honourable, but we are despised. [11] Even unto this present hour we both hunger, and thirst, and are naked, and are buffeted, and have no certain dwellingplace; [12] And labour, working with our own hands: being reviled, we bless; being persecuted, we suffer it: [13] Being defamed, we intreat: we are made as the filth of the world, and are the offscouring of all things unto this day.

2 Timothy 3:12
Yea, and all that will live godly in Christ Jesus shall suffer persecution.

Philippians 3:14
I press toward the mark for the prize of the high calling of God in Christ Jesus.

Acts 7:58
And cast him out of the city, and stoned him: and the witnesses laid down their clothes at a young man's feet, whose name was Saul.

Eye Problems?
Lesson 8

Some people teach that Paul had a sickness that God refused to heal him of, and therefore we can't expect to be healed of all sicknesses today. That's not true. It's not a consistent interpretation with the whole of God's Word. As we saw in the previous **Lesson,** Paul's thorn in the flesh wasn't sickness but rather a demonic messenger sent from Satan to stir up persecution.

People who teach that Paul's thorn in the flesh was sickness often misinterpret Galatians 4. They theorize that he had some kind of eye disease that caused runny, puffy eyes and gave him constant eye problems. They attempt to verify this with a passage in this chapter:

> *Brethren, I beseech you, be as I am; for I am as ye are: ye have not injured me at all. Ye know how through infirmity of the flesh I preached the gospel unto you at the first. And my temptation which was in my flesh ye despised not, nor rejected; but received me as an angel of God, even as Christ Jesus. Where is then the blessedness ye spake of? for I bear you record, that, if it had been possible, ye would have plucked out your own eyes, and have given them to me.*
>
> **Galatians 4:12-15**

"Infirmity of the Flesh"

Notice the terminology in verse 13, **"infirmity of the flesh."** This wasn't just an "infirmity"; it was an **"infirmity of the flesh."** Paul wasn't talking about a lack of understanding (as in not knowing how to pray, Rom. 8:26) or a hardship that he endured (like the shipwrecks and perils mentioned in 2 Cor. 11:25-26). This is literally talking about some kind of physical problem. Since he used the terminology **"infirmity of the flesh,"** he qualified it. He basically used this same terminology again in verse 14 of Galatians 4.

Some people look at this and argue, "Paul said right here that he did have an infirmity!" Yes, he did mention a problem here. But notice what he said in verse 13:

> *Ye know how through infirmity of the flesh I preached the gospel unto you at the first.*
>
> **Galatians 4:13**

"At the first" implies that it wasn't something long-term that God wouldn't heal him of. It was something temporary. Paul went on to say,

Where is then the blessedness ye spake of? for I bear you record, that, if it had been possible, ye would have plucked out your own eyes, and have given them to me.

Galatians 4:15

Some people say, "Look, now Paul's talking about an eye problem. That's his infirmity of the flesh." So they theorize that this was an ancient Aramaic disease of runny, puffy eyes that lasted throughout Paul's entire life. If you can swallow that, then you can make the Bible say anything you want. That is a flimsy basis of interpretation!

Left for Dead

Let's consider a much more accurate interpretation. In order to do so, we need to look at Acts 14. Paul was preaching in Lystra and Derbe. For a while, the people there thought he was a god:

And when the people saw what Paul had done, they lifted up their voices, saying in the speech of Lycaonia, The gods are come down to us in the likeness of men. And they called Barnabas, Jupiter; and Paul, Mercurius, because he was the chief speaker.

Acts 14:11-12

Paul and Barnabas restrained the people from offering a sacrifice and worshiping them. However, the very next day, those same people became mad at them:

And there came thither certain Jews from Antioch and Iconium, who persuaded the people, and, having stoned Paul, drew him out of the city, supposing he had been dead. Howbeit, as the disciples stood round about him, he rose up, and came into the city: and the next day he departed with Barnabas to Derbe.

Acts 14:19-20

This was the instance when Paul was stoned and left for dead. He had referred to this in 2 Corinthians 11:

Once was I stoned.

2 Corinthians 11:25

Personally, I believe he was dead. If he wasn't dead, he was so close to it that the people who were trying to kill him supposed that **"he had been dead"** (Acts 14:19). Whether he was dead or very close to it, the Word says that as the disciples stood round about him, he rose up and came into the city. The next day he departed with Barnabas to Derbe, twenty to fifty miles away (the exact distance is disputed; see Note 3 at Acts 14:20 and Note 5 at Acts 14:6 of *Life for Today Study Bible and Commentary*: the Acts of the Apostles Edition). Paul walked (and/or rode) to the next town, and the next day preached to the people there (Acts 14:20-21). Can you guess where the cities Iconium, Lystra, and Derbe were located? They were all part of a region called Galatia. These are the people Paul was writing to in Galatians 4 when he said, "At first you took pity on me because of this infirmity in my flesh. You would have plucked out your own eyes for me."

Instead of pulling out of the clear blue sky that Paul had some kind of an ancient eye disease, it's much more honest with Scripture to recognize that Galatians 4 is referring to the exact same time period when Paul had been stoned, left for dead, rose up, traveled over twenty miles the next day, and began preaching to the people in the next city. Since Paul went from being stoned to death to preaching in the next city in less than twenty-four hours, is it so inconceivable that his eyes might have been hurting him due to the rocks that had repeatedly struck his head the day before?

If Paul was talking about the fact that he had some damage to his eyes from the stoning the day before, it was only temporary. Paul said it was only **"at the first"** that this **"infirmity of the flesh"** bothered him (Gal. 4:13). Although it's obvious that God's miraculous healing power was at work in his body, it probably took him some time to fully mend. It was something temporary in his body that healed over time. Paul got over it.

Swallowing a Camel

It's also possible that when Paul said "You would have plucked out your own eyes and given them to me," he was using a figure of speech. People say, "You'd give your right arm for me." Does that mean they have bad right arms? No. It's just a figure of speech people use to say that this person would sacrifice anything for them. So Paul saying "You would have plucked out your own eye and given it to me" may not have had anything to do with him having anything wrong with his eyes.

The people who contend that Paul's thorn in the flesh was sickness in the form of some eye disease go on to Galatians 6:

Ye see how large a letter I have written unto you with mine own hand.

Galatians 6:11

I've actually heard someone use this verse to argue that Paul was so nearly blind because of his eyesight problem that his handwriting was three or four inches tall. They said he had to write huge letters to be able to communicate. If that were true and Paul was referring to large-size letters, can you imagine how big this letter to the Galatians had to have been? It would have been volumes and volumes. Nobody could have carried it! He would have had only one or two words on a page. Just count how many words there are in Galatians. That's not what Paul was talking about here.

There are different words for talking about size or quantity in the Greek language. The word translated **"large"** in Galatians 6:11 is the one for quantity. Paul wasn't talking about how big and tall each individual letter of each word was; he was saying, "This letter—this piece of correspondence—that I've written you has become so long." In my Bible, Paul's letter to the

Galatians takes up four pages of small print. If you were to print Galatians out in twelve-point type (Times New Roman font), double-spaced on regular sheets of 8.5 x 11 paper, it would be more than eight pages long. I would consider that a large letter, in the sense that it's long. Most personal notes are only a page long, or less.

The people who argue that Paul was saying that every individual letter of each word he wrote was so big are straining at a gnat and swallowing a camel (Matt. 23:24). People who use these scriptures to say that Paul had an eye disease are breaking every rule of sound Bible interpretation. They're just taking some reference and interpreting it any way they want. If Paul did have any eye problems, referred to in Galatians 4, it was because he was stoned and left for dead the day before, and it was only temporary. That would be the only correlation between what Paul was saying in Galatians 4 and his mentioning of the thorn in the flesh in 2 Corinthians 12:7.

Paul's thorn in the flesh was not some type of sickness; it was a demonic messenger sent from Satan to stir up persecution wherever he went. We are redeemed from sickness but not from persecution.

Eye Problems?
Lesson 8 – Outline

I. Some people teach that Paul had a sickness that God refused to heal him of, and therefore we can't expect to be healed of all sicknesses today.

   A. They attempt to verify this with Galatians 4:

   > *Brethren, I beseech you, be as I am; for I am as ye are: ye have not injured me at all. Ye know how through infirmity of the flesh I preached the gospel unto you at the first. And my temptation which was in my flesh ye despised not, nor rejected; but received me as an angel of God, even as Christ Jesus. Where is then the blessedness ye spake of? for I bear you record, that, if it had been possible, ye would have plucked out your own eyes, and have given them to me.*
   >
   > **Galatians 4:12-15**

   B. Notice the terminology in verse 13, **"infirmity of the flesh."** This is literally talking about some kind of physical problem.

   C. So people theorize that this was an ancient Aramaic disease of runny, puffy eyes that lasted throughout Paul's entire life.

   D. If you can swallow that, then you can make the Bible say anything you want.

II. Let's consider a much more accurate interpretation.

   A. In order to do so, we need to look at Acts 14:11-12 and 19-21.

   B. Paul was preaching in Lystra and Derbe.

   C. This was the instance when he was stoned and left for dead (2 Cor. 11:25).

   D. Can you guess where the cities Iconium, Lystra, and Derbe were located? They were all part of a region called Galatia.

   E. These are the people Paul was writing to in Galatians 4 when he said, "At first you took pity on me because of this infirmity in my flesh. You would have plucked out your own eyes for me."

   F. Instead of pulling out of the clear blue sky that Paul had some kind of an ancient eye disease, it's much more honest with Scripture to recognize that Galatians 4 is referring to the exact same time period when Paul had been stoned, left for dead, rose up, traveled over twenty miles the next day, and began preaching to the people in the next city.

III. If Paul was talking about the fact that he had some damage to his eyes from the stoning the day before, it was only temporary.

    A. Paul said it was only **"at the first"** that this **"infirmity of the flesh"** bothered him.

    B. It was something temporary in his body that healed over time.

    C. Paul got over it.

IV. It's also possible that when Paul said "You would have plucked out your own eyes and given them to me," he was using a figure of speech.

    A. People say, "You'd give your right arm for me."

    B. Does that mean they have bad right arms? No.

    C. It's just a figure of speech people use to say that this person would sacrifice anything for them.

V. The people who contend that Paul's thorn in the flesh was sickness in the form of some eye disease go on to Galatians 6:

Ye see how large a letter I have written unto you with mine own hand.

Galatians 6:11

    A. I've actually heard someone use this verse to argue that Paul was so nearly blind because of his eyesight problem that his handwriting was three or four inches tall.

    B. That's not what Paul was talking about here.

    C. There are different words for talking about size or quantity in the Greek language.

    D. The word translated **"large"** in Galatians 6:11 is the one for quantity.

    E. If you were to print Galatians out in twelve-point type (Times New Roman font), double-spaced on regular sheets of 8.5 x 11 paper, it would be more than eight pages long.

    F. I would consider that a large letter, in the sense that it's long.

VI. If Paul did have any eye problems, referred to in Galatians 4, it was because he was stoned and left for dead the day before, and it was only temporary.

    A. That would be the only correlation between what Paul was saying in Galatians 4 and his mentioning of the thorn in the flesh in 2 Corinthians 12:7.

    B. Paul's thorn in the flesh was not some type of sickness; it was a demonic messenger sent from Satan to stir up persecution wherever he went.

    C. We are redeemed from sickness but not from persecution.

Eye Problems?
Lesson 8 – Teacher's Guide

1. Some people teach that Paul had a sickness that God refused to heal him of, and therefore we can't expect to be healed of all sicknesses today. They attempt to verify this with Galatians 4:12-15. Notice the terminology in verse 13, **"infirmity of the flesh."** This is literally talking about some kind of physical problem. So people theorize that this was an ancient Aramaic disease of runny, puffy eyes that lasted throughout Paul's entire life. If we can swallow that, then we can make the Bible say anything we want.

2. Let's consider a much more accurate interpretation. In order to do so, we need to look at Acts 14:11-12 and 19-21. Paul was preaching in Lystra and Derbe. This was the instance when he was stoned and left for dead (2 Cor. 11:25). Can you guess where the cities Iconium, Lystra, and Derbe were located? They were all part of a region called Galatia. These are the people Paul was writing to in Galatians 4 when he said, "At first you took pity on me because of this infirmity in my flesh. You would have plucked out your own eyes for me."

   Instead of pulling out of the clear blue sky that Paul had some kind of an ancient eye disease, it's much more honest with Scripture to recognize that Galatians 4 is referring to the exact same time period when Paul had been stoned, left for dead, rose up, traveled over twenty miles the next day, and began preaching to the people in the next city.

3. If Paul was talking about the fact that he had some damage to his eyes from the stoning the day before, it was only temporary. Paul said it was only **"at the first"** that this **"infirmity of the flesh"** bothered him. It was something temporary in his body that healed over time. Paul got over it.

1. A. Read Galatians 4:12-15. Is this talking about some kind of physical problem? (Yes)
   B. What do some people theorize? (That this was an ancient Aramaic disease of runny, puffy eyes that lasted throughout Paul's entire life)
2. A. Where were Iconium, Lystra, and Derbe located? (In Galatia)
   B. Read Acts 14:11-12 and 19-21. Instead of pulling out of the clear blue sky that Paul had some kind of an ancient eye disease, what is much more honest with Scripture? (To recognize that Galatians 4 is referring to the exact same time period when Paul had been stoned, left for dead, rose up, traveled over twenty miles the next day, and began preaching to the people in the next city)
3. A. If Paul was talking about the fact that he had some damage to his eyes from the stoning the day before, it was only what? (Temporary)
   B. Did Paul get over it? (Yes)

4.	It's also possible that when Paul said "You would have plucked out your own eyes and given them to me," he was using a figure of speech. People say, "You'd give your right arm for me." Does that mean they have bad right arms? No. It's just a figure of speech people use to say that this person would sacrifice anything for them.

5.	The people who contend that Paul's thorn in the flesh was sickness in the form of some eye disease go on to Galatians 6:11. I've actually heard someone use this verse to argue that Paul was so nearly blind because of his eyesight problem that his handwriting was three or four inches tall. That's not what Paul was talking about here. There are different words for talking about size or quantity in the Greek language. The word translated **"large"** in Galatians 6:11 is the one for quantity. If we were to print Galatians out in twelve-point type (Times New Roman font), double-spaced on regular sheets of 8.5 x 11 paper, it would be more than eight pages long. I would consider that a large letter, in the sense that it's long.

6.	If Paul did have any eye problems, referred to in Galatians 4, it was because he was stoned and left for dead the day before, and it was only temporary. That would be the only correlation between what Paul was saying in Galatians 4 and his mentioning of the thorn in the flesh in 2 Corinthians 12:7. Paul's thorn in the flesh was not some type of sickness; it was a demonic messenger sent from Satan to stir up persecution wherever he went. We are redeemed from sickness but not from persecution.

4.	A.	It's also possible that when Paul said "You would have plucked out your own eyes and given them to me," he was using what? (A figure of speech)
	B.	When people use this figure of speech, what does it mean? (That this person would do anything for them)
5.	A.	Read Galatians 6:11. What did I hear someone use this verse to argue? (That Paul was so nearly blind because of his eyesight problem that his handwriting was three or four inches tall)
	B.	Is the word translated "large" in this verse the one for size or quantity? (Quantity)
6.	A.	If Paul did have any eye problems, referred to in Galatians 4, what was it because of? (He was stoned and left for dead the day before)
	B.	Were his eye problems permanent? (No)
	C.	If Paul's thorn in the flesh was not some type of sickness, what was it? (A demonic messenger sent from Satan to stir up persecution wherever he went)

Eye Problems?
Lesson 8 – Discipleship Questions

1. Read Galatians 4:12-15. Even though Paul had an infirmity of the flesh, what did he do?

2. What would the people of Galatia have done for Paul?

3. According to Romans 8:26, what does the Spirit make for us?

4. According to 2 Corinthians 11:25-26, was Paul rarely persecuted?

5. Read Acts 14:11-12. Why did the people think Paul and Barnabas were gods come down in the likeness of men?

6. Read Acts 14:19-21. What happened when the disciples stood round about Paul after he had been stoned?

7. In Derbe, Paul and Barnabas preached the Gospel to that city and taught _____.

    A. No one.

    B. A few people.

    C. Algebra.

    D. Everyone.

    E. Many.

8. According to Acts 14:6, where did Paul and Barnabas flee to?

9. Read Galatians 6:11. Whose hand wrote the letter to the Galatians?

10. According to Matthew 23:24, what kind of guides were Jesus talking to?

11. Were they physically blind?

12. Read 2 Corinthians 12:7. Paul was given a messenger of _____, lest he should be exalted above measure.

Eye Problems?
Lesson 8 – Answer Key

1. He preached the Gospel.

2. They would have plucked out their own eyes and given them to him.

3. Intercession.

4. No.

5. Because of what they saw Paul do.

6. He stood up and came into the city.

7. E. Many.

8. Lystra, Derbe, and the surrounding region.

9. Paul's.

10. Blind guides.

11. No.

12. Satan.

Eye Problems?
Lesson 8 – Scriptures

Galatians 4:12-15
Brethren, I beseech you, be as I am; for I am as ye are: ye have not injured me at all. [13] Ye know how through infirmity of the flesh I preached the gospel unto you at the first. [14] And my temptation which was in my flesh ye despised not, nor rejected; but received me as an angel of God, even as Christ Jesus. [15] Where is then the blessedness ye spake of? for I bear you record, that, if it had been possible, ye would have plucked out your own eyes, and have given them to me.

Romans 8:26
Likewise the Spirit also helpeth our infirmities: for we know not what we should pray for as we ought: but the Spirit itself maketh intercession for us with groanings which cannot be uttered.

2 Corinthians 11:25-26
Thrice was I beaten with rods, once was I stoned, thrice I suffered shipwreck, a night and a day I have been in the deep; [26] In journeyings often, in perils of waters, in perils of robbers, in perils by mine own countrymen, in perils by the heathen, in perils in the city, in perils in the wilderness, in perils in the sea, in perils among false brethren.

Acts 14:11-12
And when the people saw what Paul had done, they lifted up their voices, saying in the speech of Lycaonia, The gods are come down to us in the likeness of men. [12] And they called Barnabas, Jupiter; and Paul, Mercurius, because he was the chief speaker.

Acts 14:19-21
And there came thither certain Jews from Antioch and Iconium, who persuaded the people, and, having stoned Paul, drew him out of the city, supposing he had been dead. [20] Howbeit, as the disciples stood round about him, he rose up, and came into the city: and the next day he departed with Barnabas to Derbe. [21] And when they had preached the gospel to that city, and had taught many, they returned again to Lystra, and to Iconium, and Antioch.

Acts 14:6
They were ware of it, and fled unto Lystra and Derbe, cities of Lycaonia, and unto the region that lieth round about.

Galatians 6:11
Ye see how large a letter I have written unto you with mine own hand.

Matthew 23:24
Ye blind guides, which strain at a gnat, and swallow a camel.

2 Corinthians 12:7
And lest I should be exalted above measure through the abundance of the revelations, there was given to me a thorn in the flesh, the messenger of Satan to buffet me, lest I should be exalted above measure.

Redeemed from the Curse
Lesson 9

I've given these different interpretations much thought, study, and prayer. I've listened to other people and considered their positions. Yet I believe that what I have shared with you is more honest and more consistent with the whole of Scripture than any of those others. Grabbing at Paul's thorn in the flesh and making it sickness is a convenient theology. In other words, we don't really have to produce. We can just live carnally. We don't have to seek God. We just pray a prayer, and if the person doesn't get healed, we say, "Well, it must be like Paul's thorn in the flesh. God just wants you to bear it." That's a cop-out!

The truth is that the Lord wants us healed. But He has to have someone who can operate in faith, use their God-given authority, exercise His power, and make it manifest. This puts responsibility on us, and many of us have become masters at dodging responsibility.

"Don't Drink the Water"

Some people have tried to use 1 Timothy 5 to counter the truth that it's always God's will to heal. Paul was talking to his son in the faith, Timothy, saying,

> *Drink no longer water, but use a little wine for thy stomach's sake and thine often infirmities.*
>
> **1 Timothy 5:23**

I've actually heard people teach from this that Timothy had some chronic sickness that he never got healed of. Therefore, they teach that if Timothy, who was Paul's right-hand man, didn't get healed, then it's not God's will to heal us either.

This is just one verse of Scripture. It's the only verse in the entire New Testament that talks about Timothy and taking a little wine for his stomach's sake. There is nothing else to compare this with. Therefore, anything anyone says about this is supposition. It's a supposition that he had some chronic sickness that he never got healed of. To offer this verse based on that supposition as proof that God doesn't want to heal us is an inaccurate and dishonest interpretation of Scripture.

Apparently, whatever sickness Timothy had was a stomach problem, and it was related to the water. What happens when you travel to some third-world country and drink the water? That's right: stomach trouble. In Mexico, they call it Montezuma's Revenge. It's because the water isn't good for you to drink. Although I haven't personally experienced this, I have seen many people who have traveled with me to other countries get sick drinking the water. I've heard horror stories of how it bothered them. So Paul was counseling Timothy to quit drinking the water, because that's what was causing Timothy's stomach problems, and to instead drink a little wine.

This isn't some endorsement for medicine. Some people argue that wine has medicinal qualities, and therefore Paul was advising Timothy to take medicine for his stomach problems.

No, it's very clear that this stomach problem was related to the water. So Paul was saying, "Quit drinking the water and drink wine instead." If they had had sodas back then, he could have said, "Stop drinking the water and have a soda instead." But they didn't have sodas back then, just wine. This is not saying that Timothy had some chronic problem from which he never received healing; this is just Paul telling Timothy, "Quit drinking the water. That's what is causing you to have an upset stomach. Drink something else instead." It's like me saying to a Bible college student while we're on a missions trip in a foreign country, "Don't drink the tap water here. Drink bottled water or have a soda instead, but don't drink the water." That's all he's saying.

From this verse, 1 Timothy 5:23, people have invented some kind of a doctrine that makes it look like God wants us to be sick. That's inaccurate. It's not being honest with Scripture.

You Have to Believe

Erastus abode at Corinth: but Trophimus have I left at Miletum sick.

2 Timothy 4:20

Some folks argue, "Even one of Paul's companions, Trophimus, didn't get healed. Therefore, it must not be God's will to heal everybody." It's true that not everyone receives healing, but that doesn't mean it's because God doesn't want them to be healed. Not everyone receives salvation, but it's very obvious that God wants everyone to be saved. Just because people are sick doesn't mean that God willed them to be ill. People infer that, because Trophimus was traveling with the Apostle Paul. They say, "If it was God's will for him to be healed, he would have received."

People say the same thing to me because an associate or an employee of mine is ill, has some kind of a sickness that they get an operation for, or they wear glasses. These people will ask, "If it was God's will to heal them, then how come they aren't healed?" I can't get another person healed only on my faith. A person doesn't get healed just by being around someone who has faith. It doesn't come by osmosis. Each individual has to believe.

Trophimus had to believe. The Word doesn't tell us why he was left at Miletum. Possibly, he was believing God, and it just took a period of time for healing to manifest in his body. Perhaps Paul didn't want to wait for the healing to manifest and went on ahead. It's possible that Trophimus was healed and caught up with Paul later on or ministered in some other way.

It's also possible that Trophimus just quit believing God, so Paul decided to leave him there sick.

There are other possibilities, but there is no reason to interpret Paul leaving Trophimus sick at Miletum as some indication that God doesn't want us to be healed.

Never a Blessing

If we're honest with the Scripture, we've debunked the misinterpretations people use to undermine healing. It's not true to say that God wants certain people sick. You may still be wondering about some scriptures like Romans 8:28, which says that God works all things together for good.

Because of a wrong understanding of God's sovereignty, some people think that the Lord controls everything and that a person couldn't be sick unless God allowed it. That is not what the Word teaches. Again, God doesn't allow people to go to hell. In one sense, you could say that He allows it because of His high regard for our free will. But it's not His desire, wish, or plan. God puts roadblocks in our way, inviting us to repent and be born again, but ultimately He gives us the choice. God doesn't control us like pawns in a chess game. Those who go to hell have to climb over mountains of obstacles that the Lord placed in their path.

Although there are several Old Testament references for when God struck people with sickness, not once was it ever considered a blessing. Both Miriam (Num. 12) and King Uzziah (2 Chr. 26) became leprous. A plague killed 185,000 people (2 Kin. 19). The angel of the Lord went through and killed all the firstborn of the Egyptians in one night (Ex. 12). Yes, God put sickness on people under the Old Covenant, but it was never a blessing.

Prior to being struck with leprosy, Miriam had been a great leader among the children of Israel. After this incident, the only thing said about her in the Word was that she died, and the people mourned for her. Her ministry was over. The leprosy was a punishment and a curse, but not a blessing.

Uzziah had been a king that was mightily used of God. But after being struck with leprosy, it was as if the anointing lifted. He just suffered the whole time. Sickness was a curse, not a blessing. It didn't help him; it hurt him.

The 185,000 people killed by the death angel didn't benefit. It didn't do them any good. It may have made an example out of them, but it wasn't a blessing for them.

In the New Covenant

Deuteronomy 28 states very clearly that sickness is a curse—not good—and health is a blessing. There were times that God smote people with curses, but Galatians 3 reveals that...

> *Christ hath redeemed us from the curse of the law, being made a curse for us: for it is written, Cursed is every one that hangeth on a tree: That the blessing of Abraham might come on the Gentiles through Jesus Christ; that we might receive the promise of the Spirit through faith.*
>
> **Galatians 3:13-14**

Christ redeemed us from the curse of the Law. Yes, there are instances where God smote people with sickness, leprosy, disease, blindness, and death (2 Kin. 1), but it was never a blessing (Luke 9:54-56). It was always punishment, and it was always a curse. And in the New Covenant, we are redeemed from the curse.

God's System

Some people wonder, *Well, if God doesn't chastise us with sickness and correct us with tragedy, then how will we learn?* The Bible says,

> *All scripture is given by inspiration of God, and is profitable for doctrine, for reproof, for correction, for instruction in righteousness: That the man of God may be perfect, throughly furnished unto all good works.*
>
> **2 Timothy 3:16-17**

God reproves, corrects, and instructs you through His Word. The Lord's system of correction is not sickness, disease, and tragedy; God disciplines and trains you through His Word. Notice how this passage says the correction of the Word will make you perfect, thoroughly furnished unto all good works. That means it's sufficient. You don't need some other form of correction.

Some folks argue, "Yeah, but not everyone obeys the Word. Some people only respond when everything in their lives goes sour." Tragedy, sickness, and disease are not God's system; His system is to teach you through the Word—through the Holy Spirit quickening the Word to you. You can learn other ways, but that's not God's system.

There's no doubt that certain people have become paraplegics, and because of that they've learned to turn to God. He has sustained them, and they walk in much joy and peace, blessing and ministering to many people today. That's good, but it's wrong for them to say God made them paraplegic so they could learn this. No, the Lord tried to teach them by the Holy Spirit through the Word of God.

If you don't respond to the Lord through His Word, there are other ways you can learn. You can learn by hard knocks, if you live through them. Difficult life experiences make exciting testimonies, if you survive them. Many people don't. But that's not God's system. He teaches you through His Word.

Consider These Truths

God can work for good anything that happens to you, but not everything that happens to you comes from God (John 10:10). Sickness is not from God (James 1:16-17). The Lord doesn't put sickness on you to humble you. God wants you well!

Paul was not afflicted by God. It was a messenger of Satan that came against him. The Lord didn't refuse to heal him, saying, "Just bear it." No, the Lord told him, "Paul, I'll give you grace to endure all the hardship and persecution that the devil and people throw your way." God loved those people. He didn't want to just kill them and wipe them out in order to end all of Paul's problems. There were other Sauls out there who needed to be converted and made spokesmen for God. Therefore, the Lord didn't stop the persecution against the Apostle Paul. It was a demonic messenger that stirred up hardship and persecution against him. This thorn in the flesh had been sent by Satan to try to beat Paul down and keep him from being exalted and used of God. These are powerful truths that are clearly consistent with the whole of God's Word.

It's not God's will for you to be sick, so quit hiding behind Paul's thorn in the flesh. Stop holding on to this religious bias against healing. Turn from this wrong concept that the Lord is putting sickness on you to teach you something today. You need to approach God's Word simply, honestly considering these truths I've discussed thus far. Look in the Bible for yourself. Consider the context and the meanings of the words in their original languages. As you study it out for yourself, I believe you'll prove true what I've shared with you.

It's a religious bias, prejudice, and predetermination that argues that God wants people to be sick. It's a convenient theology that dodges responsibility. Because this bias exists, people have gone to the Word of God and tried to make it say things it doesn't say.

These truths I've shared will help you establish in your heart that it's always God's will for you to be well.

Redeemed from the Curse
Lesson 9 – Outline

I. Some people have tried to use 1 Timothy 5 to counter the truth that it's always God's will to heal:

> *Drink no longer water, but use a little wine for thy stomach's sake and thine often infirmities.*
>
> **1 Timothy 5:23**

   A. I've actually heard people teach from this that Timothy had some chronic sickness that he never got healed of. Therefore, they teach that if Timothy, who was Paul's right-hand man, didn't get healed, then it's not God's will to heal us either.

   B. To offer this verse based on that supposition as proof that God doesn't want to heal us is an inaccurate and dishonest interpretation of Scripture.

   C. Apparently, whatever sickness Timothy had was a stomach problem, and it was related to the water.

   D. So Paul was counseling Timothy to quit drinking the water, because that's what was causing Timothy's stomach problems, and to instead drink a little wine.

II. Some people argue, "Even one of Paul's companions, Trophimus, didn't get healed. Therefore, it must not be God's will to heal everybody":

> *Erastus abode at Corinth: but Trophimus have I left at Miletum sick.*
>
> **2 Timothy 4:20**

   A. It's true that not everyone receives healing, but that doesn't mean it's because God doesn't want them to be healed.

   B. Each individual has to believe. Trophimus had to believe.

   C. Possibly, he was believing God, and it just took a period of time for healing to manifest in his body.

   D. Perhaps Paul didn't want to wait for the healing to manifest and went on ahead.

   E. It's also possible that Trophimus just quit believing God, so Paul decided to leave him there sick.

III. Although there are several Old Testament references for when God struck people with sickness, not once was it ever considered a blessing.

   A. Deuteronomy 28 states very clearly that sickness is a curse—not good—and health is a blessing.

B. There were times that God smote people with curses, but Galatians 3 reveals that...

> *Christ hath redeemed us from the curse of the law, being made a curse for us: for it is written, Cursed is every one that hangeth on a tree: That the blessing of Abraham might come on the Gentiles through Jesus Christ; that we might receive the promise of the Spirit through faith.*
>
> **Galatians 3:13-14**

C. Christ redeemed us from the curse of the Law.

IV. God reproves, corrects, and instructs you through His Word:

> *All scripture is given by inspiration of God, and is profitable for doctrine, for reproof, for correction, for instruction in righteousness: That the man of God may be perfect, throughly furnished unto all good works.*
>
> **2 Timothy 3:16-17**

A. Some folks argue, "Yeah, but not everyone obeys the Word. Some people only respond when everything in their lives goes sour."

B. Tragedy, sickness, and disease are not God's system; His system is to teach you through the Word—through the Holy Spirit quickening the Word to you.

C. If you don't respond to the Lord through His Word, there are other ways you can learn.

D. But that's not God's system. He teaches you through His Word.

V. God can work for good anything that happens to you, but not everything that happens to you comes from God (John 10:10).

A. Stop holding on to this religious bias against healing.

B. It's a convenient theology that dodges responsibility.

C. Because this bias exists, people have gone to the Word of God and tried to make it say things it doesn't say.

D. These truths I've shared will help you establish in your heart that it's always God's will for you to be well.

Redeemed from the Curse
Lesson 9 – Teacher's Guide

1. Some people have tried to use 1 Timothy 5:23 to counter the truth that it's always God's will to heal. I've actually heard people teach from this that Timothy had some chronic sickness that he never got healed of. Therefore, they teach that if Timothy, who was Paul's right-hand man, didn't get healed, then it's not God's will to heal us either. To offer this verse based on that supposition as proof that God doesn't want to heal us is an inaccurate and dishonest interpretation of Scripture. Apparently, whatever sickness Timothy had was a stomach problem, and it was related to the water. So Paul was counseling Timothy to quit drinking the water, because that's what was causing Timothy's stomach problems, and to instead drink a little wine.

2. Some people argue, "Even one of Paul's companions, Trophimus, didn't get healed. Therefore, it must not be God's will to heal everybody" (2 Tim. 4:20). It's true that not everyone receives healing, but that doesn't mean it's because God doesn't want them to be healed. Each individual has to believe. Trophimus had to believe. Possibly, he was believing God, and it just took a period of time for healing to manifest in his body. Perhaps Paul didn't want to wait for the healing to manifest and went on ahead. It's also possible that Trophimus just quit believing God, so Paul decided to leave him there sick.

3. Although there are several Old Testament references for when God struck people with sickness, not once was it ever considered a blessing. Deuteronomy 28 states very clearly that sickness is a curse—not good—and health is a blessing. There were times that God smote people with curses, but Galatians 3:13-14 reveal that Christ redeemed us from the curse of the Law.

1. A. Read 1 Timothy 5:23. What do some people teach from this verse? (That Timothy had some chronic sickness that he never got healed of)
    B. Why did Paul counsel Timothy to quit drinking the water? (Because that's what was causing Timothy's stomach problems)
2. A. Since not everyone receives healing, does that mean God doesn't want them to be healed? (No)
    B. What does each individual have to do? (Believe)
    C. Is this true of Trophimus? (Yes)
3. A. In the Old Testament, not once was sickness considered a _____. (Blessing)
    B. Read Galatians 3:13-14. What does this passage reveal we are redeemed from? (The curse of the Law)

4. God reproves, corrects, and instructs us through His Word (2 Tim. 3:16-17). Some folks argue, "Yeah, but not everyone obeys the Word. Some people only respond when everything in their lives goes sour." Tragedy, sickness, and disease are not God's system; His system is to teach us through the Word—through the Holy Spirit quickening the Word to us. If we don't respond to the Lord through His Word, there are other ways we can learn. But that's not God's system. He teaches us through His Word.

5. God can work for good anything that happens to us, but not everything that happens to us comes from God (John 10:10). We need to stop holding on to this religious bias against healing. It's a convenient theology that dodges responsibility. Because this bias exists, people have gone to the Word of God and tried to make it say things it doesn't say. These truths I've shared will help us establish in our hearts that it's always God's will for us to be well.

4. A. Read 2 Timothy 3:16-17. What does God reprove, correct, and instruct us through? (His Word)
    B. What is God's system? (To teach us through the Word—through the Holy Spirit quickening the Word to us)
5. A. What can God work for good? (Anything that happens to us)
    B. Because of a religious bias, what have people done with the Word? (Tried to make it say things it doesn't say)
    C. What will these truths I've shared help us establish in our hearts? (That it's always God's will for us to be well)

Redeemed from the Curse
Lesson 9 – Additional Information

I encourage you to check out my teaching entitled "The Sovereignty of God." I've dealt with that verse (and others) there more thoroughly than I can here.

Redeemed from the Curse
Lesson 9 – Discipleship Questions

1. According to 1 Timothy 5:23, because of the water, Timothy had infirmities _____.

2. According to 2 Timothy 4:20, whom did Paul leave at Miletum sick?

   A. Erastus.

   B. Timothy.

   C. Trophimus.

   D. All of the above.

   E. None of the above.

3. Read Romans 8:28. All things work together for good to them that what?

4. Read Galatians 3:13-14. What was Christ made for us?

5. **"That the _____ of Abraham might come on the Gentiles through Jesus Christ."**

6. That we might receive what?

7. According to Luke 9:54-56, what did James and John ask the Lord?

8. What did He turn and do?

9. What did He say?

10. Read 2 Timothy 3:16-17. How much of Scripture is given by inspiration of God?

11. What is Scripture profitable for?

12. According to John 10:10, the thief comes only to what?

13. Jesus has come that what?

14. Read James 1:16-17. **"Every _____ gift and every _____ gift is from above."**

15. Is there any variableness or shadow of turning with the Father of lights?

Redeemed from the Curse
Lesson 9 – Answer Key

1.   Often.

2.   C. Trophimus.

3.   Love God, to them who are called according to His purpose.

4.   A curse.

5.   **"Blessing."**

6.   The promise of the Spirit through faith.

7.   "Wilt thou that we command fire to come down from heaven, and consume them, even as Elias did?"

8.   He rebuked them.

9.   "Ye know not what manner of spirit ye are of."

10.   All Scripture.

11.   Reproof, correction, and instruction in righteousness.

12.   To steal and to kill and to destroy.

13.   That they might have life and that they might have it more abundantly.

14.   **"Good", "Perfect."**

15.   No.

Redeemed from the Curse
Lesson 9 – Scriptures

1 Timothy 5:23

Drink no longer water, but use a little wine for thy stomach's sake and thine often infirmities.

2 Timothy 4:20

Erastus abode at Corinth: but Trophimus have I left at Miletum sick.

Romans 8:28

And we know that all things work together for good to them that love God, to them who are the called according to his purpose.

Galatians 3:13-14

Christ hath redeemed us from the curse of the law, being made a curse for us: for it is written, Cursed is every one that hangeth on a tree: [14] That the blessing of Abraham might come on the Gentiles through Jesus Christ; that we might receive the promise of the Spirit through faith.

Luke 9:54-56

And when his disciples James and John saw this, they said, Lord, wilt thou that we command fire to come down from heaven, and consume them, even as Elias did? [55] But he turned, and rebuked them, and said, Ye know not what manner of spirit ye are of. [56] For the Son of man is not come to destroy men's lives, but to save them. And they went to another village.

2 Timothy 3:16-17

All scripture is given by inspiration of God, and is profitable for doctrine, for reproof, for correction, for instruction in righteousness: [17] That the man of God may be perfect, throughly furnished unto all good works.

John 10:10

The thief cometh not, but for to steal, and to kill, and to destroy: I am come that they might have life, and that they might have it more abundantly.

James 1:16-17

Do not err, my beloved brethren. [17] Every good gift and every perfect gift is from above, and cometh down from the Father of lights, with whom is no variableness, neither shadow of turning.

Jesus Healed Them All
Lesson 10

Healing is part of Christ's Atonement (Is. 53:4-5). Therefore, it's not an add-on or in addition to salvation. It's a done deal (1 Pet. 2:24). Through Christ's death, burial, and resurrection, healing has already been provided. Paul's thorn in the flesh was a demonic messenger that stirred up persecution (2 Cor. 12:7). It wasn't sickness. The Lord isn't putting sickness or disease on anyone today. Under the New Covenant, we've been redeemed from the curse of the Law (Deut. 28:15-68 and Gal. 3:13-14). Through faith in Christ and what He's done, every blessing—including health—is now ours in Him (Deut. 28:1-14 and Eph. 1:3). Hopefully, you've already come into agreement with the Word.

If Satan can get you to believe that God wants you sick, that there is some purpose in you being ill, that the Lord is using it for some reason, then it is impossible for you to truly fight against it lest you think you're fighting against God. So it renders you passive.

James 4:7 says,

Submit yourselves therefore to God. Resist the devil, and he will flee from you.

We must resist the devil. "Resist" means to actively fight against. If Satan can get us into a passive position where we're just saying "Well, whatever God wills" and we aren't actively fighting against the devil, then he can overcome us with sickness and disease. We need to know that when we are fighting sickness, we are doing God's will and that we aren't fighting against Him or being rebellious toward some type of correction or punishment that He's sent into our lives. Basically, religion today has said that sickness comes from God, that He uses it to work His will in our lives, and that it's wrong to believe for healing. This has to be totally eradicated from our hearts and minds before we can truly believe and receive our healing. These are the foundations.

Now, once that's established and we really believe, that doesn't mean we're just automatically going to be healed. We do have to believe that it's God's will, but then there are other factors that are involved in seeing healing manifest. That's what we are going to look into in these next few **Lessons**. If it is God's will to heal and if He's not the one who puts sickness on us, then why aren't we all healed?

Jesus Hasn't Changed

First of all, when Jesus was here on this earth, every person who would allow Him to minister to them was healed. Jesus healed them all, and He didn't do that just once; He did it on a number of occasions. Jesus was the express image of the Father. He said, "I do always those things that I see my Father do." The very fact that Jesus healed all, never refusing to heal a single person, never putting sickness on anyone, should be proof enough that God is not the author of sickness.

In the Gospels alone, there are seventeen times where Jesus healed all of the sick that were present. Although Mark, Luke, and John all have examples of this as well, let's look at this truth through the book of Matthew. Jesus did heal them all, and He hasn't changed:

Jesus Christ the same yesterday, and to day, and for ever.

Hebrews 13:8

Christ isn't the one who has changed; His followers have. We aren't representing Him the way He really wants to be represented. It's not God who isn't healing the sick today; it's His followers. We've really fallen in this area.

Matthew 4:23-24 says that…

Jesus went about all Galilee, teaching in their synagogues, and preaching the gospel of the kingdom, and healing all manner of sickness and all manner of disease among the people. And his fame went throughout all Syria: and they brought unto him all sick people that were taken with divers diseases and torments, and those which were possessed with devils, and those which were lunatic, and those that had the palsy; and he healed them.

People with all kinds of sicknesses, diseases, and torments were brought to Jesus and He healed them. He didn't just heal some; He healed them all!

Every Sickness & Every Disease

When the even was come, they brought unto him many that were possessed with devils: and he cast out the spirits with his word, and healed all that were sick: That it might be fulfilled which was spoken by Esaias the prophet, saying, Himself took our infirmities, and bare our sicknesses.

Matthew 8:16-17

This passage states very clearly that Jesus healed all that were sick—not some of them, but all of them.

Jesus went about all the cities and villages, teaching in their synagogues, and preaching the gospel of the kingdom, and healing every sickness and every disease among the people.

Matthew 9:35

What a powerful statement! Jesus was healing every sickness and every disease among the people. He didn't just have a few people who received, and then others who went away still sick; Jesus healed them all.

But when Jesus knew it, he withdrew himself from thence: and great multitudes followed him, and he healed them all.

Matthew 12:15

Even with great multitudes, He healed them all. It is God's will for you to be well! The life and example of Jesus is clear: He healed them all. The Lord never refused to heal a single person. There were some who refused to receive healing, which I'll deal with later, but He healed all who would receive His ministry.

Jesus went forth, and saw a great multitude, and was moved with compassion toward them, and he healed their sick.

Matthew 14:14

And when they were gone over, they came into the land of Gennesaret. And when the men of that place had knowledge of him, they sent out into all that country round about, and brought unto him all that were diseased; And besought him that they might only touch the hem of his garment: and as many as touched were made perfectly whole.

Matthew 14:34-36

Glory to God, Not the Devil

And great multitudes came unto him, having with them those that were lame, blind, dumb, maimed, and many others, and cast them down at Jesus' feet; and he healed them.

Matthew 15:30

Again, this implies that He healed every single one of them. Verse 31 shows the results:

Insomuch that the multitude wondered, when they saw the dumb to speak, the maimed to be whole, the lame to walk, and the blind to see: and they glorified the God of Israel.

Something that brought glory to God is not of the devil. How people can say that people being miraculously healed is of the devil is nothing but a copout. It's an excuse for their powerlessness. It's a way to justify themselves, and to do it, they have to condemn those who are following the example of Jesus.

And great multitudes followed him; and he healed them there.

Matthew 19:2

And the blind and the lame came to him in the temple; and he healed them.

Matthew 21:14

These are just a few of the seventeen separate examples in the Gospels where Jesus healed all that came to Him (the rest are listed at the end of this **Study Guide** in the section called Is it Always God's Will to Heal?). Since He said He did exactly what He saw His Father do and Hebrews 1:3 says He was the express image of the Father, this shows that it is God's will to heal us all.

"Then why don't we see every single person healed?" That's a simple question, but it has a complex answer, which we're going to spend the next few **Lessons** dealing with.

Jesus Healed Them All
Lesson 10 – Outline

I. When Jesus was here on this earth, every person who would allow Him to minister to them was healed.

   A. And He didn't do that just once; He did it on a number of occasions.

   B. Christ isn't the one who has changed (Heb. 13:8); His followers have.

   C. It's not God who isn't healing the sick today; it's His followers.

II. People with all kinds of sicknesses, diseases, and torments were brought to Jesus and He healed them.

   A. He didn't just heal some; He healed them all (Matt. 4:23-24; 8:16-17; 9:35; 12:15; 14:14, 34-36; 15:30; 19:2; and 21:14)!

   B. Even with great multitudes, He healed them all. It is God's will for you to be well!

III. Matthew 15:31 shows the results:

   Insomuch that the multitude wondered, when they saw the dumb to speak, the maimed to be whole, the lame to walk, and the blind to see: and they glorified the God of Israel.

   A. Something that brought glory to God is not of the devil.

   B. How people can say that people being miraculously healed is of the devil is nothing but a cop-out.

   C. It's an excuse for their powerlessness.

   D. It's a way to justify themselves, and to do it, they have to condemn those who are following the example of Jesus.

IV. Since Jesus said He did exactly what He saw His Father do and Hebrews 1:3 says He was the express image of the Father, this shows that it is God's will to heal us all.

   A. "Then why don't we see every single person healed?"

   B. That's a simple question, but it has a complex answer, which we're going to spend the next few **Lessons** dealing with.

Jesus Healed Them All
Lesson 10 – Teacher's Guide

1. When Jesus was here on this earth, every person who would allow Him to minister to them was healed. And He didn't do that just once; He did it on a number of occasions. Christ isn't the one who has changed (Heb. 13:8); His followers have. It's not God who isn't healing the sick today; it's His followers.

2. People with all kinds of sicknesses, diseases, and torments were brought to Jesus and He healed them. He didn't just heal some; He healed them all (Matt. 4:23-24; 8:16-17; 9:35; 12:15; 14:14, 34-36; 15:30; 19:2; and 21:14)! Even with great multitudes, He healed them all. It is God's will for us to be well!

3. Matthew 15:31 shows the results. Something that brought glory to God is not of the devil. How people can say that people being miraculously healed is of the devil is nothing but a cop-out. It's an excuse for their powerlessness. It's a way to justify themselves, and to do it, they have to condemn those who are following the example of Jesus.

4. Since Jesus said He did exactly what He saw His Father do and Hebrews 1:3 says He was the express image of the Father, this shows that it is God's will to heal us all. "Then why don't we see every single person healed?" That's a simple question, but it has a complex answer, which we're going to spend the next few **Lessons** dealing with.

1. A. Did Jesus heal every person who would allow Him to minister to them on only one occasion? (No)
   B. Who is not healing the sick today? (God's followers)
2. What did Jesus do with great multitudes? (He healed them all)
3. A. Read Matthew 15:31. Who was glorified as a result of these healings? (The God of Israel)
   B. What is nothing but a cop-out? (Saying that people being miraculously healed is of the devil)
4. A. Since Jesus said He did exactly what He saw His Father do and Hebrews 1:3 says He was the express image of the Father, what does this show? (That it is God's will to heal us all)
   B. The reason everyone isn't healed is a _____. (Complex answer)

Jesus Healed Them All
Lesson 10 – Discipleship Questions

1. Read Isaiah 53:4-5. Who is this passage describing?

2. Read 1 Peter 2:24. Who are dead to sins?

3. Read 2 Corinthians 12:7. How was Paul to be exalted above measure?

4. The warnings and curses of Deuteronomy 28:15-68 are of the _____ Covenant.

    A. Old.

    B. Marital.

    C. Blood.

    D. All of the above.

    E. None of the above.

5. Read Galatians 3:13-14. For whose benefit did Christ suffer?

6. According to Deuteronomy 28:1-14, these blessings would come upon the people if they did how many of God's commandments?

7. According to Ephesians 1:3, where are the spiritual blessings God has blessed us with?

8. Read James 4:7. What does this passage say to do before we resist the devil?

9. According to Hebrews 13:8, for how long is Jesus the same?

10. Read Matthew 4:23-24. What did Jesus do besides heal the people?

11. According to Matthew 8:16-17, Jesus did these things fulfilling the prophecy of whom?

12. Read Matthew 9:35, 12:15, and 14:14. What is common among these verses?

13. Read Matthew 14:34-36. The men of that place sent out into all that country and brought unto Him all that were diseased when what?

14. According Matthew 15:30-31, what did Jesus do when the great multitudes cast the lame, the blind, the dumb, maimed, and many others at His feet?

15. Read Matthew 19:2. What kind of multitudes followed Jesus?

16. According to Matthew 21:14, where did the blind and lame come to Jesus?

17. According to Hebrews 1:3, what is upheld by the word of God's power?

Jesus Healed Them All
Lesson 10 – Answer Key

1. Jesus.

2. We are.

3. Through the abundance of the revelations.

4. A. Old.

5. Ours.

6. All of them.

7. In heavenly places in Christ.

8. Submit to God.

9. Forever.

10. He preached the Gospel of the kingdom to them.

11. Esaias (Isaiah).

12. That Jesus healed them all.

13. When they had knowledge of Him.

14. He healed them.

15. Great multitudes.

16. In the temple.

17. All things.

Jesus Healed Them All
Lesson 10 – Scriptures

Isaiah 53:4-5
Surely he hath borne our griefs, and carried our sorrows: yet we did esteem him stricken, smitten of God, and afflicted. [5] But he was wounded for our transgressions, he was bruised for our iniquities: the chastisement of our peace was upon him; and with his stripes we are healed.

I Peter 2:24
Who his own self bare our sins in his own body on the tree, that we, being dead to sins, should live unto righteousness: by whose stripes ye were healed.

2 Corinthians 12:7
And lest I should be exalted above measure through the abundance of the revelations, there was given to me a thorn in the flesh, the messenger of Satan to buffet me, lest I should be exalted above measure.

Deuteronomy 28:1-68
And it shall come to pass, if thou shalt hearken diligently unto the voice of the LORD thy God, to observe and to do all his commandments which I command thee this day, that the LORD thy God will set thee on high above all nations of the earth: [2] And all these blessings shall come on thee, and overtake thee, if thou shalt hearken unto the voice of the LORD thy God. [3] Blessed shalt thou be in the city, and blessed shalt thou be in the field. [4] Blessed shall be the fruit of thy body, and the fruit of thy ground, and the fruit of thy cattle, the increase of thy kine, and the flocks of thy sheep. [5] Blessed shall be thy basket and thy store. [6] Blessed shalt thou be when thou comest in, and blessed shalt thou be when thou goest out. [7] The LORD shall cause thine enemies that rise up against thee to be smitten before thy face: they shall come out against thee one way, and flee before thee seven ways. [8] The LORD shall command the blessing upon thee in thy storehouses, and in all that thou settest thine hand unto; and he shall bless thee in the land which the LORD thy God giveth thee. [9] The LORD shall establish thee an holy people unto himself, as he hath sworn unto thee, if thou shalt keep the commandments of the LORD thy God, and walk in his ways. [10] And all people of the earth shall see that thou art called by the name of the LORD; and they shall be afraid of thee. [11] And the LORD shall make thee plenteous in goods, in the fruit of thy body, and in the fruit of thy cattle, and in the fruit of thy ground, in the land which the LORD sware unto thy fathers to give thee. [12] The LORD shall open unto thee his good treasure, the heaven to give the rain unto thy land in his season, and to bless all the work of thine hand: and thou shalt lend unto many nations, and thou shalt not borrow. [13] And the LORD shall make thee the head, and not the tail; and thou shalt be above only, and thou shalt not be beneath; if that thou hearken unto the commandments of the LORD thy God, which I command thee this day, to observe and to do them: [14] And thou shalt not

go aside from any of the words which I command thee this day, to the right hand, or to the left, to go after other gods to serve them. [15] But it shall come to pass, if thou wilt not hearken unto the voice of the LORD thy God, to observe to do all his commandments and his statutes which I command thee this day; that all these curses shall come upon thee, and overtake thee: [16] Cursed shalt thou be in the city, and cursed shalt thou be in the field. [17] Cursed shall be thy basket and thy store. [18] Cursed shall be the fruit of thy body, and the fruit of thy land, the increase of thy kine, and the flocks of thy sheep. [19] Cursed shalt thou be when thou comest in, and cursed shalt thou be when thou goest out. [20] The LORD shall send upon thee cursing, vexation, and rebuke, in all that thou settest thine hand unto for to do, until thou be destroyed, and until thou perish quickly; because of the wickedness of thy doings, whereby thou hast forsaken me. [21] The LORD shall make the pestilence cleave unto thee, until he have consumed thee from off the land, whither thou goest to possess it. [22] The LORD shall smite thee with a consumption, and with a fever, and with an inflammation, and with an extreme burning, and with the sword, and with blasting, and with mildew; and they shall pursue thee until thou perish. [23] And thy heaven that is over thy head shall be brass, and the earth that is under thee shall be iron. [24] The LORD shall make the rain of thy land powder and dust: from heaven shall it come down upon thee, until thou be destroyed. [25] The LORD shall cause thee to be smitten before thine enemies: thou shalt go out one way against them, and flee seven ways before them: and shalt be removed into all the kingdoms of the earth. [26] And thy carcase shall be meat unto all fowls of the air, and unto the beasts of the earth, and no man shall fray them away.[27] The LORD will smite thee with the botch of Egypt, and with the emerods, and with the scab, and with the itch, whereof thou canst not be healed. [28] The LORD shall smite thee with madness, and blindness, and astonishment of heart: [29] And thou shalt grope at noonday, as the blind gropeth in darkness, and thou shalt not prosper in thy ways: and thou shalt be only oppressed and spoiled evermore, and no man shall save thee. [30] Thou shalt betroth a wife, and another man shall lie with her: thou shalt build an house, and thou shalt not dwell therein: thou shalt plant a vineyard, and shalt not gather the grapes thereof. [31] Thine ox shall be slain before thine eyes, and thou shalt not eat thereof: thine ass shall be violently taken away from before thy face, and shall not be restored to thee: thy sheep shall be given unto thine enemies, and thou shalt have none to rescue them. [32] Thy sons and thy daughters shall be given unto another people, and thine eyes shall look, and fail with longing for them all the day long: and there shall be no might in thine hand. [33] The fruit of thy land, and all thy labours, shall a nation which thou knowest not eat up; and thou shalt be only oppressed and crushed alway: [34] So that thou shalt be mad for the sight of thine eyes which thou shalt see. [35] The LORD shall smite thee in the knees, and in the legs, with a sore botch that cannot be healed, from the sole of thy foot unto the top of thy head. [36] The LORD shall bring thee, and thy king which thou shalt set over thee, unto a nation which neither thou nor thy fathers have known; and there shalt thou serve other gods, wood and stone. [37] And thou shalt become an astonishment, a proverb, and a byword, among all nations whither the LORD shall lead thee.[38] Thou shalt carry much seed out into the field, and shalt gather but little in; for the locust shall consume it. [39] Thou shalt plant vineyards, and dress them, but shalt neither drink of the wine, nor gather the grapes; for the worms shall eat them. [40] Thou shalt have olive trees throughout all thy coasts, but thou shalt not anoint thyself with the oil; for thine olive shall cast his fruit. [41] Thou shalt beget sons and daughters, but thou shalt not enjoy them; for they shall go into captivity. [42] All thy trees and fruit of thy land shall the locust consume. [43] The stranger that is within thee shall get up above thee very high; and thou shalt come down very low. [44] He shall lend to thee, and thou shalt not lend to him: he shall be the head, and thou shalt be the tail. [45] Moreover all these curses shall come upon thee, and shall pursue thee, and overtake thee, till thou be destroyed; because thou hearkenedst not unto the voice of the LORD thy God, to keep his commandments and his statutes which he commanded thee: [46] And they shall be upon thee for a sign and for a wonder, and upon thy seed for ever.[47] Because thou servedst not the LORD thy God with joyfulness, and with gladness of heart, for the abundance of all things; [48] Therefore shalt thou serve thine enemies which the LORD shall send against thee, in hunger, and in thirst, and in nakedness, and in want of all things: and he shall put a yoke of iron upon thy neck, until he have destroyed thee. [49] The LORD shall bring a nation against thee from far, from the end of the earth, as swift as the eagle flieth; a nation whose tongue thou shalt not understand; [50] A nation of fierce countenance, which shall not regard the person of the old, nor shew favour to the young: [51] And he shall eat the fruit of thy cattle, and the fruit of thy land, until thou be destroyed: which also shall not leave thee either corn, wine, or oil, or the increase of thy kine, or flocks of thy sheep, until he have destroyed thee. [52] And he shall besiege thee in all thy gates, until thy high and fenced walls come down, where-in thou trustedst, throughout all thy land: and he shall besiege thee in all thy gates throughout all thy land, which the LORD thy God hath given thee. [53] And thou shalt eat the fruit of thine own body, the flesh of thy sons and of thy daughters, which the LORD thy God hath given thee, in the siege, and in the straitness, wherewith thine enemies shall distress thee: [54] So that the man that is tender among you, and very delicate, his eye shall be evil toward his brother, and toward the wife of his bosom, and toward the remnant of his children which he shall leave: [55] So that he will not give to any of them of the flesh of his children whom he shall eat: because he hath nothing left him in the siege, and in the straitness, wherewith thine enemies shall distress thee in all thy gates. [56] The tender and delicate woman among you, which would not adventure to set the sole of her foot upon the ground for delicate-ness and tenderness, her eye shall be evil toward the husband of her bosom, and toward her son, and toward her daughter, [57] And toward her young one that co-meth out from between her feet, and toward her children which she shall bear: for she shall eat them for want of all things secretly in the siege and straitness, where-with thine enemy shall distress thee in thy gates. [58] If thou wilt not observe to do all the words of this law that are written in this book, that thou mayest fear this glorious and fearful name, THE LORD THY GOD; [59] Then the LORD will make thy plagues wonderful, and the plagues of thy seed, even great plagues, and of long continuance, and sore sicknesses, and of long continuance. [60] Moreover he will bring upon thee all the diseases of Egypt, which thou wast afraid of; and they shall cleave unto thee. [61] Also every sickness, and every plague, which is not written in the book of this law, them will the LORD bring upon thee, until thou be destroyed.

[62] And ye shall be left few in number, whereas ye were as the stars of heaven for multitude; because thou wouldest not obey the voice of the LORD thy God. [63] And it shall come to pass, that as the LORD rejoiced over you to do you good, and to multiply you; so the LORD will rejoice over you to destroy you, and to bring you to nought; and ye shall be plucked from off the land whither thou goest to possess it. [64] And the LORD shall scatter thee among all people, from the one end of the earth even unto the other; and there thou shalt serve other gods, which neither thou nor thy fathers have known, even wood and stone. [65] And among these nations shalt thou find no ease, neither shall the sole of thy foot have rest: but the LORD shall give thee there a trembling heart, and failing of eyes, and sorrow of mind: [66] And thy life shall hang in doubt before thee; and thou shalt fear day and night, and shalt have none assurance of thy life: [67] In the morning thou shalt say, Would God it were even! and at even thou shalt say, Would God it were morning! for the fear of thine heart wherewith thou shalt fear, and for the sight of thine eyes which thou shalt see. [68] And the LORD shall bring thee into Egypt again with ships, by the way whereof I spake unto thee, Thou shalt see it no more again: and there ye shall be sold unto your enemies for bondmen and bondwomen, and no man shall buy you.

Galatians 3:13-14
Christ hath redeemed us from the curse of the law, being made a curse for us: for it is written, Cursed is every one that hangeth on a tree: [14] That the blessing of Abraham might come on the Gentiles through Jesus Christ; that we might receive the promise of the Spirit through faith.

Ephesians 1:3
Blessed be the God and Father of our Lord Jesus Christ, who hath blessed us with all spiritual blessings in heavenly places in Christ.

James 4:7
Submit yourselves therefore to God. Resist the devil, and he will flee from you.

Hebrews 13:8
Jesus Christ the same yesterday, and to day, and for ever.

Matthew 4:23-24
And Jesus went about all Galilee, teaching in their synagogues, and preaching the gospel of the kingdom, and healing all manner of sickness and all manner of disease among the people. [24] And his fame went throughout all Syria: and they brought unto him all sick people that were taken with divers diseases and torments, and those which were possessed with devils, and those which were lunatick, and those that had the palsy; and he healed them.

Matthew 8:16-17

When the even was come, they brought unto him many that were possessed with devils: and he cast out the spirits with his word, and healed all that were sick: [17] That it might be fulfilled which was spoken by Esaias the prophet, saying, Himself took our infirmities, and bare our sicknesses.

Matthew 9:35

And Jesus went about all the cities and villages, teaching in their synagogues, and preaching the gospel of the kingdom, and healing every sickness and every disease among the people.

Matthew 12:15

But when Jesus knew it, he withdrew himself from thence: and great multitudes followed him, and he healed them all.

Matthew 14:14

And Jesus went forth, and saw a great multitude, and was moved with compassion toward them, and he healed their sick.

Matthew 14:34-36

And when they were gone over, they came into the land of Gennesaret. [35] And when the men of that place had knowledge of him, they sent out into all that country round about, and brought unto him all that were diseased; [36] And besought him that they might only touch the hem of his garment: and as many as touched were made perfectly whole.

Matthew 15:30-31

And great multitudes came unto him, having with them those that were lame, blind, dumb, maimed, and many others, and cast them down at Jesus' feet; and he healed them: [31] Insomuch that the multitude wondered, when they saw the dumb to speak, the maimed to be whole, the lame to walk, and the blind to see: and they glorified the God of Israel.

Matthew 19:2

And great multitudes followed him; and he healed them there.

Matthew 21:14

And the blind and the lame came to him in the temple; and he healed them.

Hebrews 1:3

Who being the brightness of his glory, and the express image of his person, and upholding all things by the word of his power, when he had by himself purged our sins, sat down on the right hand of the Majesty on high.

Why Isn't Everyone Healed?
Lesson 11

If it's God's will to heal us all, why isn't everyone healed? Jesus' disciples basically asked Him the exact same question in Matthew 17:

> *Then came the disciples to Jesus apart, and said, Why could not we cast him out?*
>
> **Matthew 17:19**

In the first part of Matthew 17, Jesus had taken three of His disciples—Peter, James, and John—and gone up onto a mountain. This is where He was transfigured. He literally began to radiate the light of the *shekinah* glory of God. A cloud overshadowed Jesus and these three disciples, and an audible voice came out of the cloud, saying,

> *This is my beloved Son, in whom I am well pleased; hear ye him.*
>
> **Matthew 17:5**

Elijah and Moses appeared and spoke with Jesus about His crucifixion, which was coming up shortly. These disciples saw all this and had a miraculous, glorious time. Then they came down from the mountain to the rest of the disciples and the crowd that had gathered there.

> *And when they were come to the multitude, there came to him a certain man, kneeling down to him, and saying, Lord, have mercy on my son: for he is lunatic, and sore vexed: for ofttimes he falleth into the fire, and oft into the water. And I brought him to thy disciples, and they could not cure him.*
>
> **Matthew 17:14-16**

While Jesus was on the mountain with Peter, James, and John, the rest of the disciples were down below. A man had a son whom the Scripture says was lunatic. He suffered from seizures, probably something like epilepsy. This is described in Mark's account of this same instance (Mark 9:17-29). So the father brought this boy to Jesus' disciples to cast this demon out, but they couldn't do it.

> *Then Jesus answered and said, O faithless and perverse generation, how long shall I be with you? how long shall I suffer you? bring him hither to me.*
>
> **Matthew 17:17**

Jesus wasn't pleased with His disciples' inability to effect this healing. If the Lord had been there, He would have healed this boy, which later on He did. Jesus wasn't at all pleased with His disciples' inability to deal with this situation. This is a completely different attitude than what most people have today.

"I've Failed"

As a matter of fact, some people will be critical of my teaching in this **Study Guide** because I'm saying that it's God's will to heal everyone all the time. One of the obvious reasons we don't see people healed today is that we aren't believing God for it. We are operating in unbelief. Rather than accept that, some folks will criticize me, saying, "You aren't being compassionate. You're just criticizing people you ought to be compassionate toward. You should tell them they're doing the best they can, and that's fine."

Well, how did Jesus respond? When He found out His disciples couldn't heal the demoniac boy, He declared, "O faithless and perverse generation! How long shall I be with you? How long shall I put up with you? Bring him here to Me." Do you really think that Jesus would have a more compassionate response to you today? Do you think that the Lord has changed, and now He doesn't want you to minister healing to people? Absolutely not!

I've failed. I don't always see healing manifest. I've seen some people very close to me die—family and friends that I loved with all of my heart. I've had to accept partial responsibility. It's a complex issue. I'm not saying that it was all my fault, all their fault, or all anybody's fault. We're still learning. But I am saying that I know it was God's will for these people to be healed.

I saw my dad die after praying for him for several months to get well. I was only twelve years old at the time. A few years later, I saw a girl die that I was unofficially engaged to. (I wasn't really engaged to her, but we had thought about it. I was a soldier in Vietnam, and her family told people I was engaged to her, which allowed me emergency leave to come home during that time.) I remember being with her as she strangled to death on her own blood. We stood there for hours praying and believing for her to be raised from the dead.

I understand people wanting to dodge responsibility because they just can't cope. If they think there was something they could have done to have stopped this, then it would make them feel so guilty. They'd have to say, "I've failed." Well, I believe I did fail. I believe that not only I, but this girl, my father, and others, we didn't appropriate what Jesus had provided for us. So, yes, we were wrong. But am I condemned by that? No, I'm not condemned at all. I believe that God loves me. He has comforted me. But knowing the truth has motivated me to learn what His Word says and not allow it to happen again. Believe me: I am motivated! I realize it's not God who is letting people die; it's us, and it's because of our unbelief.

We Are Responsible

Jesus said, "You faithless and perverse generation." When people come to the church today with financial problems, we send them to the lenders, saying, "Have you been to the bank? Have you checked in with the social workers?" If they're sick, we ask, "Have you been to the doctor? Does he need to operate? Have you taken medication?" If they are depressed and discouraged, we ask, "Have you taken any medicine for this? Have you gone to a psychiatrist? You need a shrink and some therapy." In other words, the church has basically abdicated its authority and responsibility for meeting the needs of people. And today, people feel like you are inconsiderate and uncompassionate if you tell people, "We are responsible for ministering to the sick, the poor, and the demonized."

Jesus wasn't pleased that His disciples couldn't effect this cure. The Lord is not pleased today that His disciples aren't seeing all the sick healed. It's God's will to heal every single person every single time. The reason this doesn't happen isn't because God fails to do it; it's because His representatives aren't operating in the fullness of what He has provided for them.

Yes, this puts responsibility on me. Yes, this means I've missed it. Yes, this means other people have missed it too. I'd rather maintain God's integrity than my own. God is a good God, and He isn't causing people to die. God is not the one who is putting terminal diseases on people like cancer and AIDS. That's not the way that it is.

Sin

There are three main reasons people get sick. One of them is sin.

After healing the man at the pool of Bethesda, Jesus said to him,

Behold, thou art made whole: sin no more, lest a worse thing come unto thee.

John 5:14

Jesus made it very clear in this verse that this man's sickness returning, and even something worse than what he'd had, could come on him if he sinned. Therefore, Jesus linked sickness with sin. Now, this isn't the only reason people get sick, but it is one reason.

When alcoholics drink all of their lives and get liver disease, they did that to themselves. Satan used their actions to gain access to them. They have liver disease not because God did it, not because the devil did it directly, but because they're reaping the results of their sin (Rom. 6:21-23). Drug abusers get brain damage. They often contract diseases that are transmitted through shared needles. Sexually promiscuous people get sexually transmitted diseases. This isn't happening because Satan is judging them; they're doing it to themselves. They've opened up a door through sin.

A Direct Attack

The second major reason we get sick is because we are in a battle with the devil. Some of us aren't aware of this, but not everything that goes on is merely physical. There is a spiritual battle raging with godly angels carrying out the Lord's will and demonic spirits carrying out Satan's will. Sometimes our Enemy just fights us, and it's not based on an individual sin we've committed. In a sense, it is sin-based because Satan was loosed into this earth through sin, but the sickness isn't necessarily from our individual sins.

Jesus spoke of this as He walked by a man who had been born blind:
And his disciples asked him, saying, Master, who did sin, this man, or his parents, that he was born blind? Jesus answered, Neither hath this man sinned, nor his parents: but that the works of God should be made manifest in him.

John 9:2-3

The Lord wasn't saying that neither this man nor his parents had ever sinned. The Bible is clear about this point:

All have sinned, and come short of the glory of God.

Romans 3:23

Even though they had sin in their lives, Jesus was saying that neither this man's sins nor his parents' sins had caused this blindness; it just happened. There is a spiritual battle going on, and Satan is going about seeking whom he may devour (1 Pet. 5:8).

Sin is one reason we get sick. Another reason is that we're living in a fallen world, and there are spiritual battles. Sometimes Satan just attacks us with things. An illness could be nothing but a direct attack from the devil.

Natural Things

The third main reason people get sick is simply natural things. This is something many Spirit-filled Christians haven't really taken into account. They recognize the first two reasons—that sin is an inroad of Satan into their lives, allowing him to do things and that they're in a spiritual battle, and sometimes the devil just fights them. However, Spirit-filled Christians will often so spiritualize everything that they don't recognize that there are just some things that happen naturally.

If you aren't paying attention while walking down stairs, you could trip, fall, and break your leg, neck, or collarbone. You could have all kinds of negative things happen. Yet it's not sin or the devil; it was just something natural. You could hurt yourself, catch a cold, get an infection, have swelling—all kinds of things—for purely natural reasons.

I've heard of people who dove off a cliff and hit a rock in a pool of water. Now they're quadriplegic. It wasn't necessarily the devil that did that to them. He may have enticed them to go against their better judgment and do something that wasn't wise, but it was natural. When someone loses a limb due to a car wreck, it's not so much the devil but something natural.

Since mankind fell and sin tainted the earth, all kinds of things like germs, bacteria, viruses, and fungi that were good became corrupted and now fight against our human bodies. In this fallen world, some things are just natural.

One time, a man I knew had an accident while putting a roof on a house. He hit a nail, and it broke, ricocheted off the roof, and stuck in his eye. Many people would say "Well, that's the devil," but mistakes happen. People aren't perfect. Sometimes things are just natural.

There's Always Something We Can Do About it!

You can give an inroad to sickness through sin.

It could be natural. When you fall off your house, you're going to hurt yourself. You might hurt something or break something. It's not necessarily demonic. It's not sin. It's just natural. Sometimes stuff like that just happens.

Or the devil could be attacking you through no fault of your own. In fact, when Satan fights against you, it's a very good sign that you're doing something right. The Enemy seeks to hinder people who are responsive to God and fighting him. You can tell you've arrived at the Promised Land when you meet the giants. When problems are staring you in the face, sometimes it's an indication that you're doing things right instead of wrong.

The good news is that no matter what caused the sickness—sin, the devil, or something natural—there's always something we can do about it. Since the Lord has redeemed us from sickness and disease, we can take our authority, exercise our faith, and effect a cure. Even if our own sin opened a door and brought the sickness on us, we can repent and release the forgiveness and healing power of God in our lives. Regardless of how these sicknesses and diseases come, there's always something we as believers can do about it.

Why Isn't Everyone Healed?
Lesson 11 – Outline

I. One of the obvious reasons we don't see people healed today is that we aren't believing God for it.

    A. We are operating in unbelief.

    B. Rather than accept that, some folks will criticize me, saying, "You aren't being compassionate. You're just criticizing people you ought to be compassionate toward. You should tell them they're doing the best they can, and that's fine."

    C. Well, how did Jesus respond? When He found out His disciples couldn't heal the demoniac boy, He declared, "O faithless and perverse generation!" (Matt. 17:17).

    D. Do you really think that Jesus would have a more compassionate response to you today? Absolutely not!

II. I've failed. I don't always see healing manifest.

    A. I've had to accept partial responsibility.

    B. Am I condemned by that? No, I'm not condemned at all. I believe that God loves me. He has comforted me.

    C. But knowing the truth has motivated me to learn what His Word says and not allow it to happen again.

III. It's God's will to heal every single person every single time.

    A. The reason this doesn't happen isn't because God fails to do it; it's because His representatives aren't operating in the fullness of what He has provided for them.

    B. I'd rather maintain God's integrity than my own. God is a good God, and He isn't causing people to die.

IV. There are three main reasons people get sick. One of them is sin.

    A. After healing the man at the pool of Bethesda, Jesus said to him,

> **Behold, thou art made whole: sin no more, lest a worse thing come unto thee.**
>
> **John 5:14**

    B. Jesus made it very clear in this verse that this man's sickness returning, and even something worse than what he'd had, could come on him if he sinned.

    C. When alcoholics drink all of their lives and get liver disease, they did that to themselves—not because God did it, not because the devil did it directly, but because they're reaping the results of their sin (Rom. 6:21-23).

V. The second major reason we get sick is because we are in a battle with the devil.

    A. Sometimes our Enemy just fights us, and it's not based on an individual sin we've committed.

> *And his disciples asked him, saying, Master, who did sin, this man, or his parents, that he was born blind? Jesus answered, Neither hath this man sinned, nor his parents: but that the works of God should be made manifest in him.*
>
> **John 9:2-3**

    B. Jesus was saying that neither this man's sins nor his parents' sins had caused this blindness.

    C. Sometimes Satan just attacks us with things.

VI. The third main reason people get sick is simply natural things.

    A. Spirit-filled Christians will often so spiritualize everything that they don't recognize that there are just some things that happen naturally.

    B. I've heard of people who dove off a cliff and hit a rock in a pool of water. Now they're quadriplegic.

    C. It wasn't necessarily the devil that did that to them. He may have enticed them to go against their better judgment and do something that wasn't wise, but it was natural.

VII. The good news is that no matter what caused the sickness—sin, the devil, or something natural—there's always something we can do about it.

    A. Since the Lord has redeemed us from sickness and disease, we can take our authority, exercise our faith, and effect a cure.

    B. Even if our own sin opened a door and brought the sickness on us, we can repent and release the forgiveness and healing power of God in our lives.

Why Isn't Everyone Healed?
Lesson 11 – Teacher's Guide

1. One of the obvious reasons we don't see people healed today is that we aren't believing God for it. We are operating in unbelief. Rather than accept that, some folks will criticize me, saying, "You aren't being compassionate. You're just criticizing people you ought to be compassionate toward. You should tell them they're doing the best they can, and that's fine." Well, how did Jesus respond? When He found out His disciples couldn't heal the demoniac boy, He declared, "O faithless and perverse generation!" (Matt. 17:17). Do we really think that Jesus would have a more compassionate response to us today? Absolutely not!

2. I've failed. I don't always see healing come to pass. I've had to accept partial responsibility. Am I condemned by that? No, I'm not condemned at all. I believe that God loves me. He has comforted me. But knowing the truth has motivated me to learn what His Word says and not allow it to happen again.

3. It's God's will to heal every single person every single time. The reason this doesn't happen isn't because God fails to do it; it's because we as His representatives aren't operating in the fullness of what He has provided for them. I'd rather maintain God's integrity than my own. God is a good God, and He isn't causing people to die.

1. A. What is one of the obvious reasons we don't see people healed today? (We aren't believing for it)
    B. What are we operating in? (Unbelief)
2. A. Do I always see healing manifest? (No)
    B. What has knowing the truth motivated me to do? (Learn what God's Word says and not allow it to happen again)
3. A. What's the reason that every single person is not healed every single time? (We as God's representatives aren't operating in the fullness of what He has provided for us)
    B. What kind of God is He? (A good God)
    C. He isn't what? (Causing people to die)

4.   There are three main reasons we get sick. One of them is sin (John 5:14). Jesus made it very clear in this verse that this man's sickness returning, and even something worse than what he'd had, could come on him if he sinned. When alcoholics drink all of their lives and get liver disease, they did that to themselves—not because God did it, not because the devil did it directly, but because they're reaping the results of their sin (Rom. 6:21-23).

5.   The second major reason we get sick is because we are in a battle with the devil. Sometimes our Enemy just fights us, and it's not based on an individual sin we've committed (John 9:2-3). Jesus was saying that neither this man's sins nor his parents' sins had caused this blindness. Sometimes Satan just attacks us with things.

6.   The third main reason we get sick is simply natural things. Many of us as Spirit-filled Christians will often so spiritualize everything that we don't recognize that there are just some things that happen naturally. I've heard of people who dove off a cliff and hit a rock in a pool of water. Now they're quadriplegic. It wasn't necessarily the devil that did that to them. He may have enticed them to go against their better judgment and do something that wasn't wise, but it was natural.

7.   The good news is that no matter what caused the sickness—sin, the devil, or something natural—there's always something we can do about it. Since the Lord has redeemed us from sickness and disease, we can take our authority, exercise our faith, and effect a cure. Even if our own sin opened a door and brought the sickness on us, we can repent and release the forgiveness and healing power of God in our lives.

4.   A. Read John 5:14. What is first main reason we get sick? (Sin)
     B. If it's not because God did it or because the devil did it directly, what are people reaping when they sin? (The results of their sin)
5.   A. Read John 9:2-3. What is the second major reason we get sick? (Because we are in a battle with the devil. Sometimes our Enemy just fights us)
     B. Is this him fighting us based on an individual sin we did? (No)
6.   A. What is the third main reason we get sick? (Natural things)
     B. Was it necessarily the devil? (No)
7.   A. What is the good news? (That no matter what caused the sickness—sin, the devil, or something natural—there's always something we can do about it)
     B. What if our own sin opened a door and brought the sickness on us? (We can repent and release the forgiveness and healing power of God in our lives)

Why Isn't Everyone Healed?
Lesson 11 – Discipleship Questions

1. Read Matthew 17:19. Did the disciples ask Jesus this question in front of the multitude?

2. Read Matthew 17:5. How pleased is God with His beloved Son?

3. According to Matthew 17:14-17, what was the first thing the father asked Jesus?

    A. Why they couldn't cast the demon out.

    B. If "Christ" was His last name.

    C. If He would have mercy on his son.

    D. All of the above.

    E. None of the above.

4. What did Jesus call faithless and perverse?

5. According Mark 9:17-29, what did Jesus do when He saw the people coming?

6. What did many say after Jesus cast the spirit out of the boy?

7. But Jesus did what?

8. Read John 5:14. Where did Jesus find the man after he had been made whole?

9. Read to Romans 6:21-23. **"But now being _____ free from sin."**

10. What is the gift of God?

11. According to John 9:2-3, what did Jesus' disciples call Him?

12. Read Romans 3:23. How many have sinned and come short of the glory of God?

13. According to 1 Peter 5:8, why should we be sober and vigilant?

Why Isn't Everyone Healed?
Lesson 11 – Answer Key

1. No.

2. Well pleased.

3. C. If He would have mercy on his son.

4. The generation.

5. He rebuked the foul spirit, saying unto him, "You dumb and deaf spirit, I charge you, come out of him, and enter no more into him."

6. That the boy was dead.

7. He took the boy by the hand and lifted him up.

8. In the temple.

9. **"Made."**

10. Eternal life through Jesus Christ our Lord.

11. Master.

12. All.

13. Because our Adversary, the devil, walks about as a roaring lion seeking whom he may devour.

Why Isn't Everyone Healed?
Lesson 11 – Scriptures

Matthew 17:19
Then came the disciples to Jesus apart, and said, Why could not we cast him out?

Matthew 17:5
While he yet spake, behold, a bright cloud overshadowed them: and behold a voice out of the cloud, which said, This is my beloved Son, in whom I am well pleased; hear ye him.

Matthew 17:14-17
And when they were come to the multitude, there came to him a certain man, kneeling down to him, and saying, [15] Lord, have mercy on my son: for he is lunatick, and sore vexed: for ofttimes he falleth into the fire, and oft into the water. [16] And I brought him to thy disciples, and they could not cure him. [17] Then Jesus answered and said, O faithless and perverse generation, how long shall I be with you? how long shall I suffer you? bring him hither to me.

Mark 9:17-29
And one of the multitude answered and said, Master, I have brought unto thee my son, which hath a dumb spirit; [18] And wheresoever he taketh him, he teareth him: and he foameth, and gnasheth with his teeth, and pineth away: and I spake to thy disciples that they should cast him out; and they could not. [19] He answereth him, and saith, O faithless generation, how long shall I be with you? how long shall I suffer you? bring him unto me. [20] And they brought him unto him: and when he saw him, straightway the spirit tare him; and he fell on the ground, and wallowed foaming. [21] And he asked his father, How long is it ago since this came unto him? And he said, Of a child. [22] And ofttimes it hath cast him into the fire, and into the waters, to destroy him: but if thou canst do any thing, have compassion on us, and help us. [23] Jesus said unto him, If thou canst believe, all things are possible to him that believeth. [24] And straightway the father of the child cried out, and said with tears, Lord, I believe; help thou mine unbelief. [25] When Jesus saw that the people came running together, he rebuked the foul spirit, saying unto him, Thou dumb and deaf spirit, I charge thee, come out of him, and enter no more into him. [26] And the spirit cried, and rent him sore, and came out of him: and he was as one dead; insomuch that many said, He is dead. [27] But Jesus took him by the hand, and lifted him up; and he arose. [28] And when he was come into the house, his disciples asked him privately, Why could not we cast him out? [29] And he said unto them, This kind can come forth by nothing, but by prayer and fasting.

John 5:14
Afterward Jesus findeth him in the temple, and said unto him, Behold, thou art made whole: sin no more, lest a worse thing come unto thee.

Romans 6:21-23

What fruit had ye then in those things whereof ye are now ashamed? for the end of those things is death. [22] But now being made free from sin, and become servants to God, ye have your fruit unto holiness, and the end everlasting life. [23] For the wages of sin is death; but the gift of God is eternal life through Jesus Christ our Lord.

John 9:2-3

And his disciples asked him, saying, Master, who did sin, this man, or his parents, that he was born blind? [3] Jesus answered, Neither hath this man sinned, nor his parents: but that the works of God should be made manifest in him.

Romans 3:23

For all have sinned, and come short of the glory of God.

1 Peter 5:8

Be sober, be vigilant; because your adversary the devil, as a roaring lion, walketh about, seeking whom he may devour.

"Because of Your Unbelief"
Lesson 12

After Jesus rebuked His disciples (Matt. 17:17), He turned and healed the demonized boy:

And Jesus rebuked the devil; and he departed out of him: and the child was cured from that very hour.

Matthew 17:18

The disciples immediately pulled Jesus aside and asked,

Why could not we cast him out?

Matthew 17:19

This is the question we're dealing with. If it's God's will to heal and Jesus healed this boy, why couldn't the disciples get him healed? If we believe it's God's will for everyone to be healed, how come we don't always see every person healed? What are the reasons someone isn't healed?

Why They Were Confused

The disciples who asked Jesus this question, **"Why could we not cast him out?"** believed it was God's will to heal. They knew they had the power to cast these demons out. They had already been given power and authority to heal the sick and cast out devils. The Bible reveals that seven chapters earlier:

And when he had called unto him his twelve disciples, he gave them power against unclean spirits, to cast them out, and to heal all manner of sickness and all manner of disease...Heal the sick, cleanse the lepers, raise the dead, cast out devils.

Matthew 10:1 and 8

The parallel accounts of this passage record that these disciples...

Cast out many devils, and anointed with oil many that were sick, and healed them.

Mark 6:13

And they departed, and went through the towns, preaching the gospel, and healing every where.

Luke 9:6

Upon their return, there isn't a single question recorded. This means these same disciples who were asking "Why couldn't we cast this demon out?" in Matthew 17 had believed God in the past and successfully exercised this power and authority in Mark 6. They didn't ask this question because they didn't believe. They *did* believe. They had already exercised that power and seen the desired results. This is why they were confused.

If these disciples had thought *We just don't believe that you can heal a person with this ailment. We don't believe God can do that*, they wouldn't have asked this question. The very fact that they asked this question shows that they did believe, and yet they didn't get the results they desired.

Simple, but Profound

This is important. People who don't believe that God wants us well don't spend much time wondering, *Why isn't everyone healed?* That's because they don't believe it's God's will to heal everyone. The people who are perplexed are those who *do* believe it's God's will but aren't seeing every single person—perhaps even themselves—healed. Why does that happen?

The answer Jesus gave in the first part of Matthew 17:20 is very revealing:

Because of your unbelief.

Matthew 17:20

This is simple, but it's profound. **"Because of your unbelief."**

This is different than what most people would say. If I hadn't led up to this by taking you through this particular passage of Scripture, you probably wouldn't have answered what Jesus did. If I asked you "Why isn't everyone healed?" you probably would have said something like, "Well, they just don't have enough faith." That's the typical answer most people would say.

Now, it's true that if people don't have faith, then that will affect their ability to receive healing. Every instance where Jesus ministered healing, some degree of faith was involved. Some people may argue, "What about in Luke 7:11-16 where Jesus raised the boy from the dead in the city of Nain?" It was faith for this widow mother to allow Jesus to interrupt the funeral procession and her grief. She then responded positively to His command, "Do not weep." If faith wasn't present, she and the others there would have reacted very differently. In every instance that Jesus ministered healing, somebody had to be in faith to some degree.

Reach Out and Take

Sometimes people came to Jesus like the woman in Mark 5:

For she said, If I may touch but his clothes, I shall be whole.

Mark 5:28

She touched the hem of His garment in faith, the power of God flowed, and this woman was healed. The Lord told her, "Your faith has made you whole" (Mark 5:34). Now, that's strong faith. That's a faith that reaches out and takes what God has made available.

Not everyone who received healing exhibited that type of faith, but they had to have at least what I call a "passive" faith. You may not have the faith that reaches out and takes it, but if you are going to receive healing off of my prayer and faith, then you must have at least a passive faith that will receive it if I will bring it to you.

We just saw that if we were to ask the average person "Why isn't everyone healed," most people would answer, "Well, it's because they don't have enough faith." It's true that if a person isn't operating in faith, it will hinder them from receiving, but that's not what the Lord said:

Jesus said unto them, Because of your unbelief.

Matthew 17:20

Jesus didn't say it was because they had little faith; He said it was because they had unbelief.

Believe & Disbelieve

Now, certain versions of the Bible render this verse inaccurately, saying, "Because you have so little faith." That's a terrible translation! It's not what this verse says. If you were to look at the majority of the translations, especially the more literal ones, this verse is rendered **"Because of your unbelief,"** not "Because you have so little faith."

You may be wondering, *Well, what's the difference? If you have unbelief, then that means you don't have faith. If you have faith, you won't have any unbelief.* No, that's not true.

Most people have this concept that if they are believing God, that automatically means they don't have any unbelief. They think that if they did have any unbelief, that automatically means they don't have any faith, because if they were truly in faith, there would be zero unbelief. This is not what the Word teaches:

For verily I say unto you, That whosoever shall say unto this mountain, Be thou removed, and be thou cast into the sea; and shall not doubt in his heart, but shall believe that those things which he saith shall come to pass; he shall have whatsoever he saith.

Mark 11:23

Jesus said you have to speak to this mountain. It's understood that you must speak in faith and not doubt in your heart. If being in faith truly meant you automatically had zero unbelief, why did Jesus include this part about not doubting in your heart? The truth is, you can believe and disbelieve at the same time.

At the Same Time

Consider the parallel passage of this father and his demonized boy in Mark 9:

And they brought him unto him: and when he saw him, straightway the spirit tare him; and he fell on the ground, and wallowed foaming. And he asked his father, How long is it ago since this came unto him? And he said, Of a child. And ofttimes it hath cast him into the fire, and into the waters, to destroy him: but if thou canst do any thing, have compassion on us, and help us. Jesus said unto him, If thou canst believe, all things are possible to him that believeth.

Mark 9:20-23

In other words, as the father saw the manifestation of this boy having a seizure, he felt exasperated and frustrated. Finally, he looked at Jesus and said, "If you can do anything, help us." He began to doubt and despair. He was looking at the situation and saying, "God, I don't know if You can even handle this." Instead of accepting all of the responsibility for this healing Himself, Jesus turned back to this father and declared, "If you can believe, all things are possible to him that believes."

Now look at how this father responded:

And straightway the father of the child cried out, and said with tears, Lord, I believe; help thou mine unbelief.

Mark 9:24

Jesus' reply to this wasn't, "Well, that's a stupid statement. If you truly believe, you can't have unbelief. If you have any unbelief, then you aren't really believing." The Lord didn't correct him, rebuke him, or say anything like that; He just cured the boy. This shows that you can have faith and unbelief at the same time.

Faith Canceled Out

Imagine a team of horses hooked up to a wagon. Under normal circumstances, they would have enough power to move that wagon. But if an equal team of horses was hooked to the other side of the wagon and both teams were pulling at the same time in the opposite direction, the net effect would be zero. With both teams of horses pulling on that wagon with all their strength, it wouldn't move, because they're canceling each other out. One team is negating the other. They're counterbalancing each other.

This is what Jesus was saying in the first part of Matthew 17:20. He didn't tell His disciples, "It's because you don't have enough faith"; He said, "It's because of your unbelief. Your unbelief canceled out the faith you had."

These guys had been in faith before. They had seen demons cast out, and they had seen people healed and set free. This time, they did the same thing as before but didn't get the same results. That's why they were confused. They knew they were believing God. So they asked Him, "Why could we not cast him out?" Jesus didn't answer, "Because of your little faith." He said, "It's because of your unbelief."

A Tiny, Little Mustard Seed

Translating this "Because you have so little faith" makes no sense when you look at the rest of Matthew 17:20:

> *For verily I say unto you, If ye have faith as a grain of mustard seed,*
> *ye shall say unto this mountain, Remove hence to yonder place; and it*
> *shall remove; and nothing shall be impossible unto you.*

Jesus was saying, "If your faith is only the size of a mustard seed, nothing would be impossible to you." A mustard seed is one of the tiniest seeds there are. It's like one of those poppy seeds on a bun. The point our Lord was making is that even if your faith is tiny, it's enough to cast a mountain into the sea. You don't need big faith; you just need a faith that isn't canceled out, counterbalanced, or negated by unbelief pulling in the opposite direction. A faith the size of a tiny little mustard seed is all you need to speak to a mountain and see it cast into the sea without even physically having to touch it.

If Jesus had really been saying "It's because you have so little faith," then He would have contradicted and counteracted the very point He made in the rest of the verse, about faith the size of a mustard seed making a mountain move. Do you see how that doesn't fit? It doesn't make sense. Jesus was saying, "Guys, it's not that you didn't believe; it's that your unbelief negated your faith. That's why you didn't see the desired results."

"Because of Your Unbelief"
Lesson 12 – Outline

I. If it's God's will to heal and Jesus healed this boy (Matt. 17:18), why couldn't the disciples get him healed?

    A. The disciples who asked Jesus this question, **"Why could we not cast him out?"** believed it was God's will to heal.

    B. They had already been given power and authority to heal the sick and cast out devils (Matt. 10:1 and 8).

    C. This is why the disciples were confused.

    D. The answer Jesus gave in the first part of Matthew 17:20 is very revealing:

Because of your unbelief.

Matthew 17:20a

    E. This is simple, but it's profound.

II. Every instance where Jesus ministered healing, some degree of faith was involved.

    A. Some people may argue, "What about in Luke 7:11-16 where Jesus raised the boy from the dead in the city of Nain?"

    B. It was faith for this widow mother to allow Jesus to interrupt the funeral procession and her grief.

    C. If faith wasn't present, she and the others there would have reacted very differently.

III. We just saw that if we were to ask the average person "Why isn't everyone healed," most people would answer, "Well, it's because they don't have enough faith."

    A. It's true that if a person isn't operating in faith, it will hinder them from receiving, but that's not what the Lord said.

    B. He said it was because they had unbelief.

IV. Certain versions of the Bible render Matthew 17:20 inaccurately, saying, "Because you have so little faith."

    A. If you were to look at the majority of the translations, especially the more literal ones, this verse is rendered **"Because of your unbelief,"** not "Because you have so little faith."

    B. Most people have this concept that if they are believing God, that automatically means they don't have any unbelief.

    C. This is not what the Word teaches:

For verily I say unto you, That whosoever shall say unto this mountain, Be thou removed, and be thou cast into the sea; and shall not doubt in his heart, but shall believe that those things which he saith shall come to pass; he shall have whatsoever he saith.

Mark 11:23

   D. If being in faith truly meant you automatically had zero unbelief, why did Jesus include this part about not doubting in your heart?

   E. The truth is, you can believe and disbelieve at the same time.

  V. Consider the parallel passage of this father and his demonized boy in Mark 9:

And they brought him unto him: and when he saw him, straightway the spirit tare him; and he fell on the ground, and wallowed foaming. And he asked his father, How long is it ago since this came unto him? And he said, Of a child. And ofttimes it hath cast him into the fire, and into the waters, to destroy him: but if thou canst do any thing, have compassion on us, and help us. Jesus said unto him, If thou canst believe, all things are possible to him that believeth.

Mark 9:20-23

   A. Now look at how this father responded:

And straightway the father of the child cried out, and said with tears, Lord, I believe; help thou mine unbelief.

Mark 9:24

   B. The Lord didn't correct him, rebuke him, or say anything like that; He just cured the boy.

   C. This shows that you can have faith and unbelief at the same time.

   D. Imagine a team of horses hooked up to a wagon. Under normal circumstances, they would have enough power to move that wagon. But if an equal team of horses was hooked to the other side of the wagon and both teams were pulling at the same time in the opposite direction, the net effect would be zero.

   E. This is what Jesus was saying in the first part of Matthew 17:20.

   F. He didn't tell His disciples, "It's because you don't have enough faith"; He said, "It's because of your unbelief. Your unbelief canceled out the faith you had."

 VI. Translating this "Because you have so little faith" makes no sense when you look at the rest of Matthew 17:20:

For verily I say unto you, If ye have faith as a grain of mustard seed, ye shall say unto this mountain, Remove hence to yonder place; and it shall remove; and nothing shall be impossible unto you.

A. Jesus was saying, "If your faith is only the size of a mustard seed, nothing would be impossible to you."

B. You don't need big faith; you just need a faith that isn't canceled out, counterbalanced, or negated by unbelief pulling in the opposite direction.

"Because of Your Unbelief"
Lesson 12 – Teacher's Guide

1. If it's God's will to heal and Jesus healed this boy (Matt. 17:18), why couldn't the disciples get him healed? The disciples who asked Jesus this question, **"Why could we not cast him out?"** believed it was God's will to heal. They had already been given power and authority to heal the sick and cast out devils (Matt. 10:1 and 8). This is why the disciples were confused. The answer Jesus gave in the first part of Matthew 17:20 is very revealing: **"Because of your unbelief."** This is simple, but it's profound.

2. Every instance where Jesus ministered healing, some degree of faith was involved. Some people may argue, "What about in Luke 7:11-16 where Jesus raised the boy from the dead in the city of Nain?" It was faith for this widow mother to allow Jesus to interrupt the funeral procession and her grief. If faith wasn't present, she and the others there would have reacted very differently.

3. We just saw that if we were to ask the average person "Why isn't everyone healed," most people would answer, "Well, it's because they don't have enough faith." It's true that if a person isn't operating in faith, it will hinder them from receiving, but that's not what the Lord said. He said it was because they had unbelief.

1. A. Did the disciples believe it was God's will to heal? (Yes)
    B. What had they already been given? (Power and authority to heal the sick and cast out devils)
    C. What was Jesus' answer to the disciples' question? (**"Because of your unbelief"**)
2. A. Was some degree of faith involved in every instance Jesus ministered healing? (Yes)
    B. How do we know faith was present when Jesus raised the widow mother's son from the dead? (Because the widow mother allowed Jesus to interrupt the funeral procession and her grief)
3. If a person isn't operating in faith, what will this hinder? (Them from receiving healing)

4. Certain versions of the Bible render Matthew 17:20 inaccurately, saying, "Because you have so little faith." If we were to look at the majority of the translations, especially the more literal ones, this verse is rendered "Because of your unbelief," not "Because you have so little faith." Most people have this concept that if they are believing God, that automatically means we don't have any unbelief. This is not what the Word teaches (Mark 11:23). If being in faith truly meant we automatically had zero unbelief, why did Jesus include this part about not doubting in our hearts? The truth is, we can believe and disbelieve at the same time.

5. Consider the parallel passage of this father and his demonized boy in Mark 9:20-23. Now look at how this father responded in verse 24. The Lord didn't correct him, rebuke him, or say anything like that; He just cured the boy. This shows that we can have faith and unbelief at the same time. Let's imagine a team of horses hooked up to a wagon. Under normal circumstances, they would have enough power to move that wagon. But if an equal team of horses was hooked to the other side of the wagon and both teams were pulling at the same time in the opposite direction, the net effect would be zero. This is what Jesus was saying in the first part of Matthew 17:20. He didn't tell His disciples, "It's because you don't have enough faith"; He said, "It's because of your unbelief. Your unbelief canceled out the faith you had."

6. Translating this "Because you have so little faith" makes no sense when we look at the rest of Matthew 17:20: "For verily I say unto you, If ye have faith as a grain of mustard seed, ye shall say unto this mountain, Remove hence to yonder place; and it shall remove; and nothing shall be impossible unto you." Jesus was saying, "If your faith is only the size of a mustard seed, nothing would be impossible to you." We don't need big faith; we just need a faith that isn't canceled out, counterbalanced, or negated by unbelief pulling in the opposite direction.

4. A. Read Matthew 17:20. If we were to look at the majority of the translations, especially the more literal ones, this verse would be rendered what? ("Because of your unbelief," not "Because you have so little faith")
   B. If we are believing God, does that automatically mean we don't have any unbelief? (No)
5. A. Read Mark 9:20-24. What did Jesus do when the father asked, "Help thou mine unbelief"? (He cured the boy)
   B. What canceled out the faith the disciples had? (Unbelief)
6. A. Translating this "Because you have so little faith" makes no sense when what? (When we look at the rest of Matthew 17:20)
   B. What would be impossible to us if we had faith only the size of a mustard seed? (Nothing)

"Because of Your Unbelief"
Lesson 12 – Discipleship Questions

1. Read Matthew 17:17-20. What happened when Jesus rebuked the devil?

2. **"The child was _____ from that very hour."**

3. When Jesus says **"For verily I say unto you,"** what does that mean about what follows?

    A. It's absolutely true.

    B. It shouldn't be taken literally.

    C. Get ready for a good joke.

    D. It's a parable.

    E. Don't believe it.

4. Read Matthew 10:1. Could the disciples heal only a few manner of sickness and disease?

5. Read Matthew 10:8. Jesus' instruction here was _____.

    A. Irrelevant.

    B. Debatable.

    C. A command.

    D. All of the above.

    E. None of the above.

6. According to Mark 6:13, did the disciples have experience casting out devils?

7. Read Luke 9:6. What did the disciples do besides heal people everywhere?

8. According to Luke 7:11-16, what did Jesus have when He saw the widow mother?

9. What did Jesus tell the young man to do?

10. The people glorified God, saying "A great _____ is risen among us."

11. According to Mark 5:28, what was this woman certain of?

    A. That God would heal her demonized daughter.

    B. That God wanted her well.

    C. That she needed a new perm.

    D. All of the above.

    E. None of the above.

12. According to Mark 11:23, what Jesus says here applies to _____.

13. Read Mark 9:20-24. How frequently did the spirit cast the boy into the fire and the water to destroy him?

14. What did Jesus say was possible to those who believe?

"Because of Your Unbelief"
Lesson 12– Answer Key

1. The devil departed out of the child.

2. **"Cured."**

3. A. It's absolutely true.

4. No.

5. C. A command.

6. Yes.

7. They preached the Gospel.

8. Compassion.

9. Arise.

10. "Prophet."

11. B. That God wanted her well.

12. Whosever.

13. Ofttimes (often).

14. All things.

"Because of Your Unbelief"
Lesson 12 – Scriptures

Matthew 17:17-20
Then Jesus answered and said, O faithless and perverse generation, how long shall I be with you? how long shall I suffer you? bring him hither to me. [18] And Jesus rebuked the devil; and he departed out of him: and the child was cured from that very hour. [19] Then came the disciples to Jesus apart, and said, Why could not we cast him out? [20] And Jesus said unto them, Because of your unbelief: for verily I say unto you, If ye have faith as a grain of mustard seed, ye shall say unto this mountain, Remove hence to yonder place; and it shall remove; and nothing shall be impossible unto you.

Matthew 10:1
And when he had called unto him his twelve disciples, he gave them power against unclean spirits, to cast them out, and to heal all manner of sickness and all manner of disease.

Matthew 10:8
Heal the sick, cleanse the lepers, raise the dead, cast out devils: freely ye have received, freely give.

Mark 6:13
And they cast out many devils, and anointed with oil many that were sick, and healed them.

Luke 9:6
And they departed, and went through the towns, preaching the gospel, and healing every where.

Luke 7:11-16
And it came to pass the day after, that he went into a city called Nain; and many of his disciples went with him, and much people. [12] Now when he came nigh to the gate of the city, behold, there was a dead man carried out, the only son of his mother, and she was a widow: and much people of the city was with her. [13] And when the Lord saw her, he had compassion on her, and said unto her, Weep not. [14] And he came and touched the bier: and they that bare him stood still. And he said, Young man, I say unto thee, Arise. [15] And he that was dead sat up, and began to speak. And he delivered him to his mother. [16] And there came a fear on all: and they glorified God, saying, That a great prophet is risen up among us; and, That God hath visited his people.

Mark 5:28
For she said, If I may touch but his clothes, I shall be whole.

Mark 5:34

And he said unto her, Daughter, thy faith hath made thee whole; go in peace, and be whole of thy plague.

Mark 11:23

For verily I say unto you, That whosoever shall say unto this mountain, Be thou removed, and be thou cast into the sea; and shall not doubt in his heart, but shall believe that those things which he saith shall come to pass; he shall have whatsoever he saith.

Mark 9:20-24

And they brought him unto him: and when he saw him, straightway the spirit tare him; and he fell on the ground, and wallowed foaming. [21] And he asked his father, How long is it ago since this came unto him? And he said, Of a child. [22] And oft-times it hath cast him into the fire, and into the waters, to destroy him: but if thou canst do any thing, have compassion on us, and help us. [23] Jesus said unto him, If thou canst believe, all things are possible to him that believeth. [24] And straight-way the father of the child cried out, and said with tears, Lord, I believe; help thou mine unbelief.

Faith Negated
Lesson 13

Not long after the first time God used me to raise someone from the dead, I was excited. I was pumped. I thought, *If I can see someone raised from the dead, then I can see blind eyes opened, deaf ears healed, people come out of wheelchairs—anything!* As I was holding a service in Omaha, Nebraska, on my left, in the front, there was a man sitting in a wheelchair. I was so excited. I thought, *God, I've seen You raise someone from the dead, so I know this guy is going to be healed.* I could hardly wait for me to get finished preaching so I could go over and minister to this fellow. So I went over to him, grabbed him by the hand, and declared, "In the name of Jesus Christ of Nazareth, rise up and walk!" When I yanked him out of the wheelchair, he came up, over, and then fell flat on his face. Since he was paralyzed, he couldn't stand up or catch himself.

When that happened, you could hear the gasps and groans of unbelief and shock from the people. I was shocked. I felt embarrassed and humiliated. I thought, *Look what I've done to this man. I've embarrassed and humiliated him.* It felt terrible. So I got down on my hands and knees, grabbed this guy around his chest, wrestled him back into the wheelchair, and said the equivalent of, **"Depart in peace, be ye warmed and filled"** (James 2:16). Yet I didn't give him what he needed. This man left in his wheelchair.

When I returned to the hotel room, I remember asking God, "Why did that happen?" What confused me was that I knew I had faith. Some people may think, *No, if you had faith, he would have been healed.* No, I had faith. I used my faith, as far as I could tell, just the same as I did on that man who was raised from the dead. I had just as much faith. It wasn't that I wasn't believing God. You don't go up, grab someone, and pull them out of their wheelchair unless you believe they're going to walk. I didn't expect that man to fall on his face; I expected him to walk. There was faith present, and because I had faith, I was confused. I wouldn't ever have done that if faith wasn't present, but why didn't I see the right results?

Fear of Man

So I asked God, "Why wasn't this man healed?" It took about three years for my lightning-fast mind to finally figure this out. The Lord showed me, "Andrew, you did have faith, but you also had unbelief." When the people responded in shock and I panicked, that was unbelief. I was more concerned about what other people said than I was about what God had to say.

Jesus said,

How can ye believe, which receive honour one of another, and seek not the honour that cometh from God only?

John 5:44

If you have to have other people validate you to feel good about yourself, you're a man pleaser. Worrying about other people's opinions is the fear of man. Fear is the opposite of faith. Fear is actually faith in a negative direction.

I was worried about what people thought of me. I was embarrassed and humiliated. That unbelief and fear negated my faith. Yes, I had faith. But I also had unbelief. I was still swayed by what people thought about me, and it canceled my faith.

"Let Her Go!"

God began to reveal this truth to me while I was reading a book about Smith Wigglesworth. Smith used to start each one of his meetings by standing up on the platform and boldly declaring, "Whoever gets up here first will be healed of whatever disease they've got." Then he would minister to that person and see them healed. This would get everybody's attention, and he would teach on how it happened. Then he'd have a prayer line and pray for multitudes of people.

A couple of ladies in the front row knew his pattern, so they popped right up as soon as he made this invitation. Between them, they had an elderly friend who was so weak and frail that she hadn't even been able to sit up by herself, much less stand. There had to be one lady on each side of her to hold her up. The large tumor she had on her belly made her appear to be nine months pregnant. This lady was in bad, bad shape. So at Smith's declaration, these two ladies grabbed her and took her up on the platform.

There these two women were—one on either side, holding up the woman who had this huge tumor. Wigglesworth looked at them and said, "Let her go."

These ladies explained, "We can't let her go. She's too weak and can't stand up on her own."

Smith yelled at them, "I said let her go!"

So they did. And she fell flat on her face on top of that tumor and let out a loud groan of pain. The audience gasped, full of shock and unbelief, which was the same response I had received when I pulled that man out of his wheelchair. In this similar situation, I had responded with guilt, shame, and fear of what other people thought. I was thinking *Lawsuit!* and all of these other terrible things. How did Smith Wigglesworth respond? He said, "Pick her up."

So they picked this woman up, and once they had her standing again between them, Smith said, "Let her go." It didn't faze him one bit. He wasn't moved off of his faith.

Less Unbelief

They answered, "We will not let her go! We can't let her go. She'll fall."

He yelled at them, saying, "Let her go!" So they let her go. A second time, this lady fell on her face, on top of that tumor again. The people in the audience were shocked. Moans and groans of unbelief rippled throughout the entire audience. Smith said, "Pick her up." So they picked her up. Then he said, "Let her go."

These women protested, "We will not let her go!"

Smith yelled, "You let her go!"

A man in the audience stood up and said, "You beast! Leave that poor woman alone!"

Wigglesworth answered, "I know my business. You mind your own." Then he turned back to those ladies and roared, "LET HER GO!" They let her go. She started to fall, but then caught herself. That tumor fell right out of her dress onto the stage, and she walked off perfectly healed.

The Lord showed me that Smith Wigglesworth didn't have any more faith than I had (Rom. 12:3). He didn't get any better results that first time he ministered to this woman than I got when I pulled that man out of his wheelchair. She fell flat on her face, just like he did. What was the difference? Smith didn't have any more faith than I did; he just had less unbelief. He didn't care what people thought about him.

In fact, the book said Smith was often criticized as being harsh and hard. Do you know what the word *hard* means in reference to our emotions? It means cold, insensitive, unfeeling, or unyielding to what other people think. The difference between Smith and me wasn't that he had more faith; he had less sensitivity to people's criticism. He was hardened toward what other people thought. He wasn't responding to anybody or anything except what God told him. I was still too dominated by people's opinions, by my physical realm, and what I could see, taste, hear, smell, and feel. So the difference wasn't that Smith had more faith; it was that he had less unbelief.

Decrease Your Unbelief

Most people don't understand this truth. When they pray for someone to be healed but don't immediately see the manifestation, they often think, *I just don't have enough faith.* So they start trying to build and increase their faith. They have this misconception that they need to have a huge amount of faith. However, this violates what Jesus taught in Matthew 17 when He said, "If your faith is the size of a tiny, little mustard seed, that's enough to remove a mountain into the sea." In other words, He was saying, "Guys, you don't need big faith; what you need is a pure faith that doesn't have anything contradicting, counteracting, or negating it. You need a faith that doesn't have anything pulling it in an opposite direction." Most people don't deal with unbelief in their lives. Instead, they try to build faith.

Unbelief comes very similarly to the way faith does:

So then faith cometh by hearing, and hearing by the word of God.

Romans 10:17

In other words, faith comes when we focus our attention on God and His Word. Unbelief comes in a similar way, but from the opposite direction. Unbelief comes when we focus our attention on what people have to say. It comes when we listen to all the negative things the doctor has to say. If we consider, ponder, and think on all of these negatives, they'll negate our faith. So the key to the Christian life isn't learning how to develop huge faith; it's learning how to decrease the amount of unbelief in our lives. Very few Christians have this understanding.

Most Christians will spend an extra hour a day in the Word trying to build their faith. But then, during the day, they wash it down with two or three hours' worth of "As the Stomach

Turns" on television and reading through all the bad news in the newspaper. They'll allow all the sewage from the world to flow through them—thoughts, attitudes, and concepts that are completely contrary to God's Word—and then wonder why their faith isn't working.

You don't need huge faith; you just need a pure faith that isn't counterbalanced by everything else.

How did Smith Wigglesworth get to where his faith wasn't polluted by unbelief? He resisted unbelief by refusing to focus on anything but God's Word.

One day Lester Sumrall knocked on Smith Wigglesworth's door. He asked Smith if he could come in to visit. Smith told him he could come in, but the newspaper under his arm had to stay outside. Smith never read the newspaper and refused for one to be brought into his house.

Some people say, "That's really narrow minded." Well, it is. I agree that there are some good things in the newspaper. Over the years, I've used some newspaper articles to verify points in my messages. I believe that over Smith's thirty-five-year ministry, he probably missed a dozen or so good things he could have used in his sermons. But it's certain he missed thousands of bad things that would have opened the door to unbelief. If you're going to go overboard, that's the side to do it on.

Abraham Considered Not

Consider how Abraham believed God:

Who against hope believed in hope, that he might become the father of many nations, according to that which was spoken, So shall thy seed be. And being not weak in faith, he considered not his own body now dead, when he was about an hundred years old, neither yet the deadness of Sara's womb: He staggered not at the promise of God through unbelief; but was strong in faith, giving glory to God; And being fully persuaded that, what he had promised, he was able also to perform.

Romans 4:18-21

This passage of Scripture reveals that Abraham wasn't weak in faith, because **"he considered not his own body now dead."** He didn't have huge faith, but he did have a faith that wasn't negated and counterbalanced by unbelief. Abraham simply didn't consider anything that was contrary to what God had said.

Speaking also of Abraham, Hebrews 11 says,

And truly, if they had been mindful of that country from whence they came out, they might have had opportunity to have returned.

Hebrews 11:15

If Abraham's and Sarah's minds had been full of thoughts of the country they had left behind in obedience to God, they would have been tempted to return. In other words, your temptation is linked to what you think.

You need to understand this. It will change your life if you understand and apply it. You cannot be tempted with what you don't think. You have to think about something before you can be tempted with it. Therefore, you cannot be tempted with unbelief unless you think thoughts of unbelief. You need to quit listening to everyone else and all of their unbelief. You need to stop considering the negativism, cynicism, and anti-God/anti-Christ sentiment of this world. If you didn't listen to those thoughts, you wouldn't be tempted to disbelieve God.

Through many years of ministry, I've found that the hardest people to be healed out of all the professions are doctors, nurses, and those who have received medical training. Personally, I believe this is because of what they have been taught. It's not that everything medical professionals are taught is evil; it's just that it is presented to and hammered into them as fact. "Here's what happens when a person gets a tumor. When it gets to this stage, then they will die." But they never say, "Unless they receive healing from God." They don't ever present it in a spiritual context and show that God is capable of overcoming anything. No, they just hear these thoughts, *When a tumor is at this stage, they will die. They will have so many weeks to live, and that's it. It's incurable.* And they hear these things over and over again for years at a time. I've had some medical professionals try to receive healing, and they just can't understand why it is so hard for them. It's because they have been taught so much unbelief, and it negates their little mustard seed of faith.

Faith Negated
Lesson 13 – Outline

I. Not long after the first time God used me to raise someone from the dead, I was excited.

    A. As I was holding a service in Omaha, Nebraska, there was a man sitting in a wheelchair.

    B. So I went over to him, grabbed him by the hand, and declared, "In the name of Jesus Christ of Nazareth, rise up and walk!"

    C. He came up, over, and then fell flat on his face.

    D. When that happened, you could hear the gasps and groans of unbelief and shock from the people.

    E. I felt embarrassed and humiliated.

    F. What confused me was that I knew I had faith.

    G. The Lord showed me, "Andrew, you did have faith, but you also had unbelief."

    H. When the people responded in shock and I panicked, that was unbelief. I was more concerned about what other people said than I was about what God had to say.

> *How can ye believe, which receive honour one of another, and seek not the honour that cometh from God only?*
>
> **John 5:44**

II. God began to reveal this truth to me while I was reading a book about Smith Wigglesworth.

    A. The book said Smith was often criticized as being harsh and hard.

    B. The difference between Smith and me wasn't that he had more faith; he had less sensitivity to people's criticism. He was hardened toward what other people thought.

    C. It was that he had less unbelief.

III. The key to the Christian life isn't learning how to develop huge faith; it's learning how to decrease the amount of unbelief in our lives.

    A. Most Christians will spend an extra hour a day in the Word trying to build their faith. But then they wash it down with two or three hours' worth of "As the Stomach Turns" on television and reading through all the bad news in the newspaper.

    B. They'll allow all the sewage from the world to flow through them—thoughts, attitudes, and concepts that are completely contrary to God's Word—and then wonder why their faith isn't working.

IV. One day Lester Sumrall knocked on Smith Wigglesworth's door.

    A. Smith told him he could come in, but the newspaper under his arm had to stay outside.

    B. Smith never read the newspaper and refused for one to be brought into his house.

    C. I believe that over Smith's thirty-five-year ministry, he probably missed a dozen or so good things from newspapers that he could have used in his sermons.

    D. But it's certain he missed thousands of bad things that would have opened the door to unbelief.

    E. If you're going to go overboard, that's the side to do it on.

V. Consider how Abraham believed God (Rom. 4:18-21).

    A. This passage of Scripture reveals that Abraham wasn't weak in faith, **"because he considered not his own body now dead."**

    B. Abraham simply didn't consider anything that was contrary to what God had said.

VI. If Abraham's and Sarah's minds had been full of thoughts of the country they had left behind in obedience to God, they would have been tempted to return (Heb. 11:15).

    A. In other words, your temptation is linked to what you think.

    B. Therefore, you cannot be tempted with unbelief unless you think thoughts of unbelief.

    C. You need to quit listening to everyone else and all of their unbelief.

    D. You need to stop considering the negativism, cynicism, and anti-God/anti-Christ sentiment of this world.

    E. If you didn't listen to those thoughts, you wouldn't be tempted to disbelieve God.

Faith Negated
Lesson 13 – Teacher's Guide

1. Not long after the first time God used me to raise someone from the dead, I was excited. As I was holding a service in Omaha, Nebraska, there was a man sitting in a wheelchair. So I went over to him, grabbed him by the hand, and declared, "In the name of Jesus Christ of Nazareth, rise up and walk!" He came up, over, and then fell flat on his face. When that happened, you could hear the gasps and groans of unbelief and shock from the people. I felt embarrassed and humiliated. What confused me was that I knew I had faith. The Lord showed me, "Andrew, you did have faith, but you also had unbelief." When the people responded in shock and I panicked, that was unbelief. I was more concerned about what other people said than I was about what God had to say (John 5:44).

2. God began to reveal this truth to me while I was reading a book about Smith Wigglesworth. The book said Smith was often criticized as being harsh and hard. The difference between Smith and me wasn't that he had more faith; he had less sensitivity to people's criticism. He was hardened toward what other people thought. It was that he had less unbelief.

3. The key to the Christian life isn't learning how to develop a huge faith; it's learning how to decrease the amount of unbelief in our lives. Most Christians will spend an extra hour a day in the Word trying to build their faith. But then they wash it down with two or three hours' worth of "As the Stomach Turns" on television and reading through all the bad news in the newspaper. They'll allow all the sewage from the world to flow through them— thoughts, attitudes, and concepts that are completely contrary to God's Word—and then wonder why their faith isn't working.

1. Read John 5:44. If we receive honor from others and not from God, what can we not do? (Believe)
2. What did Smith Wigglesworth have that I didn't? (Less sensitivity to people's criticism. He was hardened toward what other people thought. He had less unbelief)
3. A. What do we have to learn to do? (Decrease the amount of unbelief in our lives)
   B. If we'll allow all the sewage from the world to flow through us—thoughts, attitudes, and concepts that are completely contrary to God's Word—is it a wonder why our faith isn't working? (No)

4. One day Lester Sumrall knocked on Smith Wigglesworth's door. Smith told him he could come in, but the newspaper under his arm had to stay outside. Smith never read the newspaper and refused for one to be brought into his house. I believe that over Smith's thirty-five-year ministry, he probably missed a dozen or so good things from newspapers that he could have used in his sermons. But it's certain he missed thousands of bad things that would have opened the door to unbelief. If we're going to go overboard, that's the side to do it on.

5. Consider how Abraham believed God (Rom. 4:18-21). This passage of Scripture reveals that Abraham wasn't weak in faith, because **"he considered not his own body now dead."** Abraham simply didn't consider anything that was contrary to what God had said.

6. If Abraham's and Sarah's minds had been full of thoughts of the country they had left behind in obedience to God, they would have been tempted to return (Heb. 11:15). In other words, our temptation is linked to what we think. Therefore, we cannot be tempted with unbelief unless we think thoughts of unbelief. We need to quit listening to everyone else and all of their unbelief. We need to stop considering the negativism, cynicism, and anti-God/anti-Christ sentiment of this world. If we didn't listen to those thoughts, we wouldn't be tempted to disbelieve God.

4. Even though Smith might have missed a dozen or so good things from newspapers that he could have used in his sermons, what is certain? (That he missed thousands of bad things that would have opened the door to unbelief)

5. A. Read Romans 4:18-21. What does this passage of Scripture reveal about Abraham? (That he wasn't weak in faith, because **"he considered not his own body now dead"**)
   B. What didn't Abraham consider? (Anything that was contrary to what God had said)

6. A. Read Hebrews 11:15. We can't be tempted with unbelief unless what? (We think thoughts of unbelief)
   B. What do we need to quit listening to? (Everyone else and all their unbelief)
   C. What do we need to stop considering? (The negativism, cynicism, and anti-God/anti-Christ sentiment of this world)
   D. If we didn't listen to those thoughts, what wouldn't we be tempted to do? (Disbelieve God)

Faith Negated
Lesson 13 – Discipleship Questions

1. Read James 2:16. It profits to give someone the things _____ for the body.

2. According to John 5:44, it's better to seek the honor that comes from _____.

   A. People.

   B. God.

   C. The pastor.

   D. All of the above.

   E. None of the above.

3. Read Romans 12:3. What was given to Paul?

4. How are we not to think of ourselves?

5. According to Romans 10:17, does faith come by hearing just anything?

6. What do we have to hear before we can have faith?

7. Read Romans 4:18-21. Abraham didn't stagger at _____ through unbelief.

8. How persuaded was Abraham that He that had promised was also able to perform?

9. According to Hebrews 11:15, if they had been mindful of the country they came from, what would they have had?

Faith Negated
Lesson 13 – Answer Key

1. Needful.

2. B. God.

3. Grace.

4. More highly than we ought to think.

5. No.

6. The Word of God.

7. The promise of God.

8. He was fully persuaded.

9. Opportunity to return.

Faith Negated
Lesson 13 – Scriptures

James 2:16
And one of you say unto them, Depart in peace, be ye warmed and filled; notwithstanding ye give them not those things which are needful to the body; what doth it profit?

John 5:44
How can ye believe, which receive honour one of another, and seek not the honour that cometh from God only?

Romans 12:3
For I say, through the grace given unto me, to every man that is among you, not to think of himself more highly than he ought to think; but to think soberly, according as God hath dealt to every man the measure of faith.

Romans 10:17
So then faith cometh by hearing, and hearing by the word of God.

Romans 4:18-21
Who against hope believed in hope, that he might become the father of many nations, according to that which was spoken, So shall thy seed be. [19] And being not weak in faith, he considered not his own body now dead, when he was about an hundred years old, neither yet the deadness of Sara's womb: [20] He staggered not at the promise of God through unbelief; but was strong in faith, giving glory to God; [21] And being fully persuaded that, what he had promised, he was able also to perform.

Hebrews 11:15
And truly, if they had been mindful of that country from whence they came out, they might have had opportunity to have returned.

A Pure, Strong Faith
Lesson 14

In Matthew 17:20, Jesus was saying to His disciples, "Guys, you don't have a faith problem; what you have is an unbelief problem." The parallel account in Mark 9 says that...

They brought him unto him: and when he saw him, straightway the spirit tare him; and he fell on the ground, and wallowed foaming.

Mark 9:20

Personally, I believe this is what caused the disciples' unbelief. If you've ever seen an epileptic seizure, it's a frightful experience, especially if they start biting or swallowing their tongue. It's terrible. I've seen it before. It'll make all the hair rise up on the back of your head.

These disciples had faith: they had seen other demons cast out, and they had seen people healed. But this time, when they went to pray for this boy, there was this physical manifestation of these demons. The same thing happened to Jesus when He went to minister to this lad. The difference was that Jesus had zero unbelief to counter His faith. So He was able to effect a cure. But these disciples had responded in unbelief, which negated their faith. So when they asked the Lord "Why could we not cast him out? We know we were believing. We've seen it happen before, but how come it didn't work this time?" He told them, "It's because of your unbelief. Your unbelief negated, canceled out, and counterbalanced your faith."

Then in Matthew 17:21, Jesus continued by saying,

Howbeit this kind [of unbelief] goeth not out but by prayer and fasting.

Brackets mine

Contrary to much popular teaching, and now even a few erroneous Bible versions, the true subject of verse 21 is the unbelief mentioned in verse 20, not the demon(s) talked about in verse 19. Some people teach that certain demons are stronger than others and that you must pray and fast in order to be able to cast them out. There are all kinds of variations on this. That is not what Matthew 17:21 is saying. If you look carefully, you'll see that the subject of the previous sentence (Matt. 17:20) was unbelief, not demons. Unbelief was what stopped the disciples from casting out this demon and seeing the boy healed. And since the Lord said "This kind only goes out through much prayer and fasting," apparently there are different kinds of unbelief.

Let me quickly mention that one of the same translations that substitutes "little faith" for **"unbelief"** in verse 20, totally leaves out verse 21. I'm not quick to criticize translations. I'm aware that many people don't like the *King James Version*, which is the version I use. However, any translation that omits verses is not what I consider good. You need a good translation of the Bible. Check yours to see if Matthew 17:21 and Mark 16:17-20 are there.

Three Kinds of Unbelief

This is just Andy-ology, but through my study of the Word and experience in ministry, it seems to me that there are three different kinds of unbelief.

First, there is unbelief that comes from ignorance. Sometimes people oppose what God says, not because of anything specific, but because of a lack of knowledge. They just don't know any better. They don't know that God wants them well. They've never heard that truth before. It's ignorance, but nonetheless it's unbelief.

The way to overcome this first kind of unbelief—ignorance—is to tell them the truth. Show them the truth of God's Word. If they respect His Word and are sensitive to His Spirit, they'll receive the knowledge they need to overcome this unbelief.

The second type of unbelief comes from wrong doctrine. Many people today have been taught wrong. They've been told, "God doesn't do miracles today. Healing isn't for us today. These things passed away with the apostles." That's not true. It's not what the Word of God teaches. However, it's what they have been taught.

This unbelief that comes from wrong teaching is harder to overcome than overcoming just ignorance. That's because you must first counter the wrong doctrine and then teach them the truth. The antidote is exactly the same. It just takes an extra step administering it, which includes sitting down with them and countering their objections. The answer for both of these first two types of unbelief is to receive the truth of God's Word.

Then there's the third type of unbelief that I call natural unbelief. It's unbelief that comes from natural information that is contrary to God's Word. If you pray for someone to be healed and they fall over dead, your eyes, your ears, and all of your senses are going to tell you, "It didn't work." That's not necessarily because of ignorance or wrong doctrine; it's just that you've learned to trust what you see, taste, hear, smell, and feel. If you pray for your body to quit hurting, yet you can still feel pain, your body is going to be giving you thoughts of natural unbelief. It's not demonic or evil. Your five senses aren't of the devil; they have an important place and function in your everyday life.

Develop Your Sixth Sense

If you were going to drive me somewhere, I wouldn't want you to drive your car by faith. I'd want you to open your eyes and see if there was another vehicle coming before proceeding through that intersection. That's not wrong or unbelief. But if you know God has spoken something to you by the Word and/or by His Spirit and your physical senses are telling you it's not going to work, then you have to be able to go beyond those five senses. When God wants you to do something contrary to what you can see, taste, hear, smell, and feel, then your five natural senses can give you thoughts of unbelief that can negate your faith.

This is what happened with the disciples in Matthew 17. They saw a physical manifestation of this demon that was contrary to what they were praying and believing for, and it caused them to fear. Their five senses ministered thoughts of unbelief that countered their faith.

It was miraculous how God used me to raise that first man from the dead. I didn't know what was wrong when I walked into the room. I was standing right in front of him before I realized he was dead. I heard his wife crying, "O God, bring Everett back from the dead." When she said that, it was the first time I had even had a thought that the guy was dead. When I heard it, I just looked at him and commanded, "Everett, in the name of Jesus, come back into your body." Then he just sat up. It was that simple.

It would have been much more difficult if I would have had thirty minutes to think about him being dead. If somebody would have told me what I was getting ready to pray for, my mind would probably have come up with enough thoughts of unbelief to negate and counterbalance my faith. Personally, I believe that one of the reasons I saw this man raised from the dead was because I just didn't have time to think about anything else.

These disciples had already seen demons cast out and people healed. Apparently, they hadn't faced a physical manifestation like this before. Therefore, they hadn't had the same temptation to unbelief. But in this instance, there was a physical manifestation contrary to what they'd prayed for, and it caused them to have thoughts of unbelief. Understanding this, Jesus told them, "The only way you can get rid of this natural kind of unbelief is through fasting and prayer. It's not by just studying the Word more; you need to get into the presence of God and renew yourself to such a degree that you develop your sixth sense, which is faith."

Fasting & Prayer

This is important. You have five senses—what you can see, taste, hear, smell, and feel. If one of those senses were to be damaged—let's say you went blind—you could still get around. What you'd have to do is depend more upon your other remaining senses, like hearing and feeling. You would have to listen to what's happening around you and use a cane to feel the variances in the ground ahead as you walked. You could still get around and walk places, but you'd have to rely more on your other senses. Some blind people memorize what their apartments are like, and where everything is. They're primarily using their ears and sense of touch. You can compensate for losing one of your senses by depending on the others more.

What happens when God reveals to you through His Word that it is His will to heal you, but all five of your senses are telling you, "It didn't work. I still feel pain. I still look sick. I still have this and that, and I can taste something in my mouth that shows me I haven't been healed yet"? If all five of your senses are telling you it didn't work, you need to develop a sixth sense that will tell you it *did* work. That sixth sense is faith.

You can get to where you actually believe you have faith, and that faith becomes as real to you as what you can see, taste, hear, smell, and feel. How do you do that? By spending time in the spiritual realm. That's what prayer and fasting are all about.

However, fasting doesn't change God. It doesn't make Him move. Fasting and prayer don't make demons leave. There is no demon that you will ever encounter that, to cast them out, will require fasting and prayer added to what Jesus has already done. If you encounter a demon and it doesn't respond to the name of Jesus and faith in His name, then your prayer and fasting aren't going to get it out either. Speaking the Word of God and the name of Jesus in faith will deal with any demon. Your fasting and prayer don't move God. Neither do they move the devil. Fasting and prayer move you. They affect you.

Your appetite is one of the strongest desires your flesh has. When you deny your flesh by fasting, it's going to rise up and rebel because it wants to be fed. Your flesh wants to be indulged and taken care of. If you tell your flesh "No! Man doesn't live by bread alone but by every word that proceeds from the mouth of God" (Matt. 4:4 and Luke 4:4), I can guarantee you that your flesh is going to rebel. Although you'll think you are dying by noon the first day, it's not true. If you persevere, your body and your senses will begin to learn. They'll say, "Hey, I didn't die at noon." As a matter of fact, after fasting about three days, you'll get to where you aren't hungry anymore. You may not have experienced this yet, but it's true. You can literally bring your five senses under control, and they'll begin to recognize that, "Hey, I'm not going to starve. Okay, this faith stuff is real." You really can be sustained by God, and not by food alone. You can teach your flesh that.

Then when you say to your body "You're healed in Jesus' name," your flesh may answer "I still hurt," but that sixth sense says, "I'm healed and I believe it. So, okay, I've experienced this before." But if you haven't spent time fasting, praying, and being in the presence of God, your body will say, "No, I still hurt." You'll say "Body, you get in line," but your flesh will answer, "Who are you to tell me what to do? I tell you when to eat, what to eat, and how much to eat." It's just like a spoiled brat. But you can train your senses to discern both good (God and His Word) and evil (what contradicts them):

> *But strong meat belongeth to them that are of full age, even those who by reason of use have their senses exercised to discern both good and evil.*
>
> **Hebrews 5:14**

You can get to the place where someone like Smith Wigglesworth lived, listening to what faith has to say more than what natural things—like your mind, emotions, senses, and circumstances—have to say. When you do that, you're decreasing in unbelief.

The Measure of Faith

According to Romans 4, it's more biblically accurate to say that depending on the level of unbelief, you either have a weak faith or a strong faith:

> *And being not weak in faith, he considered not his own body now dead, when he was about an hundred years old, neither yet the deadness of Sara's womb: He staggered not at the promise of God through unbelief; but was strong in faith, giving glory to God; And being fully persuaded that, what he had promised, he was able also to perform.*
>
> **Romans 4:19-21**

What you're doing is describing how much unbelief you have mixed with your faith. If you have a lot of unbelief, then you're weak in faith. If you have little unbelief, then you're strong in faith. That's an appropriate description. But the terms "little faith" and "big faith" aren't really appropriate. The truth is, every one of us has been given *the* faith of the Son of God:

God hath dealt to every man the measure of faith.

Romans 12:3

Knowing that a man is not justified by the works of the law, but by **the faith of Jesus Christ**, *even we have believed in Jesus Christ, that we might be justified by* **the faith of Christ**, *and not by the works of the law: for by the works of the law shall no flesh be justified...I am crucified with Christ: nevertheless I live; yet not I, but Christ liveth in me: and the life which I now live in the flesh* **I live by the faith of the Son of God**, *who loved me, and gave himself for me.*

Galatians 2:16 and 20, emphasis mine

Every born-again Christian has the exact same amount and quality of faith that Jesus had. We don't have a faith problem; what we have is an unbelief problem. Instead of trying to build bigger and bigger faith, we need to stop feeding unbelief. We need to turn off the sources of unbelief in our lives and starve our unbelief. We need to get to where we spend so much time in the spiritual world, thinking on God and the truths of His Word, that we don't even have the same thoughts of unbelief. Let's be like Abraham, who didn't even consider the fact that he was a hundred years old and his wife was ninety. He just thought about what God had promised them, which was that they were going to have a child. Romans 4 says Abraham didn't even consider **"his own body now dead...neither yet the deadness of Sarah's womb."** This enabled him to not stagger in unbelief at the promise of God.

The Key to Victory

When it comes to ministering healing, it's usually not that people don't have faith. Some don't, but most do. However, they also have unbelief. Therefore, their faith is weak. It's canceled out, negated, and counterbalanced by unbelief. That's because they haven't been spending time in the presence of God. They are so accustomed to the world, they're thinking thoughts of unbelief. They're thinking *It's flu season. Everyone else has it* or *My father died from this same thing that's fighting me.* They consider, ponder, and think about all these natural things, and that unbelief negates their faith.

So the key to victory in the Christian life isn't necessarily having huge faith; it's having a simple, pure, childlike faith—faith the size of a mustard seed—that isn't canceled out by unbelief. You need to unhook from the unbelief that is pulling you in the opposite direction and let your little mustard seed amount of faith pull you to victory.

Some folks think that the only reason people aren't healed is because they don't have any faith. That offends other people who'll argue, "No, these people loved God. They were great people of faith." They'll dismiss that criticism, saying, "It must not be God's will to heal."

However, you now know that this isn't all there is to it. You can have faith, love God, and be a great person, yet have unbelief that pulls you in the other direction.

Starve your unbelief. Get to where you are so single minded about the Lord and His Word that your little mustard seed amount of faith will be enough to accomplish anything you need. It's not that hard to do either. Like a leech or a fungus, unbelief has to be fed and nourished. Separate yourself even for a week. Fasting, praying, and focusing your attention on the Lord can do great damage to your unbelief. They don't cause God to give you more power; they just cause the faith you have to work so much better because you are diminishing the unbelief that's pulling in the opposite direction. That's good news!

Once you believe the truth that God wants you well, then all you have to do is starve your unbelief until your faith starts producing the results you desire.

A Pure, Strong Faith
Lesson 14 – Outline

I. In Matthew 17:20, Jesus was saying to His disciples, "Guys, you don't have a faith problem; what you have is an unbelief problem."

    A. Then in Matthew 17:21, Jesus continued by saying,

> *Howbeit this kind [of unbelief] goeth not out but by prayer and fasting.*
> **Brackets mine**

    B. Contrary to much popular teaching, and now even a few erroneous Bible versions, the true subject of verse 21 is the unbelief mentioned in verse 20, not the demon(s) talked about in verse 19.

    C. It's unbelief that comes from natural information that is contrary to God's Word.

    D. That's not necessarily because of ignorance or wrong doctrine; it's just that you've learned to trust what you see, taste, hear, smell, and feel.

    E. Your five senses aren't of the devil; they have an important place and function in your everyday life.

II. This is what happened with the disciples in Matthew 17.

    A. They saw a physical manifestation of this demon that was contrary to what they were praying and believing for, and it caused them to fear.

    B. Their five senses ministered thoughts of unbelief that countered their faith.

    C. Understanding this, Jesus told them, "The only way you can get rid of natural unbelief is through fasting and prayer. It's not by just studying the Word more; you need to get into the presence of God and renew yourself to such a degree that you develop your sixth sense, which is faith."

III. Fasting and prayer move you.

    A. They affect you.

    B. Then when you say to your body "You're healed in Jesus' name," your flesh may answer "I still hurt," but that sixth sense says, "I'm healed and I believe it."

    C. But if you haven't spent time fasting, praying, and being in the presence of God, your body will say, "No, I still hurt." You'll say "Body, you get in line," but your flesh will answer, "Who are you to tell me what to do? I tell you when to eat, what to eat, and how much to eat." It's just like a spoiled brat.

    D. But you can train your senses to discern both good (God and His Word) and evil (what contradicts them) (Heb. 5:14).

IV. According to Romans 4, it's more biblically accurate to say that depending on the level of unbelief, you either have a weak faith or a strong faith (Rom. 4:19-21).

  A. If you have a lot of unbelief, then you're weak in faith.

  B. If you have little unbelief, then you're strong in faith.

  C. The truth is, every one of us has been given *the* faith of the Son of God (Rom. 12:3; Gal. 2:16, and 20).

  D. Every born-again Christian has the exact same amount and quality of faith that Jesus had.

V. The key to victory in the Christian life isn't necessarily having huge faith; it's having a simple, pure, childlike faith—faith the size of a mustard seed—that isn't canceled out by unbelief.

  A. You can have faith, love God, and be a great person, yet have unbelief that pulls you in the other direction.

  B. Starve your unbelief.

  C. Get to where you are so single minded about the Lord and His Word that your little mustard seed amount of faith will be enough to accomplish anything you need.

  D. Fasting, praying, and focusing your attention on the Lord can do great damage to your unbelief.

  E. They don't cause God to give you more power; they just cause the faith you have to work so much better because you are diminishing the unbelief that's pulling in the opposite direction.

  F. That's good news!

  G. Once you believe the truth that God wants you well, then all you have to do is starve your unbelief until your faith starts producing the results you desire.

A Pure, Strong Faith
Lesson 14 – Teacher's Guide

1.   In Matthew 17:20, Jesus was saying to His disciples, "Guys, you don't have a faith problem; what you have is an unbelief problem." Then in Matthew 17:21, Jesus continued by saying, **"Howbeit this kind** [of unbelief] **goeth not out but by prayer and fasting"** (brackets mine). Contrary to much popular teaching, and now even a few erroneous Bible versions, the true subject of verse 21 is the unbelief mentioned in verse 20, not the demon(s) talked about in verse 19. It's unbelief that comes from natural information that is contrary to God's Word. That's not necessarily because of ignorance or wrong doctrine; it's just that we've learned to trust what we see, taste, hear, smell, and feel. Our five senses aren't of the devil; they have an important place and function in our everyday lives.

2.   This is what happened with the disciples in Matthew 17. They saw a physical manifestation of this demon that was contrary to what they were praying and believing for, and it caused them to fear. Their five senses ministered thoughts of unbelief that countered their faith. Understanding this, Jesus told them, "The only way you can get rid of natural unbelief is through fasting and prayer. It's not by just studying the Word more; you need to get into the presence of God and renew yourself to such a degree that you develop your sixth sense, which is faith."

3.   Fasting and prayer move us. They affect us. Then when we say to our bodies "You're healed in Jesus' name," our flesh may answer "I still hurt," but that sixth sense says, "I'm healed and I believe it." But if we haven't spent time fasting, praying, and being in the presence of God, our bodies will say, "No, I still hurt." We'll say "Body, you get in line," but our flesh will answer, "Who are you to tell me what to do? I tell you when to eat, what to eat, and how much to eat." It's just like a spoiled brat. But we can train our senses to discern both good (God and His Word) and evil (what contradicts them) (Heb. 5:14).

1.   A.   Read Matthew 17:20. What was Jesus saying to His disciples? ("Guys, you don't have a faith problem; what you have is an unbelief problem")
          B.   What is the subject of verse 21? (Unbelief)

2.   A.   What happened to the disciples in Matthew 17? (They saw a physical manifestation of this demon that was contrary to what they were praying and believing for, and it caused them to fear)
          B.   How did Jesus say they could get rid of natural unbelief? (Through fasting and prayer)

3.   A.   What do fasting and prayer move and affect? (Us)
          B.   Read Hberews 5:14. What can we train our senses to discern? (Both good [God and His Word] and evil [what contradicts them])

4.   According to Romans 4, it's more biblically accurate to say that depending on the level of unbelief, we either have a weak faith or a strong faith (Rom. 4:19-21). If we have a lot of unbelief, then we're weak in faith. If we have little unbelief, then we're strong in faith. The truth is, every one of us has been given *the* faith of the Son of God (Rom. 12:3; Gal. 2:16, and 20). Every born-again Christian has the exact same amount and quality of faith that Jesus had.

5.   The key to victory in the Christian life isn't necessarily having huge faith; it's having a simple, pure, childlike faith—faith the size of a mustard seed—that isn't canceled out by unbelief. We can have faith, love God, and be great people, yet have unbelief that pulls us in the other direction. We need to starve our unbelief. We need to get to where we are so single minded about the Lord and His Word that our little mustard seed amount of faith will be enough to accomplish anything we need. Fasting, praying, and focusing our attention on the Lord can do great damage to our unbelief. They don't cause God to give us more power; they just cause the faith we have to work so much better because we are diminishing the unbelief that's pulling in the opposite direction. That's good news! Once we believe the truth that God wants us well, then all we have to do is starve our unbelief until our faith starts producing the results we desire.

4.   A. Read Romans 4:19-21. What is more biblically accurate to say? (That depending on the level of unbelief, we either have a weak faith or a strong faith)
      B. What does every born-again Christian have? (The exact same amount and quality of faith that Jesus had)
5.   A. Even if we have faith, love God, and are great people, what can we have? (Unbelief that pulls us in the other direction)
      B. We need to get to where we are so _____ about the Lord and His Word that our little mustard seed amount of faith will be enough to accomplish anything we need. (Single minded)
      C. What can do great damage to our unbelief? (Fasting and prayer)
      D. What do we have to do once we believe the truth that God wants us well? (Starve our unbelief until our faith starts producing the results we desire)

A Pure, Strong Faith
Lesson 14 – Additional Information

For further study of this important foundational truth, I encourage you to check out my teaching entitled "The Faith of God/Mind of Christ." It's available both as a single message and as the third part of *Spirit, Soul & Body*.

A Pure, Strong Faith
Lesson 14 – Discipleship Questions

1. According to Matthew 17:19-21, to do the impossible, it takes faith as small as a what?

2. Read Mark 9:20. What happened when the boy saw Jesus?

3. According to Mark 16:17-20, who are these signs to follow?

4. What happened after the Lord had spoken to the apostles?

5. What did the apostles then do?

6. Read Matthew 4:4. What is man to live by?

7. Read Luke 4:4. What were Jesus' first three words?

   A. "The pastor said…"

   B. "Salt is good…"

   C. "Get thee behind…"

   D. "It is written…"

   E. "My experience is…"

8. Read Hebrews 5:14. Who does strong meat belong to?

9. According to Romans 4:19-21, if Abraham would have staggered, he would have staggered through _____.

10. What was Abraham strong in?

11. Read Romans 12:3. Did God lend grace to Paul?

12. What Paul says in this verse is to whom?

13. According to Galatians 2:16, how is a person justified?

14. **"For by the works of the law shall _____ be justified."**

15. Read Galatians 2:20. Who lived in Paul?

16. Who loved Paul and gave Himself for him?

A Pure, Strong Faith
Lesson 14 – Answer Key

1. Grain of mustard seed.

2. The spirit tore the boy, and the boy fell on the ground and wallowed, foaming.

3. Them that believe.

4. He was taken up into heaven and sat down at the right hand of God.

5. They went forth and preached everywhere.

6. Every word that proceeds from the mouth of God.

7. D. "It is written…"

8. Those who are of full age, even those who by reason of use have their senses exercised to discern both good and evil.

9. Unbelief.

10. Faith.

11. No.

12. Every person that was among them.

13. By the faith of Jesus Christ.

14. **"No flesh."**

15. Christ.

16. The Son of God.

A Pure, Strong Faith
Lesson 14 – Scriptures

Matthew 17:19-21
Then came the disciples to Jesus apart, and said, Why could not we cast him out? [20] And Jesus said unto them, Because of your unbelief: for verily I say unto you, If ye have faith as a grain of mustard seed, ye shall say unto this mountain, Remove hence to yonder place; and it shall remove; and nothing shall be impossible unto you. [21] Howbeit this kind goeth not out but by prayer and fasting.

Mark 9:20
And they brought him unto him: and when he saw him, straightway the spirit tare him; and he fell on the ground, and wallowed foaming.

Mark 16:17-20
And these signs shall follow them that believe; In my name shall they cast out devils; they shall speak with new tongues; [18] They shall take up serpents; and if they drink any deadly thing, it shall not hurt them; they shall lay hands on the sick, and they shall recover. [19] So then after the Lord had spoken unto them, he was received up into heaven, and sat on the right hand of God. [20] And they went forth, and preached every where, the Lord working with them, and confirming the word with signs following. Amen.

Matthew 4:4
But he answered and said, It is written, Man shall not live by bread alone, but by every word that proceedeth out of the mouth of God.

Luke 4:4
And Jesus answered him, saying, It is written, That man shall not live by bread alone, but by every word of God.

Hebrews 5:14
But strong meat belongeth to them that are of full age, even those who by reason of use have their senses exercised to discern both good and evil.

Romans 4:19-21
And being not weak in faith, he considered not his own body now dead, when he was about an hundred years old, neither yet the deadness of Sara's womb: [20] He staggered not at the promise of God through unbelief; but was strong in faith, giving glory to God; [21] And being fully persuaded that, what he had promised, he was able also to perform.

Romans 12:3

For I say, through the grace given unto me, to every man that is among you, not to think of himself more highly than he ought to think; but to think soberly, according as God hath dealt to every man the measure of faith.

Galatians 2:16

Knowing that a man is not justified by the works of the law, but by the faith of Jesus Christ, even we have believed in Jesus Christ, that we might be justified by the faith of Christ, and not by the works of the law: for by the works of the law shall no flesh be justified.

Galatians 2:20

I am crucified with Christ: nevertheless I live; yet not I, but Christ liveth in me: and the life which I now live in the flesh I live by the faith of the Son of God, who loved me, and gave himself for me.

Governed by Law
Lesson 15

Healing is part of Christ's Atonement, which means it's not optional. It's already been provided for. The Lord would no more withhold healing from us than He would withhold forgiveness of sins. Our sins have been forgiven, and our bodies have been healed by the one Atonement of our Lord Jesus Christ.

We need to get this attitude that our healing has already been accomplished. If we were to fight for it the same as we fight to resist sin, then we would see a marked difference in the number of people who receive healing. However, many folks are passive when it comes to healing. They pray a prayer like, "Lord, heal me, if it be Your will." That is absolutely inaccurate because the Word says,

Beloved, I wish above all things that thou mayest prosper and be in health, even as thy soul prospereth.

3 John 2

The word **"wish"** here means that it is His will. God's will is for us to be well. Once we see His will revealed plainly in His Word, there's no reason for us to pray any longer, "If it be Your will." It's a matter of appropriating—reaching out in faith, taking, and receiving. It's standing in faith for the full manifestation. We have to be aggressive and fight to receive what God has given. We must not allow the world, the flesh, or the devil to deny us what Jesus has already provided.

Life & Peace

Sickness is never a blessing. God's Word is very clear. We saw earlier that Deuteronomy 28:1-14 lists what God considers a blessing. Verses 15-68 reveal what He considers a curse. Sickness and disease are always a curse. For religion to come along and teach that sickness is actually a blessing from God is a perversion of what the Word of God says.

Yes, the Lord did smite some people with sickness in the Old Testament. However, there's a huge difference between the Old Covenant and the New. God doesn't smite people like that in the New Covenant. But remember, under the Law, sickness was always a curse—never a blessing. And Christ has redeemed us from the curse of the Law (Gal. 3:12-13), which includes everything listed in Deuteronomy 28:15-68.

So here's what we've found out: The reason most people aren't healed is unbelief in one form or another. Unbelief is a counterbalancing, opposing force to faith. Most people try to build and increase faith but do nothing about the amount of their unbelief. They simply don't understand that faith and unbelief are opposing forces. Jesus said in Matthew 17:20 that a mustard seed amount of faith is all we need to do anything, even see a mountain cast into the sea.

We don't have a faith problem; what we really have is an unbelief problem. We expose ourselves to all kinds of thoughts, attitudes, feelings, and emotions that war against our faith. To have strong faith, we need to decrease the amount of unbelief in our lives by taking our focus away from the world and away from anything that contradicts God's Word, especially in the area of healing. We need to quit listening to all the negative reports and focus on the Word of God. If all we are is spiritually minded, then all we'll get is life and peace (Rom. 8:6).

Constant & Universal

The kingdom of God—including faith—operates by law. Understanding this truth is essential to walking in divine health.

A law is consistent and universal. It's always the same and never fluctuates, anywhere you go. Anything that doesn't fit that criteria isn't a law, but a phenomenon. Take, for instance, gravity. Gravity is a law. We call it the law of gravity. It's always constant. It always works. It's always the same no matter where you go. If gravity only worked in the United States but in Europe, Africa, or Asia, there was weightlessness, then it would be a phenomenon, not a law. If gravity only happened sometimes and other times there was weightlessness, it would be a phenomenon. But when something is consistent and universal, then it is a law.

God created this world and the laws that govern it. In addition to gravity, there are laws concerning such things as electricity and inertia. The law of inertia specifies that once an object is in motion, it tends to stay in motion. Once inertia has built up, it takes time and effort to overcome. That's why you have to apply the brakes in order to stop a moving car. How long it takes to stop depends on how fast you're going and the size and mass of the vehicle. This is the law of inertia. It also works when you're sitting still. Inertia works against you, and it takes time to accelerate and get a car moving from a stopped position. But once it's rolling, you can coast. These are just a few examples of these different laws in effect.

God created these laws—both natural and spiritual—and He doesn't just violate them. This truth directly applies to healing.

Intended for Our Good

I constantly talk with people who simply don't understand that the spiritual realm is governed by laws. They don't look at the kingdom of God as being governed by laws. They honestly think the Lord just does anything He wants.

Many people take up an offense against God when someone in their family dies. They say, "Why didn't God heal this person? If He wanted to, He could have." They fail to understand that there are laws that govern His kingdom.

In the physical realm, the law of gravity applies even to the person who walks off the edge of a tall building. God doesn't want that person to die. He actually created gravity to be a positive force in our lives. Right now, I'm sitting in a chair. I don't have to strap myself in or hold myself down. I don't have to be bolted to the floor, because gravity is working. However, that same law that's meant for our good will kill us if we walk off a ten-story building. God didn't create gravity to harm us; He made it to help us function here on planet earth. The whole world functions that way, and it's good. But if someone violates the laws God created—like stepping off a tall building—the same force that God intended for their good will kill them.

Some folks argue that if the Lord wanted to, He could just stop that. However, God doesn't just change the laws. That's not His nature. When He created these laws as part of the original creation, He said, "It is good" (Gen. 1:31). There's nothing wrong with gravity. The problem isn't with its law; it's with the people who violate its law. If God suspended the law of gravity to save one life, think of the untold millions of other lives that would be lost because of it. People depending on gravity to hold their cars to the road while driving would suddenly careen out of control into other cars and buildings. Millions of people would die just so He could save the life of one person falling off of a building. It doesn't work that way.

Laws are constant. They don't fluctuate. God doesn't violate natural laws. He doesn't violate spiritual laws either. There are spiritual laws, and they are intended for our good. The Lord has made things so that it's not just on His whim who gets healed and who doesn't. There are laws that govern faith and healing. There are reasons things happen the way they do. Our ignorance of these laws, and of the truth that there are these laws, is a huge hindrance to receiving healing. Ignorance of what these individual laws are will even hinder people from receiving healing who understand that the kingdom of God is operated and governed by laws.

Electricity

Electricity has been around since God created the earth. There's a magnetic field in the earth and electricity in the air. You can see that especially in cold, dry climates when you walk on a carpet and then touch a doorknob. The static electricity will shock you. These kinds of things have happened since the first day God created the earth. I heard someone say that there's enough energy in a typical thunderstorm to power the city of New York for one whole year.

God didn't just choose to give electricity to man a few hundred years ago. No, electricity has been here from the beginning. It was man's ignorance of electricity that kept him from using it the way it is used today. God didn't hold him back. If man would have understood the laws that govern electricity and learned how to cooperate with them, he could have enjoyed the benefits of electricity 2,000 years ago. Jesus and His disciples could have used the air conditioners, washing machines, and dishwashers we use today. The potential has always been there; it was just ignorance that kept man from it.

Likewise, there are things that people are dreaming about inventing right now. Many of these ideas sound far-fetched to us today, but they're possible. God isn't holding us back; it's our own ignorance of the laws. We're still in the process of discovering, and many radical changes are yet to come.

Consider the huge changes in telecommunications that have taken place in just the past few years alone. Today, nearly everyone has a cell phone. There's no reason people couldn't have been talking on cell phones 2,000 years ago. Both the materials to make the cell phones and the natural laws that govern how they work have been here on the earth from the beginning of time. God wasn't holding us back; we were ignorant of the laws. The ability was there, but we had to understand how to operate it.

There is a natural fear of things we don't understand. You may understand how to flip a switch and make a light turn on, but you don't know all the laws governing electricity's use. Electricity can kill, and people who don't understand it are fearful of it.

Personally, I don't fully understand electricity. When I do electrical work, I go to the breaker box and shut off all the breakers in the whole house. Now, I know you don't have to do that. But one time when I just shut off one breaker, there happened to be an adjacent breaker box that was grounded to the one I was working on, and the electricity knocked me flat on my back!

Another time, I was helping do a total remodel on someone's bathroom. I was working on replacing all the fixtures and was about to turn off all of the breakers in the whole house. A man came in and said, "You don't even have to turn off the breakers at all." He then proceeded to work with the live wires. We had just pulled out the sink, and there was water on the floor. He just stood there in the water working with the wires, and he never got shocked. Some people think, *You can't do that!* You can if you know what you're doing. Since I don't know enough about electricity and how it works to do something like that, I have a natural fear and inability that someone who understands and operates in that knowledge doesn't have.

The Law of Faith

It's the same in the spiritual world. There are reasons some people are able to walk in the power of God and others aren't. Basically, God's Word is His manual that tells us what these laws are and how His kingdom operates.

Where is boasting then? It is excluded. By what law? of works? Nay: but by the law of faith.

Romans 3:27

Although this verse in context is actually talking about the tension between grace and faith, we can also see an important principle here in the final phrase. Notice the terminology: **"the law of faith."**

Faith is governed by law. So when a person has need of healing, it's not a matter of petitioning God, and then if He wants them healed, they'll be healed. No, that's not it. There are laws that govern how healing works. It's primarily ignorance of God's laws and how His kingdom works that keeps His power from operating. Most people simply don't see that the kingdom of God is established on laws, and laws are consistent. God doesn't change. Neither does He violate His own laws just because people don't understand this. Many people get angry at God when somebody dies or a healing doesn't manifest. They think, *If He wanted to, He could have healed them.* God certainly has the power, but that power doesn't flow independent of His laws. There are spiritual laws that govern how faith works and how the power of God flows. If they don't know that, then they stop the power of God and do without because of their ignorance.

Some people take offense when they first hear these truths. They say, "You're criticizing me!" Well, I am, but in the same way that I would criticize Leonardo da Vinci. In his day, da

Vinci was considered a genius. He actually invented many things hundreds of years before man had the ability to make them. For instance, people have applied modern technology that Leonardo didn't have, like electric motors and lighter materials, and built a working helicopter based on his designs. Although he lived in the 1400s, this man was way ahead of his time.

Many of Leonardo da Vinci's concepts and plans didn't work back then, because he didn't have access to what we know and have today; that is, he didn't use electricity. He didn't have the benefit of electrical motors, and the like. Yet this man was a genius. When I point out that he was ignorant of the laws governing electricity, I'm not saying he was stupid; I'm just stating that he lacked knowledge in certain areas. He didn't understand some of the things that we understand and take for granted today.

Still Growing

I am not criticizing or trying to put anyone down when I say that a lot of people are ignorant of the laws of God. I'm simply pointing out the truth that there are many things available to us from God that we don't receive, because we don't understand and cooperate with the laws of the kingdom of God.

Through studying the Word, I've discovered many of the laws that govern how the kingdom of God works. However, I am convinced that there are many more that I still don't understand. That's the reason things don't work any better for me than they do. Although I don't know it all, I could probably tell you at least a hundred different laws and principles that I've found concerning healing. There are other laws that I don't yet understand, which is why I don't see every single person healed, but I have seen many, many people healed. I am growing and working on this.

Governed by Law
Lesson 15 – Outline

I. We need to get this attitude that our healing has already been accomplished.

    A. Many folks are passive when it comes to healing.

    B. They pray a prayer like, "Lord, heal me, if it be Your will."

    C. That is absolutely inaccurate because the Word says,

> *Beloved, I wish above all things that thou mayest prosper and be in health, even as thy soul prospereth.*
>
> **3 John 2**

    D. The word **"wish"** here means that it is His will. God's will is for us to be well.

II. The kingdom of God—including faith—operates by law.

    A. Understanding this truth is essential to walking in divine health.

    B. Laws are constant. They don't fluctuate.

    C. There are spiritual laws, and they are intended for our good.

    D. The Lord has made things so that it's not just on His whim who gets healed and who doesn't.

    E. There are laws that govern faith and healing.

III. Our ignorance of these laws is a huge hindrance to receiving healing.

    A. God's Word is His manual that tells us what these laws are and how His kingdom operates.

> *Where is boasting then? It is excluded. By what law? of works? Nay: but by the law of faith.*
>
> **Romans 3:27**

    B. Notice the terminology: **"the law of faith."**

    C. Faith is governed by law.

    D. So when a person has need of healing, it's not a matter of petitioning God, and then if He wants them healed, they'll be healed.

    E. There are laws that govern how healing works.

IV. God doesn't change.

    A. Neither does He violate His own laws just because people don't understand this.

    B. Many people get angry at God when somebody dies or a healing doesn't manifest. They think, *If He wanted to, He could have healed them.*

    C. God certainly has the power, but that power doesn't flow independent of His laws.

    D. If people don't know that, then they stop the power of God and do without because of their ignorance.

    E. I'm not trying to put anyone down; I'm simply pointing out the truth that there are many things available to us from God that we don't receive, because we don't understand and cooperate with the laws of the kingdom of God.

V. Through studying the Word, I've discovered many of the laws that govern how the kingdom of God works.

    A. Although I don't know it all, I could probably tell you at least a hundred different laws and principles that I've found concerning healing.

    B. There are other laws that I don't yet understand, which is why I don't see every single person healed, but I have seen many, many people healed.

    C. I am growing and working on this.

Governed by Law
Lesson 15 – Teacher's Guide

1. We need to get this attitude that our healing has already been accomplished. Many of us are passive when it comes to healing. We pray a prayer like, "Lord, heal me, if it be Your will." That is absolutely inaccurate because the Word says, **"Beloved, I wish above all things that thou mayest prosper and be in health, even as thy soul prospereth"** (3 John 2). The word **"wish"** here means that it is His will. God's will is for us to be well.

2. The kingdom of God—including faith—operates by law. Understanding this truth is essential to walking in divine health. Laws are constant. They don't fluctuate. There are spiritual laws, and they are intended for our good. The Lord has made things so that it's not just on His whim which of us get healed and which of us don't. There are laws that govern faith and healing.

3. Our ignorance of these laws is a huge hindrance to receiving healing. God's Word is His manual that tells us what these laws are and how His kingdom operates (Rom. 3:27). Notice the terminology in this verse: **"the law of faith."** Faith is governed by law. So when we have need of healing, it's not a matter of petitioning God, and then if He wants us healed, we'll be healed. There are laws that govern how healing works.

1. A. What attitude do we need to get toward healing? (That healing has already been accomplished)
   B. Read 3 John 2. Why is it absolutely inaccurate to pray "Lord, heal me, if it be Your will"? (Because God wishes above all things that we are in health)
2. A. What is essential to walking in divine health? (Understanding that the kingdom of God—including faith—operates by law)
   B. Has the Lord made things so that it's just on His whim which of us get healed and which of us don't? (No)
3. A. What is a huge hindrance to receiving healing? (Our ignorance of these laws)
   B. What tells us what the laws are and how God's kingdom operates? (His Word)

4.   God doesn't change. Neither does He violate His own laws just because people don't understand this. Many people get angry at God when somebody dies or a healing doesn't manifest. They think, *If He wanted to, He could have healed them*. God certainly has the power, but that power doesn't flow independent of His laws. If people don't know that, then they stop the power of God and do without because of their ignorance. I'm not trying to put anyone down; I'm simply pointing out the truth that there are many things available to us from God that we don't receive, because we don't understand and cooperate with the laws of the kingdom of God.

5.   Through studying the Word, I've discovered many of these laws that govern how the kingdom of God works. Although I don't know it all, I could probably share at least a hundred different laws and principles that I've found concerning healing. There are other laws that I don't yet understand, which is why I don't see every single person healed, but I have seen many, many people healed. I am growing and working on this.

4.   A.   What doesn't flow independent of God's laws? (His power)
     B.   Why don't we receive the many things available to us from God? (Because we don't understand and cooperate with the laws of the kingdom of God)
5.   A.   What have I discovered through studying the Word? (Many of the laws that govern how the kingdom of God works)
     B.   Why don't I see every single person healed? (Because there are other laws he doesn't understand yet)

Governed by Law
Lesson 15 – Additional Information

My teachings, *How to Receive a Miracle* and *You've Already Got It!* go into more depth on this truth and how it applies specifically to healing. I encourage you to get these teachings.

Governed by Law
Lesson 15 – Discipleship Questions

1. Read 3 John 2. What does God call us?

2. What does He wish?

3. According to Deuteronomy 28:1-14, to receive the blessings according to the Law, we are to do all of God's _____.

4. According to Deuteronomy 28:15-68, who bears the responsibility of whether we are cursed if we don't do all the commandments?

5. Read Galatians 3:12-13. What is not of faith?

6. How did Christ redeem us from the curse of the Law?

7. Read Matthew 17:20. If we have faith as a grain of mustard seed, what did Jesus say we can we say to a mountain?

8. According to Romans 8:6, **"For to be carnally minded _____ death."**

    A. "Should be."

    B. "Might be."

    C. "Is."

    D. All of the above.

    E. None of the above.

9. **"But to be spiritually minded _____ life and peace."**

    A. "Eventually will be."

    B. "Is."

    C. "Produces."

    D. All of the above.

    E. None of the above.

10. Read Genesis 1:31. How many things were very good?

11. Read Romans 3:27. Why is boasting excluded?

Governed by Law
Lesson 15 – Answer Key

1. Beloved.

2. That we may prosper and be in health, even as our souls prosper.

3. Commandments.

4. We do.

5. The Law.

6. By being made a curse for us.

7. **"Remove hence to yonder place."**

8. C. **"Is."**

9. B. **"Is."**

10. Everything God had made.

11. Because of the law of faith.

Governed By Law
Lesson 15 – Scriptures

3 John 2
Beloved, I wish above all things that thou mayest prosper and be in health, even as thy soul prospereth.

Deuteronomy 28:1-68
And it shall come to pass, if thou shalt hearken diligently unto the voice of the LORD thy God, to observe and to do all his commandments which I command thee this day, that the LORD thy God will set thee on high above all nations of the earth: [2] And all these blessings shall come on thee, and overtake thee, if thou shalt hearken unto the voice of the LORD thy God. [3] Blessed shalt thou be in the city, and blessed shalt thou be in the field. [4] Blessed shall be the fruit of thy body, and the fruit of thy ground, and the fruit of thy cattle, the increase of thy kine, and the flocks of thy sheep. [5] Blessed shall be thy basket and thy store. [6] Blessed shalt thou be when thou comest in, and blessed shalt thou be when thou goest out. [7] The LORD shall cause thine enemies that rise up against thee to be smitten before thy face: they shall come out against thee one way, and flee before thee seven ways. [8] The LORD shall command the blessing upon thee in thy storehouses, and in all that thou settest thine hand unto; and he shall bless thee in the land which the LORD thy God giveth thee. [9] The LORD shall establish thee an holy people unto himself, as he hath sworn unto thee, if thou shalt keep the commandments of the LORD thy God, and walk in his ways. [10] And all people of the earth shall see that thou art called by the name of the LORD; and they shall be afraid of thee. [11] And the LORD shall make thee plenteous in goods, in the fruit of thy body, and in the fruit of thy cattle, and in the fruit of thy ground, in the land which the LORD sware unto thy fathers to give thee. [12] The LORD shall open unto thee his good treasure, the heaven to give the rain unto thy land in his season, and to bless all the work of thine hand: and thou shalt lend unto many nations, and thou shalt not borrow. [13] And the LORD shall make thee the head, and not the tail; and thou shalt be above only, and thou shalt not be beneath; if that thou hearken unto the commandments of the LORD thy God, which I command thee this day, to observe and to do them: [14] And thou shalt not go aside from any of the words which I command thee this day, to the right hand, or to the left, to go after other gods to serve them. [15] But it shall come to pass, if thou wilt not hearken unto the voice of the LORD thy God, to observe to do all his commandments and his statutes which I command thee this day; that all these curses shall come upon thee, and overtake thee: [16] Cursed shalt thou be in the city, and cursed shalt thou be in the field. [17] Cursed shall be thy basket and thy store. [18] Cursed shall be the fruit of thy body, and the fruit of thy land, the increase of thy kine, and the flocks of thy sheep. [19] Cursed shalt thou be when thou comest in, and cursed shalt thou be when thou goest out. [20] The LORD shall send upon thee cursing, vexation, and rebuke, in all that thou settest thine hand unto for to do, until thou be destroyed, and until thou

perish quickly; because of the wickedness of thy doings, whereby thou hast forsaken me. [21] The LORD shall make the pestilence cleave unto thee, until he have consumed thee from off the land, whither thou goest to possess it. [22] The LORD shall smite thee with a consumption, and with a fever, and with an inflammation, and with an extreme burning, and with the sword, and with blasting, and with mildew; and they shall pursue thee until thou perish. [23] And thy heaven that is over thy head shall be brass, and the earth that is under thee shall be iron. [24] The LORD shall make the rain of thy land powder and dust: from heaven shall it come down upon thee, until thou be destroyed. [25] The LORD shall cause thee to be smitten before thine enemies: thou shalt go out one way against them, and flee seven ways before them: and shalt be removed into all the kingdoms of the earth. [26] And thy carcase shall be meat unto all fowls of the air, and unto the beasts of the earth, and no man shall fray them away. [27] The LORD will smite thee with the botch of Egypt, and with the emerods, and with the scab, and with the itch, whereof thou canst not be healed. [28] The LORD shall smite thee with madness, and blindness, and astonishment of heart: [29] And thou shalt grope at noonday, as the blind gropeth in darkness, and thou shalt not prosper in thy ways: and thou shalt be only oppressed and spoiled evermore, and no man shall save thee. [30] Thou shalt betroth a wife, and another man shall lie with her: thou shalt build an house, and thou shalt not dwell therein: thou shalt plant a vineyard, and shalt not gather the grapes thereof. [31] Thine ox shall be slain before thine eyes, and thou shalt not eat thereof: thine ass shall be violently taken away from before thy face, and shall not be restored to thee: thy sheep shall be given unto thine enemies, and thou shalt have none to rescue them. [32] Thy sons and thy daughters shall be given unto another people, and thine eyes shall look, and fail with longing for them all the day long: and there shall be no might in thine hand. [33] The fruit of thy land, and all thy labours, shall a nation which thou knowest not eat up; and thou shalt be only oppressed and crushed alway: [34] So that thou shalt be mad for the sight of thine eyes which thou shalt see. [35] The LORD shall smite thee in the knees, and in the legs, with a sore botch that cannot be healed, from the sole of thy foot unto the top of thy head. [36] The LORD shall bring thee, and thy king which thou shalt set over thee, unto a nation which neither thou nor thy fathers have known; and there shalt thou serve other gods, wood and stone. [37] And thou shalt become an astonishment, a proverb, and a byword, among all nations whither the LORD shall lead thee. [38] Thou shalt carry much seed out into the field, and shalt gather but little in; for the locust shall consume it. [39] Thou shalt plant vineyards, and dress them, but shalt neither drink of the wine, nor gather the grapes; for the worms shall eat them. [40] Thou shalt have olive trees throughout all thy coasts, but thou shalt not anoint thyself with the oil; for thine olive shall cast his fruit. [41] Thou shalt beget sons and daughters, but thou shalt not enjoy them; for they shall go into captivity. [42] All thy trees and fruit of thy land shall the locust consume. [43] The stranger that is within thee shall get up above thee very high; and thou shalt come down very low. [44] He shall lend to thee, and thou shalt not lend to him: he shall be the head, and thou shalt be the tail. [45] Moreover all these curses shall come upon thee, and shall pursue thee, and overtake thee, till thou be destroyed; because thou hearkenedst not unto the voice of the LORD thy God, to keep his commandments and his statutes which he commanded thee: [46] And they shall be upon thee for a sign and for a wonder, and upon thy seed for ever. [47] Because thou servedst not the LORD thy God with joyfulness, and with gladness of heart, for the abundance of all things; [48] Therefore shalt thou serve thine enemies which the LORD shall send against thee, in hunger, and in thirst, and in nakedness, and in want of all things: and he shall put a yoke of iron upon thy neck, until he have destroyed thee. [49] The LORD shall bring a nation against thee from far, from the end of the earth, as swift as the eagle flieth; a nation whose tongue thou shalt not understand; [50] A nation of fierce countenance, which shall not regard the person of the old, nor shew favour to the young: [51] And he shall eat the fruit of thy cattle, and the fruit of thy land, until thou be destroyed: which also shall not leave thee either corn, wine, or oil, or the increase of thy kine, or flocks of thy sheep, until he have destroyed thee. [52] And he shall besiege thee in all thy gates, until thy high and fenced walls come down, wherein thou trustedst, throughout all thy land: and he shall besiege thee in all thy gates throughout all thy land, which the LORD thy God hath given thee. [53] And thou shalt eat the fruit of thine own body, the flesh of thy sons and of thy daughters, which the LORD thy God hath given thee, in the siege, and in the straitness, wherewith thine enemies shall distress thee: [54] So that the man that is tender among you, and very delicate, his eye shall be evil toward his brother, and toward the wife of his bosom, and toward the remnant of his children which he shall leave: [55] So that he will not give to any of them of the flesh of his children whom he shall eat: because he hath nothing left him in the siege, and in the straitness, wherewith thine enemies shall distress thee in all thy gates. [56] The tender and delicate woman among you, which would not adventure to set the sole of her foot upon the ground for delicateness and tenderness, her eye shall be evil toward the husband of her bosom, and toward her son, and toward her daughter, [57] And toward her young one that cometh out from between her feet, and toward her children which she shall bear: for she shall eat them for want of all things secretly in the siege and straitness, wherewith thine enemy shall distress thee in thy gates. [58] If thou wilt not observe to do all the words of this law that are written in this book, that thou mayest fear this glorious and fearful name, THE LORD THY GOD; [59] Then the LORD will make thy plagues wonderful, and the plagues of thy seed, even great plagues, and of long continuance, and sore sicknesses, and of long continuance. [60] Moreover he will bring upon thee all the diseases of Egypt, which thou wast afraid of; and they shall cleave unto thee. [61] Also every sickness, and every plague, which is not written in the book of this law, them will the LORD bring upon thee, until thou be destroyed. [62] And ye shall be left few in number, whereas ye were as the stars of heaven for multitude; because thou wouldest not obey the voice of the LORD thy God. [63] And it shall come to pass, that as the LORD rejoiced over you to do you good, and to multiply you; so the LORD will rejoice over you to destroy you, and to bring you to nought; and ye shall be plucked from off the land whither thou goest to possess it. [64] And the LORD shall scatter thee among all people, from the one end of the earth even unto the other; and there thou shalt serve other gods, which neither thou nor thy fathers have known, even wood and stone. [65] And among these nations shalt thou find no ease, neither shall the sole of thy foot have rest: but the LORD shall give thee there a trembling heart, and failing of eyes, and sorrow of mind: [66] And thy life shall hang in doubt before thee; and thou shalt fear day and night, and shalt have none assurance of thy life: [67] In the morning thou shalt say, Would God it were even! and at even thou shalt say, Would God it were morning! for the fear of thine heart wherewith thou shalt fear, and for the sight of thine eyes which thou shalt see. [68] And the LORD shall bring thee into Egypt again with ships, by the way whereof I spake unto thee, Thou shalt see it no more again: and there ye shall be sold unto your enemies for bondmen and bondwomen, and no man shall buy you.

Galatians 3:12-13
And the law is not of faith: but, The man that doeth them shall live in them. [13] Christ hath redeemed us from the curse of the law, being made a curse for us: for it is written, Cursed is every one that hangeth on a tree.

Matthew 17:20
And Jesus said unto them, Because of your unbelief: for verily I say unto you, If ye have faith as a grain of mustard seed, ye shall say unto this mountain, Remove hence to yonder place; and it shall remove; and nothing shall be impossible unto you.

Romans 8:6
For to be carnally minded is death; but to be spiritually minded is life and peace.

Genesis 1:31
And God saw every thing that he had made, and, behold, it was very good. And the evening and the morning were the sixth day.

Romans 3:27
Where is boasting then? It is excluded. By what law? of works? Nay: but by the law of faith.

The Spiritual World
Lesson 16

The woman with the issue of blood vividly illustrates several of the spiritual laws concerning healing. This isn't an all-inclusive list, but it's a great place to start:

And a certain woman, which had an issue of blood twelve years, And had suffered many things of many physicians, and had spent all that she had, and was nothing bettered, but rather grew worse, When she had heard of Jesus, came in the press behind, and touched his garment. For she said, If I may touch but his clothes, I shall be whole. And straightway the fountain of her blood was dried up; and she felt in her body that she was healed of that plague. And Jesus, immediately knowing in himself that virtue had gone out of him, turned him about in the press, and said, Who touched my clothes? And his disciples said unto him, Thou seest the multitude thronging thee, and sayest thou, Who touched me? And he looked round about to see her that had done this thing. But the woman fearing and trembling, knowing what was done in her, came and fell down before him, and told him all the truth. And he said unto her, Daughter, thy faith hath made thee whole; go in peace, and be whole of thy plague.

Mark 5:25-34

This passage shows us how the kingdom of God operates by law. When this woman touched the hem of Jesus' garment, He felt virtue—power—go out of Him. So He asked, "Who touched My clothes?" Immediately, His disciples began to say, "You see the crowd of people pressing in to touch You." In other words, this multitude of people wasn't just casually bumping up against Jesus; the people were trying to touch Him because they recognized the power and virtue that was in Him. Therefore, many people were touching Him. And the disciples said, "Why are You asking who touched You? Everybody is touching You." But Jesus could tell a difference.

"Who Touched Me?"

Some people think that asking this question, "Who touched Me?" was actually deceptive on God's part. They assume that since Jesus was God, He certainly knew all things, including who had touched Him. They argue that He was just saying this as a way to try to get this woman to come forward voluntarily. That's not true.

Many people don't understand this truth that Jesus was both fully God and fully man. He was 100 percent God in His spirit, but His physical body was human—sinless—but human nonetheless. Our Lord took upon Himself a human body, and Luke 2:52 reveals that...

Jesus increased in wisdom and stature, and in favour with God and man.

Jesus had to grow up and learn things. In His spirit, as God, He knew all things. But since He was living in a physical body, His physical body had to learn. He didn't come out of the womb speaking Hebrew, understanding math, and practicing carpentry. Jesus had to learn how to eat, walk, and talk just the same as other children do. He was sinless, but He was human, and He had to grow.

The physical realm of Jesus had limitations. His physical body could only be in one place at one time, and it grew tired.

Hast thou not known? hast thou not heard, that the everlasting God, the LORD, the Creator of the ends of the earth, fainteth not, neither is weary? there is no searching of his understanding.

Isaiah 40:28

Since Jesus grew tired at times, does that mean He wasn't God? No, He was God in His spirit, but His physical body had limitations. Therefore, when Jesus asked "Who touched Me?" in His physical being, He didn't know who had touched Him.

Already Approved

Many people think that God just sovereignly looks over things. When someone gets healed, it's because they gave their request to God and He granted it. People visualize God in heaven sitting behind a desk piled high with prayers. Their petition goes by, and He either stamps "Approved" or "Disapproved" on it. So when someone gets healed, it's because God had mercy on them and healed them. If they don't, it's because He chose not to heal them for whatever reason. This attitude is expressed again and again as people say, "Why didn't God heal so and so? I prayed for them. He could have done it." They think it's up to God to approve or disapprove a person's healing. The truth is, through the stripes on Jesus' back, God has already approved everyone's healing:

Who his own self bare our sins in his own body on the tree, that we, being dead to sins, should live unto righteousness: by whose stripes ye were [past tense] healed.

1 Peter 2:24, brackets mine

Through Christ's death, burial, and resurrection, He has already paid for every person's healing. He's already stamped "Approved." It's now not up to God, but there are laws through which our faith has to function. The healing He's already provided for us won't flow until we learn these laws and begin to put them into practice.

Flip the Switch

The spiritual world operates on spiritual laws the same way that the natural world operates on natural laws.

Electricity is generated by the power company. It's delivered to where you work and live by power lines. However, if you want your lights on, you don't call the electric company and ask, "Could you please turn my lights on? Andrew Wommack is coming over, and we're having a meeting here tonight." It doesn't matter what your need or desire is, because the electric company has already done their part. They have supplied you with the power, but it's at your command. The power company isn't going to send someone out to flip the switch on your wall to turn the lights on. That's not their job. They generate the power and supply it to you. They maintain and service it to keep it available to you. But you are the one who has to turn it on.

It's the same way in the spiritual world. God has already provided His healing power for everyone. Jesus has already healed you. By His stripes, you were already healed (1 Pet. 2:24). If you are just praying and waiting on God to do something, then you are violating the laws that govern faith. You aren't cooperating with the kingdom. God has already provided healing. If you are a born-again Christian, the same virtue that raised Jesus Christ from the dead already dwells on the inside of you. You don't have a problem with God generating the power and making it available to you in your born-again spirit; the problem is that you haven't learned how to activate and release it into manifestation. You haven't yet learned how to flip the switch and turn it on. You aren't cooperating with God by faith.

In the same way, you could call the power company and wait all day for them to send someone to flip the light switch, but they aren't going to do it. You could then say, "Well, electricity doesn't work." No, it works just fine. You just don't know how to work it. You don't know how to turn it on.

The Power Will Flow

Healing works. Jesus has already healed every person. He's already released the healing power. If you aren't healed, it's not Jesus who hasn't given; it's you who haven't taken. You don't know how to turn on the power of God.

The woman with the issue of blood tapped into the power of God. She touched the hem of Jesus' garment, and virtue flowed, without the Lord looking at her and sizing her up to decide whether she was serious enough or not, whether she was holy enough or not, or any other criteria that religion says about God. He didn't do any of those things. Similar to electricity, the power just flowed.

If someone picked up a live wire that didn't have any insulation on it, the power would automatically flow through and shock them. It's not that the electric company did it to them personally to teach them a lesson; it's just the laws that govern electricity. If you touch a live wire and you're grounded, you're going to get shocked.

It's the same way with healing. You don't ever have to petition God. You don't have to beg, plead, and do all the things that have been taught. All you must do is believe and reach out in faith to receive. If you are grounded in faith, the power will flow.

The woman with the issue of blood proved this. She put into motion the laws that govern faith, and the power of God flowed. Jesus didn't even know who had touched Him. Now, He did recognize the release of that power. When He turned around and the woman wasn't forthcoming right away, I believe He drew on the gifts of the Holy Spirit and knew exactly who it was. Then He was able to point out who this woman was.

But it's significant to note here that Jesus didn't know who it was until after the power of God flowed. It wasn't God dealing with her on an individual basis, saying "Yes, I will heal you" and stamping "Approved" on her prayer. No, the healing power is already generated and available. All you have to do is reach out and touch it in faith, and the power of God will flow.

Ignorance Is Deadly

This blesses and excites me. It answers a lot of questions for me. It tells me why certain good people who desired to be healed were earnest in praying for it and yet died. God didn't reject them and their petition. The Lord didn't choose not to heal them. He has set up His kingdom to operate on laws. God wanted them healed and well, but they didn't cooperate.

Leonardo da Vinci had some good ideas that he earnestly tried to invent and make work. He came close, but there are laws. God couldn't say, "Oh well, you've come close. I'll just let this helicopter work even though you don't have the right materials. Even though you don't have a real power source or even an electrical motor, you've been so sincere. Therefore, I'm going to let it work for you." No, there are natural laws that must be cooperated with. Leonardo was close, but close wasn't close enough. So it didn't work for him.

In the spiritual world, there are good people who petition God. They may be close, but they just don't understand and cooperate with how the kingdom works. It's not God who rejected them; it's just that the kingdom operates by laws. If we violate those laws, they will kill us. Ignorance is deadly. In the natural realm, we say, "Ignorance is bliss. What you don't know won't hurt you." That's not true, especially in the spiritual realm. What we don't know is killing us (Hos. 4:6). We need to understand how the kingdom of God works.

Faith Comes by Hearing

Let's take a closer look at this woman with the issue of blood. She understood and cooperated with several kingdom laws. First of all, she had to hear of Jesus:

And a certain woman, which had an issue of blood twelve years, And had suffered many things of many physicians, and had spent all that she had, and was nothing bettered, but rather grew worse, When she had heard of Jesus, came in the press behind, and touched his garment.

Mark 5:25-27

Somebody told this woman about Jesus and the miracles He was performing. This basic law of faith is also stated clearly in Romans:

So then faith cometh by hearing, and hearing by the word of God.

Romans 10:17

You have to hear about God. You must have information fed to you. God's Word feeds you information that is contrary to nearly all of the information you'll get in the natural world. You won't have faith by listening to the (bad) news at night. You aren't going to get faith by watching soap operas on television, X-rated movies, and the like. Those things produce contrary information. If you want faith, you need to be in the Word of God.

This woman with the issue of blood had heard of God. Now, she didn't necessarily hear about Jesus through reading the Scriptures. But now we have the New Testament scriptures that include the ministry of Jesus, the ministry of His apostles, and revelation knowledge. If we are going to learn about Jesus today, we need to hear God's Word. We must get into and meditate on the Word of God.

This woman had heard about Jesus. She meditated, considered, and thought on what she had heard. She could have rejected it, but she received. Faith comes by hearing, and hearing by the Word of God.

Plug into the Power Source!

If you want to receive healing, you need to get into the Word of God. Psalm 107 says,

He sent his word, and healed them, and delivered them from their destructions.

Psalm 107:20

God's Word will heal and deliver you. If you find it, it's life and health to all your flesh:

My son, attend to my words; incline thine ear unto my sayings. Let them not depart from thine eyes; keep them in the midst of thine heart. For they are life unto those that find them, and health to all their flesh.

Proverbs 4:20-22

This is one of God's laws that many people violate. They want to receive from the Lord, but they don't spend any time in His Word. They may say, "Well, I believe that the Bible says somewhere that by His stripes, we're healed, but I'm not sure if that's an exact quote or not." If that's how you are, you aren't going to get healed through the Word of God. Others might minister to you and you could get healed off their faith, but you aren't going to get healed being that vague. You need to know what the Word of God says. You need to be able to find the scriptures that you need.

If the Word of God isn't living on the inside of you, then you're violating one of the most foundational laws. That's like having an appliance that isn't plugged into an electrical outlet and yet wondering why it isn't working. It's because you aren't plugged into the power source. You need to plug into the Word of God!

The Spiritual World
Lesson 16 – Outline

I.   The woman with the issue of blood vividly illustrates several of the spiritual laws concerning healing:

> *And a certain woman, which had an issue of blood twelve years, And had suffered many things of many physicians, and had spent all that she had, and was nothing bettered, but rather grew worse, When she had heard of Jesus, came in the press behind, and touched his garment. For she said, If I may touch but his clothes, I shall be whole. And straightway the fountain of her blood was dried up; and she felt in her body that she was healed of that plague. And Jesus, immediately knowing in himself that virtue had gone out of him, turned him about in the press, and said, Who touched my clothes? And his disciples said unto him, Thou seest the multitude thronging thee, and sayest thou, Who touched me? And he looked round about to see her that had done this thing. But the woman fearing and trembling, knowing what was done in her, came and fell down before him, and told him all the truth. And he said unto her, Daughter, thy faith hath made thee whole; go in peace, and be whole of thy plague.*
>
> **Mark 5:25-34**

   A. Some people assume that since Jesus was God, He certainly knew all things, including who had touched Him.

   B. That's not true.

   C. Jesus had to grow up and learn things (Luke 2:52).

   D. He was sinless, but He was human, and He had to grow.

   E. Therefore, when Jesus asked "Who touched Me?" in His physical being, He didn't know who had touched Him.

II. If you aren't healed, it's not Jesus who hasn't given; it's you who haven't taken.

   A. The woman with the issue of blood tapped into the power of God.

   B. She touched the hem of Jesus' garment, and virtue flowed, without the Lord looking at her and sizing her up to decide whether she was serious enough or not, whether she was holy enough or not, or any other criteria that religion says about God.

   C. All you must do is believe and reach out in faith to receive.

   D. The healing power is already generated and available.

III. In the natural realm, we say, "Ignorance is bliss. What you don't know won't hurt you."

   A. That's not true, especially in the spiritual realm.

   B. What we don't know is killing us (Hos. 4:6).

   C. We need to understand how the kingdom of God works.

IV. Let's take a closer look at this woman with the issue of blood.

   A. First of all, she had to hear of Jesus (Mark 5:25-27).

   B. This basic law of faith is also stated clearly in Romans:

   So then faith cometh by hearing, and hearing by the word of God.
   Romans 10:17

   C. You have to hear about God.

   D. If you want faith, you need to be in the Word of God.

   E. If you want to receive healing, you need to get into the Word of God.

V. God's Word will heal and deliver you.

   My son, attend to my words; incline thine ear unto my sayings. Let them not depart from thine eyes; keep them in the midst of thine heart. For they are life unto those that find them, and health to all their flesh.
   Proverbs 4:20-22

   A. You need to know what the Word of God says.

   B. If the Word of God isn't living on the inside of you, then you're violating one of the most foundational laws.

   C. That's like having an appliance that isn't plugged into an electrical outlet and yet wondering why it isn't working.

   D. It's because you aren't plugged into the power source.

   E. You need to plug into the Word of God!

The Spiritual World
Lesson 16 – Teacher's Guide

1. The woman with the issue of blood vividly illustrates several of the spiritual laws concerning healing (Mark 5:25-34). Some people assume that since Jesus was God, He certainly knew all things, including who had touched Him. That's not true. Jesus had to grow up and learn things (Luke 2:52). He was sinless, but He was human, and He had to grow. Therefore, when Jesus asked "Who touched Me?" in His physical being, He didn't know who had touched Him.

2. If we aren't healed, it's not Jesus who hasn't given; it's us who haven't taken. The woman with the issue of blood tapped into the power of God. She touched the hem of Jesus' garment, and virtue flowed, without the Lord looking at her and sizing her up to decide whether she was serious enough or not, whether she was holy enough or not, or any other criteria that religion says about God. All we must do is believe and reach out in faith to receive. The healing power is already generated and available.

3. In the natural realm, we say, "Ignorance is bliss. What you don't know won't hurt you." That's not true, especially in the spiritual realm. What we don't know is killing us (Hos. 4:6). We need to understand how the kingdom of God works.

1. A. What does the woman with the issue of blood vividly illustrate? (Several of the spiritual laws concerning healing)
    B. Did Jesus actually not know who touched Him? (Yes)
2. A. If we aren't healed, it's not Jesus who hasn't given; it's us who haven't what? (Taken)
    B. What must we do? (Believe and reach out in faith to receive)
    C. What is already generated and available? (The healing power)
3. A. Read Hosea 4:6. What is not true, especially in the spiritual realm? (That ignorance is bliss, and what we don't know won't hurt us)
    B. What do we need to understand? (How the kingdom of God works)

4. Let's take a closer look at this woman with the issue of blood. First of all, she had to hear of Jesus (Mark 5:25-27). This basic law of faith is also stated clearly in Romans 10:17. We have to hear about God. If we want faith, we need to be in the Word of God. If we want to receive healing, we need to get into the Word of God.

5. God's Word will heal and deliver us (Prov. 4:20-22). We need to know what the Word of God says. If the Word of God isn't living on the inside of us, then we're violating one of the most foundational laws. That's like having an appliance that isn't plugged into an electrical outlet and yet wondering why it isn't working. It's because we aren't plugged into the power source. We need to plug into the Word of God!

4. A. If we want faith, what do we need to do? (We need to be in the Word of God)
    B. If we want to receive healing, what do we need to do? (We need to get into the Word of God)
5. A. What do we need to know? (What the Word of God says)
    B. If the Word isn't living on the inside of us, what are we violating? (One of the most foundational laws)
    C. What is it like? (It's like having an appliance that isn't plugged into an electrical outlet and yet wondering why it isn't working)

The Spiritual World
Lesson 16 – Additional Information

My teachings entitled *A Sure Foundation* and *Effortless Change* both speak about the importance of God's Word and how it works in our lives.

The Spiritual World
Lesson 16 – Discipleship Questions

1. Read Mark 5:25-34. What did this woman do when she heard of Jesus?

    A. She came to where He was.

    B. She prayed that God would send Him to her.

    C. She stayed where she was.

    D. All of the above.

    E. None of the above.

2. When she touched Jesus, how soon did the fountain of her blood dry up?

3. What had made her whole?

4. Read Luke 2:52. What did Jesus increase in with God and man?

5. According to Isaiah 40:28, does God ever get tired?

6. According to 1 Peter 2:24, where did Jesus bear our sins?

7. Read Hosea 4:6. What had God's people rejected?

8. According to Romans 10:17, if we haven't heard God's Word, what can't we have?

9. Read Psalm 107:20. God **"sent his _____, and healed them, and delivered them from their destructions."**

10. Read Proverbs 4:20-22. God's words and His sayings are life and health to whom?

    A. Those who need it most.

    B. Those who have strong wills.

    C. Those who find His words and sayings.

    D. All of the above.

    E. None of the above.

11. And His words and sayings are health to _____.

The Spiritual World
Lesson 16 – Answer Key

1. A. She came to where He was.

2. Straightway (immediately).

3. Her faith.

4. Favor.

5. No.

6. In His own body.

7. Knowledge.

8. Faith.

9. **"Word."**

10. C. Those who find His words and sayings.

11. All their flesh.

The Spiritual World
Lesson 16 – Scriptures

Mark 5:25-34

And a certain woman, which had an issue of blood twelve years, [26] And had suffered many things of many physicians, and had spent all that she had, and was nothing bettered, but rather grew worse, [27] When she had heard of Jesus, came in the press behind, and touched his garment. [28] For she said, If I may touch but his clothes, I shall be whole. [29] And straightway the fountain of her blood was dried up; and she felt in her body that she was healed of that plague. [30] And Jesus, immediately knowing in himself that virtue had gone out of him, turned him about in the press, and said, Who touched my clothes? [31] And his disciples said unto him, Thou seest the multitude thronging thee, and sayest thou, Who touched me? [32] And he looked round about to see her that had done this thing. [33] But the woman fearing and trembling, knowing what was done in her, came and fell down before him, and told him all the truth. [34] And he said unto her, Daughter, thy faith hath made thee whole; go in peace, and be whole of thy plague.

Luke 2:52

And Jesus increased in wisdom and stature, and in favour with God and man.

Isaiah 40:28

Hast thou not known? hast thou not heard, that the everlasting God, the LORD, the Creator of the ends of the earth, fainteth not, neither is weary? there is no searching of his understanding.

I Peter 2:24

Who his own self bare our sins in his own body on the tree, that we, being dead to sins, should live unto righteousness: by whose stripes ye were healed.

Hosea 4:6

My people are destroyed for lack of knowledge: because thou hast rejected knowledge, I will also reject thee, that thou shalt be no priest to me: seeing thou hast forgotten the law of thy God, I will also forget thy children.

Romans 10:17

So then faith cometh by hearing, and hearing by the word of God.

Psalm 107:20

He sent his word, and healed them, and delivered them from their destructions.

Proverbs 4:20-22

My son, attend to my words; incline thine ear unto my sayings. [21] Let them not depart from thine eyes; keep them in the midst of thine heart. [22] For they are life unto those that find them, and health to all their flesh.

Words Are Powerful
Lesson 17

When this woman with the issue of blood had heard of Jesus, she…

Came in the press behind, and touched his garment. For she said, If I may touch but his clothes, I shall be whole.

Mark 5:27-28

Here she cooperated with another law: She spoke her faith. God's Word plainly and repeatedly reveals this truth in many different places. Someone might cite Matthew's account of this same instance, where it says,

For she said within herself, If I may but touch his garment, I shall be whole.

Matthew 9:21

According to Matthew, she said this within herself, but according to Mark, she spoke with her mouth. Which is it? I believe it's both. Before we speak things out of our mouths, we say them within ourselves. The scriptures don't contradict each other. She did both, and this is one of the laws that govern faith.

A man's belly shall be satisfied with the fruit of his mouth; and with the increase of his lips shall he be filled. Death and life are in the power of the tongue: and they that love it shall eat the fruit thereof.

Proverbs 18:20-21

Our words are powerful. With our words, we can release life, and with our words, we can release death. We need to recognize that there is power in our words—not only positive power, but also negative power.

Release Your Faith

If you are whining, griping, and complaining, you are releasing the negative force of unbelief. That unbelief will cancel out, counterbalance, and negate your faith. Many people pray and ask God to heal them. Then someone comes up to them and asks "How are you?" and they answer, "Oh, I'm dying. The doctor told me this and that, and everything in me hurts." They start speaking negative—contrary to God's Word—violating the laws governing faith. That's like short-circuiting an electrical current. The power may be there, but because they constantly short-circuit it, it's not producing the desired results.

You must recognize that the words you speak are powerful. God created the heavens and the earth by words. He spoke the world into existence. He said, "Let there be light (Gen.

1:3), and let the earth bring forth fruit (Gen. 1:11)." The physical world, even your own physical body, responds to words. Your words are important.

Many of you may think *It doesn't matter what I say*, but God's Word reveals that it does matter what you say. What you say affects what you believe. It will affect your body, the devil, and even God. God uses your words. This is one of the most important ways you release your faith.

Speak God's Word

In more than forty years of ministry, I've prayed for thousands of people. Over the years, I've learned that when I'm praying for someone, it's very important that I speak faith-filled words. I don't ever speak forth my doubts. There have been times that people have come to me in such bad shape that it caused fear and doubt to rise up inside me, but I never spoke it. I only spoke my faith. I've seen people healed in spite of my unbelief because I never spoke it.

Matthew 6:31 says,

Therefore take no thought, saying…

You can't keep a thought from coming, but you can keep from taking that thought as your own. Take no thought, saying. You haven't really taken a thought until you begin to speak it forth. What you say is so very important.

So when this woman with the issue of blood said "If I could but touch His clothes, I shall be made whole," she put a law of God into motion. We just saw that there is death and life in the power of the tongue (Prov. 18:20-21). She spoke something positive, and then, when she acted on it, the power was released.

If you are fighting some type of sickness, you need to start speaking faith-filled words. You need to want the results of the words you're saying. Don't just speak what the doctor has said or how you feel; speak what the Word of God says about you, and speak it in faith. At first you may not totally believe it, but faith comes by hearing and hearing and hearing the Word of God. Speaking God's Word, and continuing to speak it, will help you believe it.

Spiritual Power

Another passage of Scripture that shows us the importance of our words is:

*Verily I say unto you, That whosoever shall **say** unto this mountain, Be thou removed, and be thou cast into the sea; and shall not doubt in his heart, but shall believe that those things which he **saith** shall come to pass; he shall have whatsoever he **saith**.*

Mark 11:23, emphasis mine

Three different times in this one verse, emphasis is given to what you say. You must speak out your faith, not unbelief. When you speak your faith, spiritual power is released. It allows God to flow.

Most doctors have adopted this philosophy that they never want to get your hopes up. They always try to give you the worst-case scenario, thinking that's the good and wise thing to do. I'm aware that they do this for liability reasons, but you need to get people's hopes up and speak positive. You don't need to speak the negative things. When you're around somebody in a hospital room, don't talk to them about dying; talk to them about living. Release life with your words. Speak the Word of God. His Word will become life and health to all their flesh (Prov. 4:22).

Speak to Your Mountain

Again, Jesus said in Mark 11,

Whosoever shall say unto this mountain, Be thou removed.

Mark 11:23

The mountain here is referring to your problem. If you're sick and have a disease, speak to that disease. Say, "Cancer, you are dead. I command you out of my body in the name of Jesus. Cancer, you are leaving my body now." The Bible says to speak to your problem, yet most people speak to God about their problems. This is simple, but it's profound, and it has revolutionized my life.

When it comes to healing, we need to learn to operate in this principle. If we have pain in our feet, we should say, "Pain in my foot, in Jesus' name I command you to leave." We shouldn't say, "God, please take away the pain in my foot." That's not what He's instructed us to do; He told us to speak to our problems, not to speak to Him about our problems. Most people aren't cooperating with this truth. They are violating this law, and because of it the power of God doesn't flow. We need to do what the Lord has told us to do.

I remember ministering this truth to a woman in Charlotte, North Carolina, who had severe health problems. She was diagnosed in 1994 with all kinds of sickness and disease. She was in constant, excruciating pain, and suffered greatly. The doctors told her in 1997 that it was impossible for her to live much longer and that she would die within a month. When I prayed for her, it was 2001. She had already gone four years beyond what they said she could live. However, she had a multitude of different things wrong with her and lived in terrible pain.

I talked with her and explained some truths from the Word concerning healing. Then I prayed with her and spoke to the pain. She had pain all throughout her body. So I commanded pain to leave. I didn't request it; I took my God-given authority as a believer and commanded pain to leave.

Take Authority and Command

This brings me to yet another important kingdom law. Since God has already done His part through Christ's Atonement, we need to take our authority as believers and command the power of God to flow (Is. 45:11). Instead of us asking with a question mark at the end of the sentence, wondering what God is going to do, we need to believe and act on the truth that the Lord has already done it. By His stripes, we were (past tense) healed (1 Pet. 2:24).

So I spoke to her body, I spoke to the pain, and I commanded it to leave. Instantly, this woman was free of pain for the first time in seven years. She started praising God, but then stopped and said, "I still have a burning in my back right along my waist. How come this burning didn't leave?"

I responded, "Well, I didn't speak to burning. You didn't tell me about a burning, so I didn't speak to that." So I prayed again, and this time I said, "Burning, in the name of Jesus, I command you to leave." And it left.

This woman was just beside herself, walking around and praising God. I spent almost half an hour telling her how to keep her healing because Satan will come to try to steal the Word away (Mark 4:15). I told her what to do if she ever had another pain, burning, or anything like that.

How the Kingdom Works

Sure enough, before she got ready to leave, she looked at me and said, "The burning has come back."

I said, "Well, I've already told you how to do it. I'm going to join hands with you and agree, but you do the praying. You take charge of this thing."

So this woman prayed a pretty good prayer, saying, "Father, I thank You that it is Your will to heal me." Thirty minutes before, she had believed that God was the one who had given her this sickness. But she had received God's Word when I countered that unbelief. She prayed, "Father, I believe that by Your stripes, I was healed. I claim my healing in the name of Jesus." Now, that's a pretty good prayer compared to where she was previously, but I knew it wouldn't work. Knowing that the burning hadn't left, I asked her, "Do you still have any burning?"

"Yes. Why didn't it leave?"

"Because you spoke to God about your burning instead of speaking to your burning." Then I opened my Bible to Mark 11:23 and shared more about this truth with her, saying, "You need to speak to your mountain."

She looked at me and said, "You mean, I'm supposed to speak to burning, call it by that name, and actually speak to it?"

"Yes. That's what the Bible says to do."

You may think this is strange, but Jesus spoke to a fig tree (Mark 11:12-26). He's the one who told us to speak to the mountain (Mark 11:23). It works. It's a law in His kingdom. You don't have to fully understand it to do it. When you flip a switch on the wall, you don't have to understand why your lights come on; you just do it and it works. Release your faith, and exercise your God-given authority by speaking to the mountain. It'll work.

So this woman prayed again, saying, "Burning, in the name of Jesus…" Immediately she stopped and exclaimed, "It's already gone!" That's all she had to say. God had set her free. I had dinner with her over a year later, and she was still walking in divine health. It was a great miracle!

One of the important keys I used was my words. Specifically, I didn't just speak positive words to God, but I spoke positive words to the situation. I took authority and commanded the situation to change. These are some of the laws of the kingdom. It may seem strange at first, but that's just how the kingdom works.

Receive it by Faith

If you have a financial problem, speak to your checkbook. Your checkbook is speaking to you, saying, "Look at all this red and hardly any black. The Word didn't work. God isn't supplying your needs." You'll have those thoughts come to you as you look at your checkbook. So speak to the mountain. Say, "In the name of Jesus, my God supplies all of my needs according to His riches in glory by Christ Jesus (Phil. 4:19). I command this red ink to leave and black ink to come. I call God's abundant provision into manifestation. My accounts receive money and increase."

Concerning physical healing, speak to your body. I recently rebuked sugar diabetes in a man at one of my meetings. I didn't ask God to rebuke it; I did. The Lord has already done His part. God had already healed this man. It's just a matter of someone here on earth releasing their faith by taking authority and speaking to the mountain.

Repair & Restore

So I commanded this man's sugar diabetes to be gone. Then I spoke to his pancreas to come back to life and begin to function properly. I did this because that was the part of his body that wasn't working properly. I commanded his insulin to come to a proper level, and so forth.

A month later, this guy came to me with an awesome report. He started clicking through the days of stored data in his electronic monitor that he used to test his blood sugar levels. I'm not exactly sure what it means, but on the day I prayed for him, he was over 1,100. Then it just started going down. He kept clicking through the data and showing me that every day, it decreased. He was down to something like 108 at that time. This positive turnaround took place because I not only rebuked and commanded sugar diabetes to leave, but I also spoke to his body to repair.

I've actually had my hands on people with tumors that instantly left—right under my hand—when I prayed and rebuked cancer. I could feel it go down. But I've also realized that diseases like that damage the body. So I'll speak to the parts of the body that were affected and release God's healing power. I'll command the organs that were eaten away to re-grow and be restored. This is how I speak to the mountain.

When I pray for people with something like arthritis, I'll rebuke arthritis by name. I believe arthritis is a demonic spirit, so I'll rebuke the spirit and command arthritis to go in Jesus' name. If I were to stop there, they could be healed of arthritis, but the damage it caused in their bodies would still be there. So I not only rebuke arthritis, but I also speak to the body to repair. I command twisted limbs to come back into proper placement. I command pain, swelling, and inflammation to be gone. Thousands and thousands of times, I've seen the good results that come from cooperating with this spiritual law.

You must speak. The woman with the issue of blood spoke and said, "If I may but touch His clothes, I'll be made whole." Then she acted on what she believed. It would have done her no good whatsoever if she said what she said but didn't follow through with actions.

Words Are Powerful
Lesson 17 – Outline

I.   When this woman with the issue of blood had heard of Jesus, she…

Came in the press behind, and touched his garment. For she said, If I may touch but his clothes, I shall be whole.

Mark 5:27-28

    A. Here she cooperated with another law: She spoke her faith.

    B. According to Matthew 9:21, she said this within herself, but according to Mark, she spoke with her mouth. Which is it?

    C. I believe it's both.

    D. Before we speak things out of our mouths, we say them within ourselves.

II.   With your words, you can release life, and with your words, you can release death.

A man's belly shall be satisfied with the fruit of his mouth; and with the increase of his lips shall he be filled. Death and life are in the power of the tongue: and they that love it shall eat the fruit thereof.

Proverbs 18:20-21

    A. You need to recognize that there is power in your words—not only positive power, but also negative power.

    B. If you are whining, griping, and complaining, you are releasing the negative force of unbelief.

    C. That unbelief will cancel out, counterbalance, and negate your faith.

    D. Many of you may think *It doesn't matter what I say*, but God's Word reveals that it does matter what you say.

    E. This is one of the most important ways you release your faith.

III.   There have been times that people have come to me in such bad shape that it caused fear and doubt to rise up inside me, but I never spoke it.

    A. I've seen people healed in spite of my unbelief because I never spoke it.

    B. Matthew 6:31 says,

Therefore take no thought, saying…

C. You can't keep a thought from coming, but you can keep from taking that thought as your own.

D. You haven't really taken a thought until you begin to speak it forth.

E. What you say is so very important.

IV. If you are fighting some type of sickness, you need to start speaking faith-filled words.

A. You need to want the results of the words you're saying.

B. Don't just speak what the doctor has said or how you feel; speak what the Word of God says about you, and speak it in faith.

C. At first you may not totally believe it, but faith comes by hearing and hearing and hearing the Word of God.

D. Speaking God's Word, and continuing to speak it, will help you believe it.

V. Another passage of Scripture that shows you the importance of your words is:

> *Verily I say unto you, That whosoever shall **say** unto this mountain, Be thou removed, and be thou cast into the sea; and shall not doubt in his heart, but shall believe that those things which he **saith** shall come to pass; he shall have whatsoever he **saith**.*
>
> **Mark 11:23, emphasis mine**

A. Three different times in this one verse, emphasis is given to what you say.

B. The mountain here is referring to your problem.

C. The Bible says to speak to your problem, yet most people speak to God about their problems.

D. This is simple, but it's profound, and it has revolutionized my life.

VI. This brings me to yet another important kingdom law.

A. Since God has already done His part through Christ's Atonement, you need to take your authority as a believer and command the power of God to flow (Is. 45:11).

B. Instead of asking with a question mark at the end of the sentence, wondering what God is going to do, you need to believe and act on the truth that the Lord has already done it.

C. You need to speak to your mountain.

D. You may think this is strange, but Jesus spoke to a fig tree (Mark 11:12-26).

E. He's the one who told you to speak to the mountain (Mark 11:23).

F. Release your faith, and exercise your God-given authority by speaking to the mountain.

G. It'll work.

VII. I've actually had my hands on people with tumors that instantly left—right under my hand—when I prayed and rebuked cancer.

A. But I've also realized that diseases like that damage the body.

B. So I'll speak to the parts of the body that were affected and release God's healing power.

C. I'll command the organs that were eaten away to re-grow and be restored.

D. This is how I speak to the mountain.

E. Thousands and thousands of times, I've seen the good results that come from cooperating with this spiritual law.

F. You must speak.

Words Are Powerful
Lesson 17 – Teacher's Guide

1. When this woman with the issue of blood had heard of Jesus, she **"came in the press behind, and touched his garment. For she said, If I may touch but his clothes, I shall be whole"** (Mark 5:27-28). Here she cooperated with another law: She spoke her faith. According to Matthew 9:21, she said this within herself, but according to Mark, she spoke with her mouth. Which is it? I believe it's both. Before we speak things out of our mouths, we say them within ourselves.

2. With our words, we can release life, and with our words, we can release death (Prov. 18:20-21). We need to recognize that there is power in our words—not only positive power, but also negative power. If we are whining, griping, and complaining, we are releasing the negative force of unbelief. That unbelief will cancel out, counterbalance, and negate our faith. Many of us may think *It doesn't matter what I say*, but God's Word reveals that it does matter what we say. This is one of the most important ways we release our faith.

3. There have been times that people have come to me in such bad shape that it caused fear and doubt to rise up inside me, but I never spoke it. I've seen people healed in spite of my unbelief because I never spoke it. Matthew 6:31 says, **"Therefore take no thought, saying…"** We can't keep a thought from coming, but we can keep from taking that thought as our own. We haven't really taken a thought until we begin to speak it forth. What we say is so very important.

4. If we are fighting some type of sickness, we need to start speaking faith-filled words. We need to want the results of the words we're saying. We shouldn't just speak what the doctor has said or how we feel; we should speak what the Word of God says about us, and we should speak it in faith. At first we may not totally believe it, but faith comes by hearing and hearing and hearing the Word of God. Speaking God's Word, and continuing to speak it, will help us believe it.

1. A. Read Mark 5:27-28. What law did this woman cooperate with? (She spoke her faith)
   B. What do we do before we speak things out of our mouths? (We say them within ourselves)
2. A. Read Proverbs 18:20-21. What do we need to recognize is in our words? (Power)
   B. What are we doing if we're whining, griping, and complaining? (We are releasing the negative force of unbelief)
3. We can't keep a thought from coming, but we can what? (Keep from taking that thought as our own)
4. A. We need to want the results of what? (The words we're saying)
   B. What should we speak? (What the Word of God says about us)
   C. Speaking God's Word, and continuing to speak it, will what? (Help us believe it)

5. Another passage of Scripture that shows us the importance of our words is Mark 11:23. Three different times in this one verse, emphasis is given to what we say. The mountain here is referring to our problems. The Bible says to speak to our problems, yet most of us speak to God about our problems. This is simple, but it's profound, and it has revolutionized my life.

6. This brings me to yet another important kingdom law. Since God has already done His part through Christ's Atonement, we need to take our authority as believers and command the power of God to flow (Is. 45:11). Instead of us asking with a question mark at the end of the sentence, wondering what God is going to do, we need to believe and act on the truth that the Lord has already done it. We need to speak to our mountains. We may think this is strange, but Jesus spoke to a fig tree (Mark 11:12-26). He's the one who told us to speak to the mountain (Mark 11:23). We need to release our faith and exercise our God-given authority by speaking to the mountain. It'll work.

7. I've actually had my hands on people with tumors that instantly left—right under my hand—when I prayed and rebuked cancer. But I've also realized that diseases like that damage the body. So I'll speak to the parts of the body that were affected and release God's healing power. I'll command the organs that were eaten away to re-grow and be restored. This is how I speak to the mountain. Thousands and thousands of times, I've seen the good results that come from cooperating with this spiritual law. We must speak.

5. Read Mark 11:23. How many times in this verse is emphasis given to what we say? (Three times)
6. A. We need to _____ our authority as believers. (Take)
   B. We need to _____ to our mountains. (Speak)
   C. How did Jesus demonstrate this? (He spoke to a fig tree)
7. A. What do I do besides speak to the sickness? (He speaks to the parts of the body that were affected and releases God's healing power)
   B. What must we do? (Speak)

Words Are Powerful
Lesson 17 – Additional Information

There is so much more I could share with you about taking your authority and speaking to the mountain. It's really important that you receive this revelation and begin to walk in it. That's why I would like to recommend to you my teachings entitled *The Believer's Authority*, *You've Already Got It!*, and *Spiritual Authority*. You have to learn that God has already done His part, and now you must take your authority and command it to come to pass.

Everything that Christ has provided through His death, burial, and resurrection is available right now in the spirit realm by grace, but in order for you to experience the manifestation of that provision in the physical realm, you must reach out and receive it by faith.

Words Are Powerful
Lesson 17 – Discipleship Questions

1. Read Mark 5:27-28. From where did this woman approach Jesus?

2. Did this woman ask Jesus if He would heal her?

3. According to Matthew 9:21, whom did this woman consult about her plan?

    A. Her doctor.

    B. Her husband.

    C. Luke, the physician.

    D. No one.

    E. The priest.

4. Read Proverbs 18:20-21. What shall a person's belly be satisfied with?

    A. The fruit of the Spirit.

    B. The fruit of their month.

    C. A double cheeseburger.

    D. All of the above.

    E. None of the above.

5. **"Death and life are in the power of the tongue: and they that love it shall eat the _____ thereof."**

6. What happened when God said, **"Let there be light?"**

7. According to Genesis 1:11, what did God do to bring into being the grass, the herb, and the fruit?

8. Read Matthew 6:31. Eating, drinking, and being clothed are all basic _____.

9. According to Mark 11:12-26, did Jesus experience hunger?

10. What did the people make God's house into?

11. After the disciples saw the fig tree dried up from the roots, what was the first thing Jesus answered?

12. Read Proverbs 4:22. If we are to experience life and health, who is it up to?

13. Read Isaiah 45:11. The Lord is the Holy One and Maker of _____.

14. According to 1 Peter 2:24, for us to be healed, what must Jesus do in addition to taking stripes?

15. Read Mark 4:15. The Word was sown in the hearts of those where?

16. Read Philippians 4:19. This verse makes it clear that God wants to supply how many of our needs according to His riches in glory by Christ Jesus?

Words Are Powerful
Lesson 17 – Answer Key

1. From behind Him.

2. No.

3. D. No one.

4. E. None of the above.

5. **"Fruit."**

6. There was light.

7. He spoke them into being.

8. Needs.

9. Yes.

10. A den of thieves.

11. **"Have faith in God."**

12. Us.

13. Israel.

14. Nothing.

15. By the wayside.

16. All of them.

Words Are Powerful
Lesson 17 – Scriptures

Mark 5:27-28
When she had heard of Jesus, came in the press behind, and touched his garment. [28] For she said, If I may touch but his clothes, I shall be whole.

Matthew 9:21
For she said within herself, If I may but touch his garment, I shall be whole.

Proverbs 18:20-21
A man's belly shall be satisfied with the fruit of his mouth; and with the increase of his lips shall he be filled. [21] Death and life are in the power of the tongue: and they that love it shall eat the fruit thereof.

Genesis 1:3
And God said, Let there be light: and there was light.

Genesis 1:11
And God said, Let the earth bring forth grass, the herb yielding seed, and the fruit tree yielding fruit after his kind, whose seed is in itself, upon the earth: and it was so.

Matthew 6:31
Therefore take no thought, saying, What shall we eat? or, What shall we drink? or, Wherewithal shall we be clothed?

Mark 11:12-26
And on the morrow, when they were come from Bethany, he was hungry: [13] And seeing a fig tree afar off having leaves, he came, if haply he might find any thing thereon: and when he came to it, he found nothing but leaves; for the time of figs was not yet. [14] And Jesus answered and said unto it, No man eat fruit of thee hereafter for ever. And his disciples heard it. [15] And they come to Jerusalem: and Jesus went into the temple, and began to cast out them that sold and bought in the temple, and overthrew the tables of the moneychangers, and the seats of them that sold doves; [16] And would not suffer that any man should carry any vessel through the temple. [17] And he taught, saying unto them, Is it not written, My house shall be called of all nations the house of prayer? but ye have made it a den of thieves. [18] And the scribes and chief priests heard it, and sought how they might destroy him: for they feared him, because all the people was astonished at his doctrine. [19] And when even was come, he went out of the city. [20] And in the morning, as they passed by, they saw the fig tree dried up from the roots. [21] And Peter calling to remembrance saith unto him, Master, behold, the fig tree which thou cursedst is withered away. [22] And Jesus

answering saith unto them, Have faith in God. [23] For verily I say unto you, That whosoever shall say unto this mountain, Be thou removed, and be thou cast into the sea; and shall not doubt in his heart, but shall believe that those things which he saith shall come to pass; he shall have whatsoever he saith. [24] Therefore I say unto you, What things soever ye desire, when ye pray, believe that ye receive them, and ye shall have them. [25] And when ye stand praying, forgive, if ye have ought against any: that your Father also which is in heaven may forgive you your trespasses. [26] But if ye do not forgive, neither will your Father which is in heaven forgive your trespasses.

Proverbs 4:22
For they are life unto those that find them, and health to all their flesh.

Isaiah 45:11
Thus saith the LORD, the Holy One of Israel, and his Maker, Ask me of things to come concerning my sons, and concerning the work of my hands command ye me.

1 Peter 2:24
Who his own self bare our sins in his own body on the tree, that we, being dead to sins, should live unto righteousness: by whose stripes ye were healed.

Mark 4:15
And these are they by the way side, where the word is sown; but when they have heard, Satan cometh immediately, and taketh away the word that was sown in their hearts.

Philippians 4:19
But my God shall supply all your need according to his riches in glory by Christ Jesus.

Act on Your Faith
Lesson 18

Faith without corresponding actions is dead:

But wilt thou know, O vain man, that faith without works is dead?

James 2:20

You must act on your faith. If you're sick, and from reading this **Study Guide**, you've started saying "I believe in the name of Jesus that I am healed" but then you continue to think sick, talk sick, and act sick, you won't see the manifestation of your healing. You need to meditate on God's Word concerning healing, speak it forth again and again until faith comes, and then act on your faith. If you've been laying in bed because you don't feel good, get up and start doing something. Move around. Begin to act on your faith.

Made Complete

I could share with you hundreds of examples of this truth in action. I've hurt my back before and suffered from excruciating pain. I didn't feel like moving, but I got up by faith and started doing exercises and sit-ups. I did everything I didn't feel like doing, resisting it (James 4:7). That was over thirty years ago. Praise God, I still have a strong and healthy back. But before I received the manifestation of healing, my back was in a very serious condition.

Another time, I felt sick while on a painting job. I came home for a lunch break and laid down on the couch, wanting to just do nothing. My wife, being the woman of faith that she is, got me up, put my arm around her neck, and made me dance with her through the house acting like I was healed. Within thirty minutes, I was over it, went back to my painting job, and got paid that day (we really needed the money then).

Many people will lie in bed, drinking sodas and popping pills. They'll let a loved one rub their fevered brow and wonder why they're still sick. Faith is perfected, made complete, by works:

> *Seest thou how faith wrought with his works, and by works was faith made perfect?*

James 2:22

Now, don't misunderstand this truth by thinking that actions produce faith. They don't, and this is where many people have missed it. Some folks, who weren't believing God, thought, *If I just act like I'm believing God, then it'll work.* So they quit taking their insulin, treatments, and medicine, and they die. Then faith gets a bad name. Works—actions—don't produce faith, but if you already have faith, then it won't be complete until you act on it.

Focus & Commitment

The woman with the issue of blood had to act on what she believed. By faith, she had spoken, "If I may but touch His clothes, I shall be made whole." So she acted on that by working her way through the multitude of people thronging Jesus until she could reach out and touch the hem of His garment.

There's no easy way for someone to reach down and touch the hem of a garment that was all the way down to the ground. That means this woman probably crawled on her hands and knees, aggressively pushing her way through this crowd of people surrounding Jesus. It shows complete commitment on her part.

According to the Old Testament Law, her issue of blood made her unclean. Any garment or person she rubbed up against became unclean too. This was considered to be very offensive. People like this, with issues of blood, could not go out in public. If they did, they had to stand on the street corner and yell, "Unclean, unclean!" People would then clear out of the way and give them a wide path to go through. By crawling and pushing her way through this crowd in order to touch Jesus' clothes, this woman was taking some serious risks. If it was discovered that she was violating the Law, she could have been stoned to death. But she wasn't going to let anything or anyone deter or stop her from receiving from God.

This illustrates another important law of the kingdom: It takes focus and commitment to receive from God.

"With All Your Heart"

Many people are very familiar with Jeremiah 29:11, which says,

> *For I know the thoughts that I think toward you, saith the LORD, thoughts of peace, and not of evil, to give you an expected end.*

But they're not as familiar with verses 12 and 13, which continue the thought, saying,

> *Then shall ye call upon me, and ye shall go and pray unto me, and I will hearken unto you. And ye shall seek me, and find me, when ye shall search for me with all your heart.*

Notice how God's Word here reveals that you'll search for Him and find Him when you search for Him with *all* of your heart. Many people passively pray "God, I'd like to be healed," but in their hearts, they believe they could still live without it. They aren't committed to the point where they're saying, "I can't live without it." Because of that, they don't see the healing power of God manifest.

As long as you can live without being healed, you will. But when you reach a place where you say in your heart *I am not going to take this anymore*, when you get the same amount of commitment that this woman with the issue of blood had—that you are literally putting your life on the line because you could be trampled or stoned to death by the crowd, when you get focused and serious enough that you'll do whatever it takes to act on what you believe—when you get that kind of attitude—the power of God will begin to flow. That's just another law that governs how faith works.

A Clean Heart

Just like unbelief, un-forgiveness toward others can short-circuit the power of God:

> *And his lord was wroth, and delivered him to the tormentors, till he should pay all that was due unto him. So likewise shall my heavenly Father do also unto you, if ye from your hearts forgive not every one his brother their trespasses.*
>
> **Matthew 18:34-35**

If you harbor un-forgiveness in your heart, you'll be turned over to the tormentors. A root of bitterness will spring up and defile your entire body:

> *Looking diligently lest any man fail of the grace of God; lest any root of bitterness springing up trouble you, and thereby many be defiled.*
>
> **Hebrews 12:15**

You need to have a clean heart—a heart that's free from un-forgiveness and bitterness.

How Faith Works

Also, faith works by love:

> *For in Jesus Christ neither circumcision availeth any thing, nor uncircumcision; but faith which worketh by love.*
>
> **Galatians 5:6**

A man and his twelve-year-old daughter came to one of my services. She was in a wheelchair and, basically, a vegetable. She was alive and breathing, but she couldn't communicate. Her mind wasn't working, and her body didn't function. At twelve years of age, she was still using diapers. During the service, I said something about it being God's will to heal every time. This father became offended and he left. But the person who had brought him to the service convinced him to stick around until after the service, saying, "Perhaps you misunderstood what Andrew said. Maybe he can explain himself." So he stayed, but he was mad at me.

I told him, "It's God's will to heal your daughter."

He answered, "God made my daughter this way. It's His will." I understood why he said that: it was a defense mechanism. It grieved him to see his daughter in that condition. I'm sure he had prayed, but he hadn't seen any results. So he just assumed it was God's will and that the Lord had some plan for his daughter to be like that.

"God Is Love"

So I began to teach this man from the Scripture that this wasn't true. He threw scriptures back at me, justifying his position. I thought he was misinterpreting his scriptures, and he thought I was misinterpreting mine. We were at a standstill, and this man was very angry.

He was standing behind his daughter at the back of the wheelchair, and she was in between us. I was desperate to get this man to understand that God wanted his daughter healed, and I figured I had nothing to lose, since he was already mad at me. So finally, I just laid into him, saying, "What kind of a father are you, anyway? What kind of a father wants his daughter to be a quadriplegic, a vegetable, bound to a wheelchair all her life? She'll never get to play, get married, or have any other joys in life. What kind of a man are you?"

This guy was already hot, but the steam just started shooting out of his ears. He could have beat me up, and I'm sure he considered it, but he looked at me with rage in his eyes, and answered, "I would do anything to help my daughter get well. If there was an operation, I would spend any amount of money. If I could take her place and become like her so that she could be normal, I would do it. I'd do anything to get her healed!"

After he spouted all that, I looked him straight in the eye, saying, "And you think God—who has all power—loves your daughter less than you do."

That stopped him stone cold. He had a doctrine and an argument. He'd been taught wrongly that God puts sickness and disease on people. He loved his daughter and would have done anything for her. There were no lengths he wouldn't go to produce healing. So I turned the tables and challenged him, saying, "You think God—whom the Bible says is love—loves your daughter less than you do." He could argue doctrine, but not when I brought it down to love.

God is love.

I John 4:8

If we really understood and believed how much God loves us, our faith would shoot through the roof believing that He is healing us. It's not the Lord who hasn't healed; it's us who haven't understood and received. We need to understand how much God loves us. We need to focus and meditate on His love for us. That alone would work wonders for our faith.

The Owner's Manual

You may be insistent and focused on healing, but may not understand how much God loves you. You think He's upset. You hate yourself. You're disappointed with yourself, and you think the Lord dislikes you even more. That is a big hindrance to God's healing power flowing in your life. Faith works by love (Gal. 5:6). It's another kingdom law. If you want to see the Lord's healing power manifest in your life, you need to start understanding how much He loves you.

On and on we could go. Like I said, I've probably seen a hundred different laws like this that govern how faith works. I've only been able to share a few of the most important ones here in this **Study Guide**. Personally, I still don't understand all there is to know about faith and healing, but it's all revealed in the Word of God.

God's Word is the owner's manual. As born-again believers, we belong to Him, and His Word tells us how His kingdom works. We need to get into it and discover the laws that govern how faith works. Then, by faith, we need to cooperate with those laws.

Study different people in the Bible, and consider how they received their healing. Meditate on the woman with the issue of blood. Study Jairus receiving his daughter back from the dead. Look at how Jesus ministered healing to others. Pray and ask the Holy Spirit to help you see things that would apply to you and to the people He wants you to minister healing to.

God wants you well. He wants you well more than you want to be well. If you aren't well, it's not because God isn't willing; it's because you haven't understood how to receive. In other words, there's something you're doing, probably some of the things I've discussed in this **Study Guide**, that is hindering you. Maybe you've been speaking forth negative things, or you've been complaining, murmuring, and saying what the doctor had to say instead of what God has to say. Perhaps you're more moved by your medical report than by God's report in the Scriptures. You need to start declaring what God says in His Word. You need to speak to your mountain—directly to your problem. You need to act on your faith. Get committed enough that nothing will deter you from receiving by faith what God has supplied. As long as you can live without being healed, you will. But once you get determined that you're not going to live like this any longer, it'll make a difference. You need to understand the love of God and start walking in forgiveness. On and on it goes.

Receive!

God is a good God. He's already provided everything you need, including healing. God wants you well. He is for you. If you'll let Him, He will guide you into all truth and show you what you need to do to be able to receive your healing.

I want to pray for you now.

Father, I pray for my friends reading this **Study Guide** *right now. I know it's Your will for them to be well. I know that You've already done it, for by Your stripes they have already been healed (1 Pet. 2:24). Lord, You've already generated the power. It's there. We just need to flip the switch. It's just learning and changing our thinking. Father, I pray that right now the Holy Spirit would quicken on the inside of my friends whatever it is that they need to change so that they can receive what You've already done.*

Your Word says that all things that pertain to life and godliness are given to us through the knowledge of Him (2 Pet. 1:3). Father, I ask You to impart to my friends the knowledge they need right now to release and experience Your healing power.

I speak to these problems now, in the name of Jesus. I command any kind of tumors, cancer, or anything else that has invaded their bodies to die. Germs, viruses, infections, and the like, die in the name of Jesus. Father, I loose Your anointing to flow through their bodies to release them from pain and all these other symptoms. I go to the root of the problem and command these things to be healed.

In Jesus' name, I command fear to be gone, faith to come, and love to flow. We agree with You that we were healed, and if we were (past tense) healed, then we are (present tense) healed. Father, we thank You that You want us well. We receive that in Jesus' name. Amen.

Act on Your Faith
Lesson 18 – Outline

I.   Faith without corresponding actions is dead:

    But wilt thou know, O vain man, that faith without works is dead?

        James 2:20

    A. If you're sick, and from reading this **Study Guide** you've started saying "I believe in the name of Jesus that I am healed" but then you continue to think sick, talk sick, and act sick, you won't see the manifestation of your healing.

    B. Begin to act on your faith.

    C. Faith is perfected, made complete, by works:

    Seest thou how faith wrought with his works, and by works was faith made perfect?

        James 2:22

II.   Don't misunderstand this truth by thinking that actions produce faith.

    A. Some folks, who weren't believing God, thought, *If I just act like I'm believing God, then it'll work.*

    B. So they quit taking their medicine and they die.

    C. Then faith gets a bad name.

    D. Works—actions—don't produce faith, but if you already have faith, then it won't be complete until you act on it.

III. The woman with the issue of blood had to act on what she believed.

    A. According to the Old Testament Law, her issue of blood made her unclean.

    B. If it was discovered that she was violating the Law, she could have been stoned to death.

    C. But she wasn't going to let anything or anyone deter or stop her from receiving from God.

IV.   This illustrates another important law of the kingdom: It takes focus and commitment to receive from God (Jer. 29:11-13).

    A. Many people passively pray "God, I'd like to be healed," but in their hearts, they believe they could still live without it.

    B. But when you reach a place where you say in your heart *I am not going to take this anymore*, when you get the same amount of commitment that this woman with the issue of blood had—that you are literally putting your life on the line because you could be trampled or stoned to death by the crowd, when you get focused and serious enough that you'll do whatever it takes to act on what you believe—when you get that kind of attitude—the power of God will begin to flow.

V. Just like unbelief, un-forgiveness toward others can short-circuit the power of God (Matt. 18:34-35).

    A. If you harbor un-forgiveness in your heart, you'll be turned over to the tormentors.

    B. A root of bitterness will spring up and defile your entire body (Heb. 12:15).

    C. You need to have a clean heart.

VI. Also, faith works by love:

> *For in Jesus Christ neither circumcision availeth any thing, nor uncircumcision; but faith which worketh by love.*
>
> **Galatians 5:6**

> *God is love.*
>
> **I John 4:8**

    A. We need to understand how much God loves us.

    B. We need to focus and meditate on His love for us.

    C. That alone would work wonders for our faith.

    D. It's another kingdom law.

VII. I've only been able to share a few of the most important laws here in this **Study Guide**.

    A. God's Word tells us how His kingdom works.

    B. Study different people in the Bible, and consider how they received their healing.

    C. Pray and ask the Holy Spirit to help you see things that would apply to you and to the people He wants you to minister healing to.

VIII. God wants you well more than you want to be well.

    A. If you aren't well, it's not because God isn't willing; it's because you haven't understood how to receive.

    B. In other words, there's something you're doing, probably some of the things I've discussed in this **Study Guide**, that is hindering you.

    C. You need to start declaring what God says in His Word.

    D. You need to speak to your mountain—directly to your problem.

E. You need to act on your faith.

F. Get committed enough that nothing will deter you from receiving by faith what God has supplied.

G. As long as you can live without being healed, you will.

H. God has already provided everything you need, including healing.

I. If you'll let Him, He will guide you into all truth and show you what you need to do to be able to receive your healing.

Act on Your Faith
Lesson 18 – Teacher's Guide

1. Faith without corresponding actions is dead (James 2:20). If we're sick, and from reading this **Study Guide** we've started saying "I believe in the name of Jesus that I am healed" but then we continue to think sick, talk sick, and act sick, we won't see the manifestation of our healing. We need to begin to act on our faith. Faith is perfected, made complete, by works (James 2:22).

2. We shouldn't misunderstand this truth by thinking that actions produce faith. Some folks, who weren't believing God, thought, *If I just act like I'm believing God, then it'll work.* So they quit taking their medicine and they die. Then faith gets a bad name. Works—actions—don't produce faith, but if we already have faith, then it faith won't be complete until we act on it.

3. The woman with the issue of blood had to act on what she believed. According to the Old Testament Law, her issue of blood made her unclean. If it was discovered that she was violating the Law, she could have been stoned to death. But she wasn't going to let anything or anyone deter or stop her from receiving from God.

4. This illustrates another important law of the kingdom: It takes focus and commitment to receive from God (Jer. 29:11-13). Many people passively pray "God, I'd like to be healed," but in their hearts, they believe they could still live without it.

    But when we reach a place where we say in our hearts *I am not going to take this anymore*, when we get the same amount of commitment that this woman with the issue of blood had—that we are literally putting our lives on the line because we could be trampled or stoned to death by the crowd, when we get focused and serious enough that we'll do whatever it takes to act on what we believe—when we get that kind of attitude—the power of God will begin to flow.

1. Read James 2:20. What is dead without corresponding actions? (Faith)
2. A. Do actions produce faith? (No)
    B. If we already have faith, then it won't be complete until when? (Until we act on it)
3. What was going to deter or stop the woman with the issue of blood from receiving from God? (Nothing)
4. A. Another important law states what? (It takes focus and commitment to receive from God)
    B. When will the power of God begin to flow? (When we reach a place where we say in our hearts *I am not going to take this anymore*, when we get the same amount of commitment that this woman with the issue of blood had—that we are literally putting our lives on the line because we could be trampled or stoned to death by the crowd, when we get focused and serious enough that we'll do whatever it takes to act on what we believe—when we get that kind of attitude)

5. Just like unbelief, un-forgiveness toward others can short-circuit the power of God (Matt. 18:34-35). If we harbor un-forgiveness in our hearts, we'll be turned over to the tormentors. A root of bitterness will spring up and defile our entire bodies (Heb. 12:15). We need to have clean hearts.

6. Also, faith works by love (Gal. 5:6). We need to understand how much God loves us (1 John 4:8). We need to focus and meditate on His love for us. That alone would work wonders for our faith. It's another kingdom law.

7. I've only been able to share a few of the most important ones here in this **Study Guide**. God's Word tells us how His kingdom works. We need to study different people in the Bible and consider how they received their healing. We need to pray and ask the Holy Spirit to help us see things that would apply to us and to the people He wants us to minister healing to.

8. God wants us well more than we want to be well. If we aren't well, it's not because God isn't willing; it's because we haven't understood how to receive. In other words, there's something we're doing, probably some of the things I've discussed in this **Study Guide**, that is hindering us.

   We need to start declaring what God says in His Word. We need to speak to our mountains—directly to our problems. We need to act on our faith. We need to get committed enough that nothing will deter us from receiving by faith what God has supplied. As long as we can live without being healed, we will. God has already provided everything we need, including healing. If we'll let Him, He will guide us into all truth and show us what we need to do to be able to receive our healing.

5. A. Read Matthew 18:34-35. Just like unbelief, what can un-forgiveness toward others do? (Short-circuit the power of God)
   B. Read Hebrews 12:15. What will a root of bitterness do? (It will defile our entire bodies)
   C. What do we need to have? (Clean hearts)
6. What would do wonders for our faith? (Focusing and meditating on God's love for us)
7. A. What does God's Word tell us? (How His kingdom works)
   B. What do we need to study and consider? (We need to study different people in the Bible and consider how they received their healing)
   C. What do we need to ask the Holy Spirit to do? (Help us see things that would apply to us and to the people He wants us to minister healing to)
8. A. Does God want us well more than we want to be well? (Yes)
   B. If we aren't well, what is probably hindering us? (Some of the things Andrew discussed in this **Study Guide**)
   C. Name two of the things we need to start doing. (1. We need to start declaring what God says in His Word. 2. We need to speak to our mountains—directly to our problems. 3. We need to act on our faith. 4. We need to get committed enough that nothing will deter us from receiving by faith what God has supplied)
   D. If we'll let Him, what will He do? (He will guide us into all truth and show us what we need to do to be able to receive our healing)

Act on Your Faith
Lesson 18 – Additional Information

If you really understood how much God loves you, your faith would go through the roof. My teachings entitled *God's Kind of Love: The Cure for What Ails Ya!* and *God's Love to You* will really help you understand the love and mercy of God. If you've been confused because of the wrath and punishment of the Old Testament, both *The True Nature of God* and *The War Is Over* will really open your eyes. When you understand how much God loves you, your faith will work.

Act on Your Faith
Lesson 18 – Discipleship Questions

1. Read James 2:20. Faith is only alive if it has what?

2. Read James 4:7. Does God make us submit to Him or resist the devil?

3. According to James 2:22, by works, faith was made _____.

4. Read Jeremiah 29:11-13. The Lord has what kinds of thoughts toward us?

5. When we pray to Him, what does He do?

    A. He ignores us.

    B. He hearkens to us.

    C. He says He's busy.

    D. He turns His back to us.

    E. He laughs at us.

6. According to Matthew 18:34-35, the lord delivered the man to the tormentors until when?

7. How are we supposed to forgive people their trespasses?

8. Read Hebrews 12:15. We should look diligently so that what?

9. Read Galatians 5:6. What avails?

10. According to 1 John 4:8, a person that does not love does not know whom?

11. Why?

12. According to 1 Peter 2:24, do we have to bear our own sins?

13. Read 2 Peter 1:3. God's divine power has given unto us all things that pertain unto life and godliness through what?

Act on Your Faith
Lesson 18 – Answer Key

1. Works.

2. No.

3. Perfect.

4. Thoughts of peace and not of evil.

5. B. He hearkens to us.

6. Until he paid all that was due to the lord.

7. From our hearts.

8. So that we won't fail of the grace of God, so that no root of bitterness will spring up and trouble us and thereby defile many.

9. Faith that works by love.

10. God.

11. Because God is love.

12. No.

13. The knowledge of Him who has called us to glory and virtue.

Act on Your Faith
Lesson 18 – Scriptures

James 2:20
But wilt thou know, O vain man, that faith without works is dead?

James 4:7
Submit yourselves therefore to God. Resist the devil, and he will flee from you.

James 2:22
Seest thou how faith wrought with his works, and by works was faith made perfect?

Jeremiah 29:11-13
For I know the thoughts that I think toward you, saith the LORD, thoughts of peace, and not of evil, to give you an expected end. [12] Then shall ye call upon me, and ye shall go and pray unto me, and I will hearken unto you. [13] And ye shall seek me, and find me, when ye shall search for me with all your heart.

Matthew 18:34-35
And his lord was wroth, and delivered him to the tormentors, till he should pay all that was due unto him. [35] So likewise shall my heavenly Father do also unto you, if ye from your hearts forgive not every one his brother their trespasses.

Hebrews 12:15
Looking diligently lest any man fail of the grace of God; lest any root of bitterness springing up trouble you, and thereby many be defiled.

Galatians 5:6
For in Jesus Christ neither circumcision availeth any thing, nor uncircumcision; but faith which worketh by love.

1 John 4:8
He that loveth not knoweth not God; for God is love.

1 Peter 2:24
Who his own self bare our sins in his own body on the tree, that we, being dead to sins, should live unto righteousness: by whose stripes ye were healed.

2 Peter 1:3
According as his divine power hath given unto us all things that pertain unto life and godliness, through the knowledge of him that hath called us to glory and virtue.

Is it Always God's Will to Heal?

There are seventeen times in the Gospels where Jesus healed all of the sick who were present. There are forty-seven other times where He healed one or two people at a time. Nowhere do we find the Lord refusing to heal anyone.

In fact, Jesus declared that He could do nothing of Himself but only what He saw the Father do.

Then answered Jesus and said unto them, Verily, verily, I say unto you, The Son can do nothing of himself, but what he seeth the Father do: for what things soever he doeth, these also doeth the Son likewise.

John 5:19

Then said Jesus unto them, When ye have lifted up the Son of man, then shall ye know that I am he, and that I do nothing of myself; but as my Father hath taught me, I speak these things. And he that sent me is with me: the Father hath not left me alone; for I do always those things that please him.

John 8:28-29

In light of these statements, Jesus' actions are proof enough that it is always God's will to heal!

Scriptures

Seventeen times in the Gospels, Jesus healed all of the sick who were present:

1.   And Jesus went about all Galilee, teaching in their synagogues, and preaching the gospel of the kingdom, and healing all manner of sickness and all manner of disease among the people. And his fame went throughout all Syria: and they brought unto him all sick people that were taken with divers diseases and torments, and those which were possessed with devils, and those which were lunatick, and those that had the palsy; and he healed them.

Matthew 4:23-24

2.   When the even was come, they brought unto him many that were possessed with devils: and he cast out the spirits with his word, and healed all that were sick: That it might be fulfilled which was spoken by Esaias the prophet, saying, Himself took our infirmities, and bare our sicknesses.

Matthew 8:16-17

3.   And Jesus went about all the cities and villages, teaching in their synagogues, and preaching the gospel of the kingdom, and healing every sickness and every disease among the people.

Matthew 9:35

4.   But when Jesus knew it, he withdrew himself from thence: and great multitudes followed him, and he healed them all.

Matthew 12:15

5.   And Jesus went forth, and saw a great multitude, and was moved with compassion toward them, and he healed their sick.

Matthew 14:14

6.   And when they were gone over, they came into the land of Gennesaret. And when the men of that place had knowledge of him, they sent out into all that country round about, and brought unto him all that were diseased; And besought him that they might only touch the hem of his garment: and as many as touched were made perfectly whole.

Matthew 14:34-36

7.   And great multitudes came unto him, having with them those that were lame, blind, dumb, maimed, and many others, and cast them down at Jesus' feet; and he healed them: Insomuch that the multitude wondered, when they saw the dumb to speak, the maimed to be whole, the lame to walk, and the blind to see: and they glorified the God of Israel.

Matthew 15:30-31

8.   And great multitudes followed him; and he healed them there.

Matthew 19:2

9.   And the blind and the lame came to him in the temple; and he healed them.

Matthew 21:14

10.   And at even, when the sun did set, they brought unto him all that were diseased, and them that were possessed with devils. And all the city was gathered together at the door. And he healed many that were sick of divers diseases, and cast out many devils; and suffered not the devils to speak, because they knew him.

Mark 1:32-34

11.   And he preached in their synagogues throughout all Galilee, and cast out devils.

Mark 1:39

12.   And whithersoever he entered, into villages, or cities, or country, they laid the sick in the streets, and besought him that they might touch if it were but the border of his garment: and as many as touched him were made whole.

Mark 6:56

13.   Now when the sun was setting, all they that had any sick with divers diseases brought them unto him; and he laid his hands on every one of them, and healed them.

Luke 4:40

14.   And he came down with them, and stood in the plain, and the company of his disciples, and a great multitude of people out of all Judaea and Jerusalem, and from the sea coast of Tyre and Sidon, which came to hear him, and to be healed of their diseases; And they that were vexed with unclean spirits: and they were healed. And the whole multitude sought to touch him: for there went virtue out of him, and healed them all.

Luke 6:17-19

15.   And in that same hour he cured many of their infirmities and plagues, and of evil spirits; and unto many that were blind he gave sight.

Luke 7:21

16.   And the people, when they knew it, followed him: and he received them, and spake unto them of the kingdom of God, and healed them that had need of healing.

Luke 9:11

17.   And as he entered into a certain village, there met him ten men that were lepers, which stood afar off: And they lifted up their voices, and said, Jesus, Master, have mercy on us. And when he saw them, he said unto them, Go show yourselves unto the priests. And it came to pass, that, as they went, they were cleansed. And one of them, when he saw that he was healed, turned back, and with a loud voice glorified God, And fell down on his face at his feet, giving him thanks: and he was a Samaritan. And Jesus answering said, Were there not ten cleansed? but where are the nine?

Luke 17:12-17

Forty-seven other times, the Gospels show that Jesus healed one or two people at a time:

1.   *When he was come down from the mountain, great multitudes followed him. And, behold, there came a leper and worshipped him, saying, Lord, if thou wilt, thou canst make me clean. And Jesus put forth his hand, and touched him, saying, I will; be thou clean. And immediately his leprosy was cleansed. And Jesus saith unto him, See thou tell no man; but go thy way, show thyself to the priest, and offer the gift that Moses commanded, for a testimony unto them.*

Matthew 8:1-4

2.   *And when Jesus was entered into Capernaum, there came unto him a centurion, beseeching him, And saying, Lord, my servant lieth at home sick of the palsy, grievously tormented. And Jesus saith unto him, I will come and heal him. The centurion answered and said, Lord, I am not worthy that thou shouldest come under my roof: but speak the word only, and my servant shall be healed. For I am a man under authority, having soldiers under me: and I say to this man, Go, and he goeth; and to another, Come, and he cometh; and to my servant, Do this, and he doeth it. When Jesus heard it, he marvelled, and said to them that followed, Verily I say unto you, I have not found so great faith, no, not in Israel. And I say unto you, That many shall come from the east and west, and shall sit down with Abraham, and Isaac, and Jacob, in the kingdom of heaven. But the children of the kingdom shall be cast out into outer darkness: there shall be weeping and gnashing of teeth. And Jesus said unto the centurion, Go thy way; and as thou hast believed, so be it done unto thee. And his servant was healed in the selfsame hour.*

Matthew 8:5-13

3.   *And when Jesus was come into Peter's house, he saw his wife's mother laid, and sick of a fever. And he touched her hand, and the fever left her: and she arose, and ministered unto them.*

Matthew 8:14-15

4.   *And when he was come to the other side into the country of the Gergesenes, there met him two possessed with devils, coming out of the tombs, exceeding fierce, so that no man might pass by that way. And, behold, they cried out, saying, What have we to do with thee, Jesus, thou Son of God? art thou come hither to torment us before the time? And there was a good way off from them an herd of many swine feeding. So the devils besought him, saying, If thou cast us out, suffer us to go away into the herd of swine. And he said unto them, Go. And when they were come out, they went into the herd of swine: and,*

behold, the whole herd of swine ran violently down a steep place into the sea, and perished in the waters. And they that kept them fled, and went their ways into the city, and told every thing, and what was befallen to the possessed of the devils. And, behold, the whole city came out to meet Jesus: and when they saw him, they besought him that he would depart out of their coasts.

Matthew 8:28-34

5.   And he entered into a ship, and passed over, and came into his own city. And, behold, they brought to him a man sick of the palsy, lying on a bed: and Jesus seeing their faith said unto the sick of the palsy; Son, be of good cheer; thy sins be forgiven thee. And, behold, certain of the scribes said within themselves, This man blasphemeth. And Jesus knowing their thoughts said, Wherefore think ye evil in your hearts? For whether is easier, to say, Thy sins be forgiven thee; or to say, Arise, and walk? But that ye may know that the Son of man hath power on earth to forgive sins, (then saith he to the sick of the palsy,) Arise, take up thy bed, and go unto thine house. And he arose, and departed to his house. But when the multitudes saw it, they marvelled, and glorified God, which had given such power unto men.

Matthew 9:1-8

6.   And, behold, a woman, which was diseased with an issue of blood twelve years, came behind him, and touched the hem of his garment: For she said within herself, If I may but touch his garment, I shall be whole. But Jesus turned him about, and when he saw her, he said, Daughter, be of good comfort; thy faith hath made thee whole. And the woman was made whole from that hour.

Matthew 9:20-22

7.   And when Jesus came into the ruler's house, and saw the minstrels and the people making a noise, He said unto them, Give place: for the maid is not dead, but sleepeth. And they laughed him to scorn. But when the people were put forth, he went in, and took her by the hand, and the maid arose. And the fame hereof went abroad into all that land.

Matthew 9:23-26

8.   And when Jesus departed thence, two blind men followed him, crying, and saying, Thou Son of David, have mercy on us. And when he was come into the house, the blind men came to him: and Jesus saith unto them, Believe ye that I am able to do this? They said unto him, Yea, Lord. Then touched he their eyes, saying, According to your faith be it unto you. And their eyes were opened; and Jesus straitly charged them, saying, See that no man know it. But they, when they were departed, spread abroad his fame in all that country.

Matthew 9:27-31

9.   *As they went out, behold, they brought to him a dumb man possessed with a devil. And when the devil was cast out, the dumb spake: and the multitudes marvelled, saying, It was never so seen in Israel.*

Matthew 9:32-33

10.   *And, behold, there was a man which had his hand withered. And they asked him, saying, Is it lawful to heal on the sabbath days? that they might accuse him. And he said unto them, What man shall there be among you, that shall have one sheep, and if it fall into a pit on the sabbath day, will he not lay hold on it, and lift it out? How much then is a man better than a sheep? Wherefore it is lawful to do well on the sabbath days. Then saith he to the man, Stretch forth thine hand. And he stretched it forth; and it was restored whole, like as the other.*

Matthew 12:10-13

11.   *Then was brought unto him one possessed with a devil, blind, and dumb: and he healed him, insomuch that the blind and dumb both spake and saw. And all the people were amazed, and said, Is not this the son of David?*

Matthew 12:22-23

12.   *Then Jesus went thence, and departed into the coasts of Tyre and Sidon. And, behold, a woman of Canaan came out of the same coasts, and cried unto him, saying, Have mercy on me, O Lord, thou Son of David; my daughter is grievously vexed with a devil. But he answered her not a word. And his disciples came and besought him, saying, Send her away; for she crieth after us. But he answered and said, I am not sent but unto the lost sheep of the house of Israel. Then came she and worshipped him, saying, Lord, help me. But he answered and said, It is not meet to take the children's bread, and to cast it to dogs. And she said, Truth, Lord: yet the dogs eat of the crumbs which fall from their masters' table. Then Jesus answered and said unto her, O woman, great is thy faith: be it unto thee even as thou wilt. And her daughter was made whole from that very hour.*

Matthew 15:21-28

13.   *And when they were come to the multitude, there came to him a certain man, kneeling down to him, and saying, Lord, have mercy on my son: for he is lunatic, and sore vexed: for ofttimes he falleth into the fire, and oft into the water. And I brought him to thy disciples, and they could not cure him. Then Jesus answered and said, O faithless and perverse generation, how long shall I be with you? how long shall I suffer you? bring him hither to me. And Jesus rebuked the devil; and he departed out of him: and the child was cured from that very hour.*

Matthew 17:14-18

14.   *And, behold, two blind men sitting by the way side, when they heard that Jesus passed by, cried out, saying, Have mercy on us, O Lord, thou Son of David. And the multitude rebuked them, because they should hold their peace: but they cried the more, saying, Have mercy on us, O Lord, thou Son of David. And Jesus stood still, and called them, and said, What will ye that I shall do unto you? They say unto him, Lord, that our eyes may be opened. So Jesus had compassion on them, and touched their eyes: and immediately their eyes received sight, and they followed him.*

Matthew 20:30-34

15.   *And they went into Capernaum; and straightway on the sabbath day he entered into the synagogue, and taught. And they were astonished at his doctrine: for he taught them as one that had authority, and not as the scribes. And there was in their synagogue a man with an unclean spirit; and he cried out, Saying, Let us alone; what have we to do with thee, thou Jesus of Nazareth? art thou come to destroy us? I know thee who thou art, the Holy One of God. And Jesus rebuked him, saying, Hold thy peace, and come out of him. And when the unclean spirit had torn him, and cried with a loud voice, he came out of him. And they were all amazed, insomuch that they questioned among themselves, saying, What thing is this? what new doctrine is this? for with authority commandeth he even the unclean spirits, and they do obey him. And immediately his fame spread abroad throughout all the region round about Galilee.*

Mark 1:21-28

16.   *And forthwith, when they were come out of the synagogue, they entered into the house of Simon and Andrew, with James and John. But Simon's wife's mother lay sick of a fever, and anon they tell him of her. And he came and took her by the hand, and lifted her up; and immediately the fever left her, and she ministered unto them.*

Mark 1:29-31

17.   And there came a leper to him, beseeching him, and kneeling down to him, and saying unto him, If thou wilt, thou canst make me clean. And Jesus, moved with compassion, put forth his hand, and touched him, and saith unto him, I will; be thou clean. And as soon as he had spoken, immediately the leprosy departed from him, and he was cleansed. And he straitly charged him, and forthwith sent him away; And saith unto him, See thou say nothing to any man: but go thy way, show thyself to the priest, and offer for thy cleansing those things which Moses commanded, for a testimony unto them. But he went out, and began to publish it much, and to blaze abroad the matter, insomuch that Jesus could no more openly enter into the city, but was without in desert places: and they came to him from every quarter.

Mark 1:40-45

18.   And again he entered into Capernaum after some days; and it was noised that he was in the house. And straightway many were gathered together, insomuch that there was no room to receive them, no, not so much as about the door: and he preached the word unto them. And they come unto him, bringing one sick of the palsy, which was borne of four. And when they could not come nigh unto him for the press, they uncovered the roof where he was: and when they had broken it up, they let down the bed wherein the sick of the palsy lay. When Jesus saw their faith, he said unto the sick of the palsy, Son, thy sins be forgiven thee. But there were certain of the scribes sitting there, and reasoning in their hearts, Why doth this man thus speak blasphemies? who can forgive sins but God only? And immediately when Jesus perceived in his spirit that they so reasoned within themselves, he said unto them, Why reason ye these things in your hearts? Whether is it easier to say to the sick of the palsy, Thy sins be forgiven thee; or to say, Arise, and take up thy bed, and walk? But that ye may know that the Son of man hath power on earth to forgive sins, (he saith to the sick of the palsy,) I say unto thee, Arise, and take up thy bed, and go thy way into thine house. And immediately he arose, took up the bed, and went forth before them all; insomuch that they were all amazed, and glorified God, saying, We never saw it on this fashion.

Mark 2:1-12

19.   And he entered again into the synagogue; and there was a man there which had a withered hand. And they watched him, whether he would heal him on the sabbath day; that they might accuse him. And he saith unto the man which had the withered hand, Stand forth. And he saith unto them, Is it lawful to do good on the sabbath days, or to do evil? to save life, or to kill? But they held their peace. And when he had looked round about on them with anger, being grieved for the hardness of their hearts, he saith unto the man,

Stretch forth thine hand. And he stretched it out: and his hand was restored whole as the other.

Mark 3:1-5

20.   *And they came over unto the other side of the sea, into the country of the Gadarenes. And when he was come out of the ship, immediately there met him out of the tombs a man with an unclean spirit, Who had his dwelling among the tombs; and no man could bind him, no, not with chains: Because that he had been often bound with fetters and chains, and the chains had been plucked asunder by him, and the fetters broken in pieces: neither could any man tame him. And always, night and day, he was in the mountains, and in the tombs, crying, and cutting himself with stones. But when he saw Jesus afar off, he ran and worshipped him, And cried with a loud voice, and said, What have I to do with thee, Jesus, thou Son of the most high God? I adjure thee by God, that thou torment me not. For he said unto him, Come out of the man, thou unclean spirit. And he asked him, What is thy name? And he answered, saying, My name is Legion: for we are many. And he besought him much that he would not send them away out of the country. Now there was there nigh unto the mountains a great herd of swine feeding. And all the devils besought him, saying, Send us into the swine, that we may enter into them. And forthwith Jesus gave them leave. And the unclean spirits went out, and entered into the swine: and the herd ran violently down a steep place into the sea, (they were about two thousand;) and were choked in the sea. And they that fed the swine fled, and told it in the city, and in the country. And they went out to see what it was that was done. And they come to Jesus, and see him that was possessed with the devil, and had the legion, sitting, and clothed, and in his right mind: and they were afraid. And they that saw it told them how it befell to him that was possessed with the devil, and also concerning the swine. And they began to pray him to depart out of their coasts. And when he was come into the ship, he that had been possessed with the devil prayed him that he might be with him. Howbeit Jesus suffered him not, but saith unto him, Go home to thy friends, and tell them how great things the Lord hath done for thee, and hath had compassion on thee. And he departed, and began to publish in Decapolis how great things Jesus had done for him: and all men did marvel.*

Mark 5:1-20

21.   *And a certain woman, which had an issue of blood twelve years, And had suffered many things of many physicians, and had spent all that she had, and was nothing bettered, but rather grew worse, When she had heard of Jesus, came in the press behind, and touched his garment. For she said, If I may touch but his clothes, I shall be whole.*

And straightway the fountain of her blood was dried up; and she felt in her body that she was healed of that plague. And Jesus, immediately knowing in himself that virtue had gone out of him, turned him about in the press, and said, Who touched my clothes? And his disciples said unto him, Thou seest the multitude thronging thee, and sayest thou, Who touched me? And he looked round about to see her that had done this thing. But the woman fearing and trembling, knowing what was done in her, came and fell down before him, and told him all the truth. And he said unto her, Daughter, thy faith hath made thee whole; go in peace, and be whole of thy plague.

Mark 5:25-34

22.   *While he yet spake, there came from the ruler of the synagogue's house certain which said, Thy daughter is dead: why troublest thou the Master any further? As soon as Jesus heard the word that was spoken, he saith unto the ruler of the synagogue, Be not afraid, only believe. And he suffered no man to follow him, save Peter, and James, and John the brother of James. And he cometh to the house of the ruler of the synagogue, and seeth the tumult, and them that wept and wailed greatly. And when he was come in, he saith unto them, Why make ye this ado, and weep? the damsel is not dead, but sleepeth. And they laughed him to scorn. But when he had put them all out, he taketh the father and the mother of the damsel, and them that were with him, and entereth in where the damsel was lying. And he took the damsel by the hand, and said unto her, Talitha cumi; which is, being interpreted, Damsel, I say unto thee, arise. And straightway the damsel arose, and walked; for she was of the age of twelve years. And they were astonished with a great astonishment. And he charged them straitly that no man should know it; and commanded that something should be given her to eat.*

Mark 5:35-43

23.   *And from thence he arose, and went into the borders of Tyre and Sidon, and entered into an house, and would have no man know it: but he could not be hid. For a certain woman, whose young daughter had an unclean spirit, heard of him, and came and fell at his feet: The woman was a Greek, a Syrophenician by nation; and she besought him that he would cast forth the devil out of her daughter. But Jesus said unto her, Let the children first be filled: for it is not meet to take the children's bread, and to cast it unto the dogs. And she answered and said unto him, Yes, Lord: yet the dogs under the table eat of the children's crumbs. And he said unto her, For this saying go thy way; the devil is gone out of thy daughter. And when she was come to her house, she found the devil gone out, and her daughter laid upon the bed.*

Mark 7:24-30

24.   And again, departing from the coasts of Tyre and Sidon, he came unto the sea of Galilee, through the midst of the coasts of Decapolis. And they bring unto him one that was deaf, and had an impediment in his speech; and they beseech him to put his hand upon him. And he took him aside from the multitude, and put his fingers into his ears, and he spit, and touched his tongue; And looking up to heaven, he sighed, and saith unto him, Ephphatha, that is, Be opened. And straightway his ears were opened, and the string of his tongue was loosed, and he spake plain. And he charged them that they should tell no man: but the more he charged them, so much the more a great deal they published it; And were beyond measure astonished, saying, He hath done all things well: he maketh both the deaf to hear, and the dumb to speak.

Mark 7:31-37

25.   And he cometh to Bethsaida; and they bring a blind man unto him, and besought him to touch him. And he took the blind man by the hand, and led him out of the town; and when he had spit on his eyes, and put his hands upon him, he asked him if he saw ought. And he looked up, and said, I see men as trees, walking. After that he put his hands again upon his eyes, and made him look up: and he was restored, and saw every man clearly. And he sent him away to his house, saying, Neither go into the town, nor tell it to any in the town.

Mark 8:22-26

26.   And when he came to his disciples, he saw a great multitude about them, and the scribes questioning with them. And straightway all the people, when they beheld him, were greatly amazed, and running to him saluted him. And he asked the scribes, What question ye with them? And one of the multitude answered and said, Master, I have brought unto thee my son, which hath a dumb spirit; And wheresoever he taketh him, he teareth him: and he foameth, and gnasheth with his teeth, and pineth away: and I spake to thy disciples that they should cast him out; and they could not. He answereth him, and saith, O faithless generation, how long shall I be with you? how long shall I suffer you? bring him unto me. And they brought him unto him: and when he saw him, straightway the spirit tare him; and he fell on the ground, and wallowed foaming. And he asked his father, How long is it ago since this came unto him? And he said, Of a child. And ofttimes it hath cast him into the fire, and into the waters, to destroy him: but if thou canst do any thing, have compassion on us, and help us. Jesus said unto him, If thou canst believe, all things are possible to him that believeth. And straightway the father of the child cried out, and said with tears, Lord, I believe; help thou mine unbelief. When Jesus saw that the people came running together, he rebuked the foul spirit,

saying unto him, Thou dumb and deaf spirit, I charge thee, come out of him, and enter no more into him. And the spirit cried, and rent him sore, and came out of him: and he was as one dead; insomuch that many said, He is dead. But Jesus took him by the hand, and lifted him up; and he arose. And when he was come into the house, his disciples asked him privately, Why could not we cast him out? And he said unto them, This kind can come forth by nothing, but by prayer and fasting.

Mark 9:14-29

27.   *And they came to Jericho: and as he went out of Jericho with his disciples and a great number of people, blind Bartimaeus, the son of Timaeus, sat by the highway side begging. And when he heard that it was Jesus of Nazareth, he began to cry out, and say, Jesus, thou Son of David, have mercy on me. And many charged him that he should hold his peace: but he cried the more a great deal, Thou Son of David, have mercy on me. And Jesus stood still, and commanded him to be called. And they call the blind man, saying unto him, Be of good comfort, rise; he calleth thee. And he, casting away his garment, rose, and came to Jesus. And Jesus answered and said unto him, What wilt thou that I should do unto thee? The blind man said unto him, Lord, that I might receive my sight. And Jesus said unto him, Go thy way; thy faith hath made thee whole. And immediately he received his sight, and followed Jesus in the way.*

Mark 10:46-52

28.   *And in the synagogue there was a man, which had a spirit of an unclean devil, and cried out with a loud voice, Saying, Let us alone; what have we to do with thee, thou Jesus of Nazareth? art thou come to destroy us? I know thee who thou art; the Holy One of God. And Jesus rebuked him, saying, Hold thy peace, and come out of him. And when the devil had thrown him in the midst, he came out of him, and hurt him not. And they were all amazed, and spake among themselves, saying, What a word is this! for with authority and power he commandeth the unclean spirits, and they come out. And the fame of him went out into every place of the country round about.*

Luke 4:33-37

29.   *And he arose out of the synagogue, and entered into Simon's house. And Simon's wife's mother was taken with a great fever; and they besought him for her. And he stood over her, and rebuked the fever; and it left her: and immediately she arose and ministered unto them.*

Luke 4:38-39

30.   *And it came to pass, when he was in a certain city, behold a man full of leprosy: who seeing Jesus fell on his face, and besought him, saying, Lord, if thou wilt, thou canst make me clean. And he put forth his hand, and touched him, saying, I will: be thou clean. And immediately the leprosy departed from him. And he charged him to tell no man: but go, and show thyself to the priest, and offer for thy cleansing, according as Moses commanded, for a testimony unto them. But so much the more went there a fame abroad of him: and great multitudes came together to hear, and to be healed by him of their infirmities.*

Luke 5:12-15

31.   *And it came to pass on a certain day, as he was teaching, that there were Pharisees and doctors of the law sitting by, which were come out of every town of Galilee, and Judaea, and Jerusalem: and the power of the Lord was present to heal them. And, behold, men brought in a bed a man which was taken with a palsy: and they sought means to bring him in, and to lay him before him. And when they could not find by what way they might bring him in because of the multitude, they went upon the housetop, and let him down through the tiling with his couch into the midst before Jesus. And when he saw their faith, he said unto him, Man, thy sins are forgiven thee. And the scribes and the Pharisees began to reason, saying, Who is this which speaketh blasphemies? Who can forgive sins, but God alone? But when Jesus perceived their thoughts, he answering said unto them, What reason ye in your hearts? Whether is easier, to say, Thy sins be forgiven thee; or to say, Rise up and walk? But that ye may know that the Son of man hath power upon earth to forgive sins, (he said unto the sick of the palsy,) I say unto thee, Arise, and take up thy couch, and go into thine house. And immediately he rose up before them, and took up that whereon he lay, and departed to his own house, glorifying God. And they were all amazed, and they glorified God, and were filled with fear, saying, We have seen strange things to day.*

Luke 5:17-26

32.   *And it came to pass also on another sabbath, that he entered into the synagogue and taught: and there was a man whose right hand was withered. And the scribes and Pharisees watched him, whether he would heal on the sabbath day; that they might find an accusation against him. But he knew their thoughts, and said to the man which had the withered hand, Rise up, and stand forth in the midst. And he arose and stood forth. Then said Jesus unto them, I will ask you one thing; Is it lawful on the sabbath days to do good, or to do evil? to save life, or to destroy it? And looking round about upon*

them all, he said unto the man, Stretch forth thy hand. And he did so: and his hand was restored whole as the other.

Luke 6:6-10

33.　　Now when he had ended all his sayings in the audience of the people, he entered into Capernaum. And a certain centurion's servant, who was dear unto him, was sick, and ready to die. And when he heard of Jesus, he sent unto him the elders of the Jews, beseeching him that he would come and heal his servant. And when they came to Jesus, they besought him instantly, saying, That he was worthy for whom he should do this: For he loveth our nation, and he hath built us a synagogue. Then Jesus went with them. And when he was now not far from the house, the centurion sent friends to him, saying unto him, Lord, trouble not thyself: for I am not worthy that thou shouldest enter under my roof: Wherefore neither thought I myself worthy to come unto thee: but say in a word, and my servant shall be healed. For I also am a man set under authority, having under me soldiers, and I say unto one, Go, and he goeth; and to another, Come, and he cometh; and to my servant, Do this, and he doeth it. When Jesus heard these things, he marvelled at him, and turned him about, and said unto the people that followed him, I say unto you, I have not found so great faith, no, not in Israel. And they that were sent, returning to the house, found the servant whole that had been sick.

Luke 7:1-10

34.　　And it came to pass the day after, that he went into a city called Nain; and many of his disciples went with him, and much people. Now when he came nigh to the gate of the city, behold, there was a dead man carried out, the only son of his mother, and she was a widow: and much people of the city was with her. And when the Lord saw her, he had compassion on her, and said unto her, Weep not. And he came and touched the bier: and they that bare him stood still. And he said, Young man, I say unto thee, Arise. And he that was dead sat up, and began to speak. And he delivered him to his mother. And there came a fear on all: and they glorified God, saying, That a great prophet is risen up among us; and, That God hath visited his people. And this rumour of him went forth throughout all Judaea, and throughout all the region round about.

Luke 7:11-17

35.　　And when he went forth to land, there met him out of the city a certain man, which had devils long time, and ware no clothes, neither abode in any house, but in the tombs. When he saw Jesus, he cried out, and fell down before him, and with a loud voice said, What *have I to do with thee, Jesus, thou Son of God most high? I beseech thee, torment me not. (For he had commanded the unclean spirit to come out of the man. For oftentimes it had caught him: and he was kept bound with chains and in fetters; and he brake the bands, and was driven of the devil into the wilderness.) And Jesus asked him, saying, What is thy name? And he said, Legion: because many devils were entered into him. And they besought him that he would not command them to go out into the deep. And there was there an herd of many swine feeding on the mountain: and they besought him that he would suffer them to enter into them. And he suffered them. Then went the devils out of the man, and entered into the swine: and the herd ran violently down a steep place into the lake, and were choked. When they that fed them saw what was done, they fled, and went and told it in the city and in the country. Then they went out to see what was done; and came to Jesus, and found the man, out of whom the devils were departed, sitting at the feet of Jesus, clothed, and in his right mind: and they were afraid. They also which saw it told them by what means he that was possessed of the devils was healed. Then the whole multitude of the country of the Gadarenes round about besought him to depart from them; for they were taken with great fear: and he went up into the ship, and returned back again. Now the man out of whom the devils were departed besought him that he might be with him: but Jesus sent him away, saying, Return to thine own house, and show how great things God hath done unto thee. And he went his way, and published throughout the whole city how great things Jesus had done unto him.*

Luke 8:27-39

36.   *And a woman having an issue of blood twelve years, which had spent all her living upon physicians, neither could be healed of any, Came behind him, and touched the border of his garment: and immediately her issue of blood stanched. And Jesus said, Who touched me? When all denied, Peter and they that were with him said, Master, the multitude throng thee and press thee, and sayest thou, Who touched me? And Jesus said, Somebody hath touched me: for I perceive that virtue is gone out of me. And when the woman saw that she was not hid, she came trembling, and falling down before him, she declared unto him before all the people for what cause she had touched him, and how she was healed immediately. And he said unto her, Daughter, be of good comfort: thy faith hath made thee whole; go in peace.*

Luke 8:43-48

37.   *While he yet spake, there cometh one from the ruler of the synagogue's house, saying to him, Thy daughter is dead; trouble not*

the Master. But when Jesus heard it, he answered him, saying, Fear not: believe only, and she shall be made whole. And when he came into the house, he suffered no man to go in, save Peter, and James, and John, and the father and the mother of the maiden. And all wept, and bewailed her: but he said, Weep not; she is not dead, but sleepeth. And they laughed him to scorn, knowing that she was dead. And he put them all out, and took her by the hand, and called, saying, Maid, arise. And her spirit came again, and she arose straightway: and he commanded to give her meat. And her parents were astonished: but he charged them that they should tell no man what was done.

Luke 8:49-56

38.   And it came to pass, that on the next day, when they were come down from the hill, much people met him. And, behold, a man of the company cried out, saying, Master, I beseech thee, look upon my son: for he is mine only child. And, lo, a spirit taketh him, and he suddenly crieth out; and it teareth him that he foameth again, and bruising him hardly departeth from him. And I besought thy disciples to cast him out; and they could not. And Jesus answering said, O faithless and perverse generation, how long shall I be with you, and suffer you? Bring thy son hither. And as he was yet a-coming, the devil threw him down, and tare him. And Jesus rebuked the unclean spirit, and healed the child, and delivered him again to his father.

Luke 9:37-42

39.   And he was casting out a devil, and it was dumb. And it came to pass, when the devil was gone out, the dumb spake; and the people wondered.

Luke 11:14

40.   And, behold, there was a woman which had a spirit of infirmity eighteen years, and was bowed together, and could in no wise lift up herself. And when Jesus saw her, he called her to him, and said unto her, Woman, thou art loosed from thine infirmity. And he laid his hands on her: and immediately she was made straight, and glorified God. And the ruler of the synagogue answered with indignation, because that Jesus had healed on the sabbath day, and said unto the people, There are six days in which men ought to work: in them therefore come and be healed, and not on the sabbath day. The Lord then answered him, and said, Thou hypocrite, doth not each one of you on the sabbath loose his ox or his ass from the stall, and lead him away to watering? And ought not this woman, being a daughter of Abraham, whom Satan hath bound, lo, these eighteen years, be loosed from this bond on the sabbath day? And when he had said these things, all his

adversaries were ashamed: and all the people rejoiced for all the glorious things that were done by him.

Luke 13:11-17

41. *And it came to pass, as he went into the house of one of the chief Pharisees to eat bread on the sabbath day, that they watched him. And, behold, there was a certain man before him which had the dropsy. And Jesus answering spake unto the lawyers and Pharisees, saying, Is it lawful to heal on the sabbath day? And they held their peace. And he took him, and healed him, and let him go; And answered them, saying, Which of you shall have an ass or an ox fallen into a pit, and will not straightway pull him out on the sabbath day?*

Luke 14:1-5

42. *And it came to pass, that as he was come nigh unto Jericho, a certain blind man sat by the way side begging: And hearing the multitude pass by, he asked what it meant. And they told him, that Jesus of Nazareth passeth by. And he cried, saying, Jesus, thou Son of David, have mercy on me. And they which went before rebuked him, that he should hold his peace: but he cried so much the more, Thou Son of David, have mercy on me. And Jesus stood, and commanded him to be brought unto him: and when he was come near, he asked him, Saying, What wilt thou that I shall do unto thee? And he said, Lord, that I may receive my sight. And Jesus said unto him, Receive thy sight: thy faith hath saved thee. And immediately he received his sight, and followed him, glorifying God: and all the people, when they saw it, gave praise unto God.*

Luke 18:35-43

43. *And Jesus answered and said, Suffer ye thus far. And he touched his ear, and healed him.*

Luke 22:51

44. *So Jesus came again into Cana of Galilee, where he made the water wine. And there was a certain nobleman, whose son was sick at Capernaum. When he heard that Jesus was come out of Judaea into Galilee, he went unto him, and besought him that he would come down, and heal his son: for he was at the point of death. Then said Jesus unto him, Except ye see signs and wonders, ye will not believe. The nobleman saith unto him, Sir, come down ere my child die. Jesus saith unto him, Go thy way; thy son liveth. And the man believed the word that Jesus had spoken unto him, and he went his way. And as he was now going down, his servants met him, and told him, saying,*

Thy son liveth. Then enquired he of them the hour when he began to amend. And they said unto him, Yesterday at the seventh hour the fever left him. So the father knew that it was at the same hour, in the which Jesus said unto him, Thy son liveth: and himself believed, and his whole house. This is again the second miracle that Jesus did, when he was come out of Judaea into Galilee.

John 4:46-54

45.   *Now there is at Jerusalem by the sheep market a pool, which is called in the Hebrew tongue Bethesda, having five porches. In these lay a great multitude of impotent folk, of blind, halt, withered, waiting for the moving of the water. For an angel went down at a certain season into the pool, and troubled the water: whosoever then first after the troubling of the water stepped in was made whole of whatsoever disease he had. And a certain man was there, which had an infirmity thirty and eight years. When Jesus saw him lie, and knew that he had been now a long time in that case, he saith unto him, Wilt thou be made whole? The impotent man answered him, Sir, I have no man, when the water is troubled, to put me into the pool: but while I am coming, another steppeth down before me. Jesus saith unto him, Rise, take up thy bed, and walk. And immediately the man was made whole, and took up his bed, and walked: and on the same day was the sabbath. The Jews therefore said unto him that was cured, It is the sabbath day: it is not lawful for thee to carry thy bed. He answered them, He that made me whole, the same said unto me, Take up thy bed, and walk. Then asked they him, What man is that which said unto thee, Take up thy bed, and walk? And he that was healed wist not who it was: for Jesus had conveyed himself away, a multitude being in that place. Afterward Jesus findeth him in the temple, and said unto him, Behold, thou art made whole: sin no more, lest a worse thing come unto thee. The man departed, and told the Jews that it was Jesus, which had made him whole.*

John 5:2-15

46.   *When he had thus spoken, he spat on the ground, and made clay of the spittle, and he anointed the eyes of the blind man with the clay, And said unto him, Go, wash in the pool of Siloam, (which is by interpretation, Sent.) He went his way therefore, and washed, and came seeing.*

John 9:6-7

47.   *And when he thus had spoken, he cried with a loud voice, Lazarus, come forth. And he that was dead came forth, bound hand and foot with graveclothes: and his face was bound about with a napkin. Jesus saith unto them, Loose him, and let him go.*

John 11:43-44

About the Author

For over four decades, Andrew Wommack has traveled America and the world teaching the truth of the Gospel. His profound revelation of the Word of God is taught with clarity and simplicity, emphasizing God's unconditional love and the balance between grace and faith. He reaches millions of people through the daily *Gospel Truth* radio and television programs, broadcast both domestically and internationally. He founded Charis Bible College in 1994 and has since established CBC extension schools in other major cities of America and around the world. Andrew has produced a library of teaching materials, available in print, audio, and visual formats. And, as it has been from the beginning, his ministry continues to distribute free audio materials to those who cannot afford them.

Receive Jesus as Your Savior

Choosing to receive Jesus Christ as your Lord and Savior is the most important decision you'll ever make!

God's Word promises, **"That if thou shalt confess with thy mouth the Lord Jesus, and shalt believe in thine heart that God hath raised him from the dead, thou shalt be saved. For with the heart man believeth unto righteousness; and with the mouth confession is made unto salvation"** (Rom. 10:9-10). **"For whosoever shall call upon the name of the Lord shall be saved"** (Rom. 10:13).

By His grace, God has already done everything to provide salvation. Your part is simply to believe and receive.

Pray out loud, *"Jesus, I confess that You are my Lord and Savior. I believe in my heart that God raised You from the dead. By faith in Your Word, I receive salvation now. Thank You for saving me!"*

The very moment you commit your life to Jesus Christ, the truth of His Word instantly comes to pass in your spirit. Now that you're born again, there's a brand-new you!

Please contact me and let me know that you've prayed to receive Jesus as your Savior or to be filled with the Holy Spirit. I would like to rejoice with you and help you understand more fully what has taken place in your life. I'll send you a free gift that will help you understand and grow in your new relationship with the Lord. *Welcome to your new life!*

Receive the Holy Spirit

As His child, your loving heavenly Father wants to give you the supernatural power you need to live this new life.

"For every one that asketh receiveth; and he that seeketh findeth; and to him that knocketh it shall be opened...how much more shall your heavenly Father give the Holy Spirit to them that ask him?" (Luke 11:10-13).

All you have to do is ask, believe, and receive!

Pray, *"Father, I recognize my need for Your power to live this new life. Please fill me with Your Holy Spirit. By faith, I receive it right now! Thank You for baptizing me. Holy Spirit, You are welcome in my life!"*

Congratulations—now you're filled with God's supernatural power!

Some syllables from a language you don't recognize will rise up from your heart to your mouth (1 Cor. 14:14). As you speak them out loud by faith, you're releasing God's power from within and building yourself up in your spirit (1 Cor. 14:4). You can do this whenever and wherever you like.

It doesn't really matter whether you felt anything or not when you prayed to receive the Lord and His Spirit. If you believed in your heart that you received, then God's Word promises that you did. **"Therefore I say unto you, What things soever ye desire, when ye pray, believe that ye receive them, and ye shall have them"** (Mark 11:24). God always honors His Word—believe it!

Please contact me and let me know that you've prayed to receive Jesus as your Savior or to be filled with the Holy Spirit. I would like to rejoice with you and help you understand more fully what has taken place in your life. I'll send you a free gift that will help you understand and grow in your new relationship with the Lord. *Welcome to your new life!*

Recommended Teachings

Mentioned in book:

You've Already Got It!
"The Sovereignty of God"
"The Faith of God/Mind of Christ"
Spirit, Soul & Body
How to Receive a Miracle
A Sure Foundation
Effortless Change
The Believer's Authority
Spiritual Authority
The True Nature of God
God's Kind of Love: The Cure for What Ails Ya!
God's Love to You
The War Is Over
Life for Today Study Bible and Commentary: The Acts of the Apostles Edition

Others:

God Wants You Well (audio)
"Healing Scriptures"
Healing Journeys (DVD video)
Hardness of Heart
A Better Way to Pray
"What to Do When Your Prayers Seem Unanswered"
Niki Ochenski: The Story of a Miracle! (DVD video)
"Niki's Healing Testimony"
"Jodie Stehouwer's Testimony"
Stillborn – Krow Family Miracle (DVD video)
Christian Survival Kit
"The Book of Job"
"All Things Work Together for Good"
Discover the Keys to Staying Full of God

Note: Titles in italics denote entire albums or videos. Titles in quotations denote single
teaching CDs.

Notes

Notes

Notes

Notes

Notes

Notes

Notes